100 CLASSIC HIKES IN
SOUTHERN CALIFORNIA

100 CLASSIC HIKES IN
SOUTHERN CALIFORNIA

San Bernardino National Forest / Angeles National Forest / Santa Lucia Mountains / Big Sur and the Sierras

Allen Riedel

THE MOUNTAINEERS BOOKS

For Sierra, Makaila, and Michael

THE MOUNTAINEERS BOOKS
*is the nonprofit publishing arm of The Mountaineers Club, an organization founded in 1906 and
dedicated to the exploration, preservation, and enjoyment of outdoor and wilderness areas.*

1001 SW Klickitat Way, Suite 201, Seattle, WA 98134

First edition, 2008

Manufactured in China

Copy Editor: Carol Poole
Cover and Book Design: The Mountaineers Books
Layout and Cartography: Jennifer Shontz, Red Shoe Design
Photographer: All photographs by the author, except where noted.

Cover photograph: *Hardy pines intermingle with desert chaparral throughout Southern California.*
Frontispiece: *A white-tailed kite soars above the skyline of Montana De Oro State Park.*

Library of Congress Cataloging-in-Publication Data
Riedel, Allen.
  100 classic hikes in Southern California / by Allen Riedel.
     p. cm.
  Includes index.
  ISBN 978-1-59485-066-0
  1. Hiking—California, Southern—Guidebooks. 2. California,
Southern—Guidebooks. I. Title. II. Title: One hundred classic hikes
in Southern California.
GV199.42.C22S686 2008
796.5109794'9—dc22
                                     2007052541

CONTENTS

ACKNOWLEDGMENTS

I would like to thank all of my friends who have hiked, trekked, backpacked, camped, and otherwise traveled and adventured with me over the past few years, especially Bruno Lucidarme, Chrissy Ziburskie, Sean Coolican, Bill Buck, Adam Mendelsohn, Tom Kashirsky, Cameron Alston, Matt Piazza, Monique Riedel, Michael Millenheft III, Eric Walther, Bob Romano, Eric Romero, Daniel Suarez, my beautiful daughters—Sierra and Makaila—Sooz Snyder, Steve Bera, Kathy Wing, and Jim Zuber.

There are several people who wrote me reference letters and were instrumental in helping me get my first book deal that I forgot to mention the first time around: Victoria Christopher Murray, Professor Chuck Mendoza, and Jim Zuber, whose website, *www.localhikes.com,* is not only an awesome service but the one that got my feet off the ground both literally and figuratively. I would like to thank all of the wonderful people at The Mountaineers Books who have been helpful and supportive every single step of the way. A show of gratitude goes out to all of the land managers, departments, and services who have helped me by courtesy checking my work, offering information, and protecting the open and beautiful spaces of this nation. I would like to thank my brother, Larry Riedel, my mom, Barbara Riedel, and my Dad, Elmer Riedel, who always encouraged me to accomplish my dreams. I wish you could see me now, Dad! I miss you! I would also like to thank everyone who has bought my books or enjoyed my writing in one way or another. Thanks to Dave Ammenheuser and Patricia Mays at the Press Enterprise, I've thoroughly enjoyed working with both of you. I would like to thank all of my friends on the staffs at Mount Vernon, John Muir, Serrano, and Lakeside Middle Schools as well as my students, it has been a pleasure teaching with all of you. I would not have been able to complete this manuscript without my personal healer, Ian MacGregor, who fixed me more than a few times with his combination of kinesiology, acupuncture, acupressure, chiropractic, and massage. Once, I saw him and could barely walk; two days later, I was on the trail for two weeks hiking over 150 miles feeling fantastic. Thanks, Ian!

Lastly, I would like to send a special thank you to Monique for teaching me that true love really does exist, even if it takes the passage of much time for it to be realized. I know how much you believe in me and in us!

TRAILS AT A GLANCE

HIKE NUMBER AND NAME	DIFFICULTY	SEASON	HIGHLIGHTS
Short day hikes			
1. Bayside Trail	Easy	All	Views of San Diego Harbor, historic lighthouse
2. Razor Trail	Easy	All	Rare pine species, wildlife, wildflowers
3. Salton Sea—Rock Hill Trail	Easy	Nov–Mar	Birdwatching, unique inland sea
4. Cottonwood Creek Falls	Easy	Nov–Mar	Waterfall, swimming holes
6. Garnet Peak	Easy	All	Clear desert vistas, nice summit
7. Stonewall Peak Trail	Easy	All	Mountaintop viewpoint
9. Pictograph Trail	Easy	Nov–Mar	Native American rock art
10. Ghost Mountain	Easy	Nov–Mar	Historic homestead, views
11. Palomar Mountain Observatory Trail	Easy	All	Hale Telescope, viewpoint, pine forest
13. Holy Jim Falls/Trabuco Canyon	Easy	Nov–May	Waterfall, riparian canyon
15. Lost Horse Mine	Easy	Nov–Mar	Historic mine and stamp mill, views
16. Ryan Mountain	Easy	Nov–Mar	Mountain views
18. Barker Dam	Easy	Nov–Mar	Boulder formations, beautiful reservoir, rock art, Joshua trees
28. Castle Rock and Champion Lodgepole Pine	Easy	All	Mammoth lodgepole pine, rock formations
37. Eaton Canyon Falls	Easy	Nov–May	Waterfall, easy city access
38. San Gabriel Peak	Easy	All	Mountain views, tunnel
39. Switzer Falls	Easy	All	Waterfall, lush forest
40. Solstice Canyon	Easy	All	Stream, ancient trees, interesting ruins
42. Zuma Dume Trail	Easy	All	Beach, coastal tide pools, overlook
44. Mugu Peak	Moderate	All	Coastal views, wildflowers
45. Anacapa Lighthouse Trail	Easy	All	Undeveloped coast views, old lighthouse
49. Forbush Flat	Easy	All	Views, oak woodland
55. Oso Flaco Lake	Easy	All	Birdwatching, pristine beach and sand dune ecosystem
57. Kelso Dunes	Moderate	Nov–May	Unique geology, views, sand dunes
58. Lava Tubes	Easy	Nov–May	Unique geology
59. Teutonia Peak	Easy	Nov–May	Unique geology, views, Joshua trees
61. Black Hill Trail	Easy	All	Coastal views, Morro Rock
63. Moonstone Beach Trail	Easy	All	Beach, wildlife
64. Limekiln State Park	Easy	All	Waterfall, redwoods, lush forest, limekilns
66. Ewoldsen Trail/McWay Falls	Moderate	All	Waterfall, redwoods, lush forest

67.	Pfeiffer Falls/Valley View	Easy	All	Waterfall, redwoods, lush forest
68.	Andrew Molera State Park Beach Trail	Easy	All	Wildlife, wildflowers, beach views
70.	Trona Pinnacles	Easy	Nov–Mar	Unique geology
72.	Trail of 100 Giants/Dome Rock	Easy	Mar–Nov	Views, giant sequoia
74.	Jordan Peak Lookout	Easy	May–Sept	Views, historic lookout
77.	Congress Trail	Easy	All	Giant sequoias
81.	Boole Tree Loop	Easy	Mar–Oct	Views, giant sequoia
84.	Badwater	Easy	All	Lowest point in North America
85.	The Racetrack	Easy	Nov–Mar	Unique geology, secluded
90.	Schulman Grove	Easy	May–Nov	Ancient trees, views
92.	Devils Postpile/Rainbow Falls	Easy	May–Nov	Unique geology, waterfalls
94.	Parker Lake	Easy	All	Beautiful alpine lake, quaking aspens, wildflowers
95.	Mono Lake—South Tufa	Easy	All	Unique scenery, mountain backdrops, odd geology and life

Half-day hikes

5.	Big Laguna Trail	Easy	All	Wide-open mountaintop views, lake
8.	Pacific Crest Trail—Laguna Mountain Ridge	Easy	All	Clear desert vistas
17.	Pine City	Easy	Nov–Mar	Historic mine settlement, pinyon pines
19.	Alta Seca Bench	Moderate	All	Views, off-trail exploration
29.	Cougar Crest	Moderate	All	Lake views, mountaintop vistas
30.	Delamar Mountain	Moderate	All	Mountain views, boulder outcroppings
33.	Pine Mountain	Strenuous	May–Nov	Secluded trail, mountaineering path, mountain views
35.	Mount Hawkins	Strenuous	All	Pine forest, mountain views
36.	Waterman Mountain	Moderate	All	Pine forest, mountain views
41.	Malibu Creek	Easy	All	Lovely lake, creek, oak-lined path, historic movie and television site
43.	Backbone Trail—Zuma Canyon	Easy	All	Wildflowers, coastal chaparral habitat
48.	Potato Harbor	Easy	All	Undeveloped coast views
54.	Gaviota Hot Springs and Peak	Strenuous	All	Hot springs, coastal views
56.	Tehachapi Mountain	Moderate	All	Views, pine forest
60.	Valencia Peak/The Bluffs Loop	Moderate	All	Views, unique geology, wildlife, wildflowers
62.	Cerro Alto	Moderate	All	Coastal views
65.	Cone Peak	Moderate	All	Views, pine forest, wildflowers
69.	High Peaks/Balconies Cave Loop	Moderate	Sept–Mar	Unique geology, condors, views
71.	Manter Meadow	Moderate	Mar–Nov	Meadow, wildlife, wildflowers, secluded
73.	The Needles	Moderate	Mar–Nov	Views, historic lookout

79.	Big Baldy Ridge	Easy	May–Sept	Views, wildflowers
80.	Sunset Trail Loop	Moderate	All	Waterfalls, streams, giant sequioa
82.	Mist Falls	Moderate	May–Nov	Waterfall, river, lush valley, flowers
93.	San Joaquin Mountain	Strenuous	May–Nov	High Sierra views, incredible ridgeline
96.	Sentinel Dome/Taft Point Loop	Easy	May–Nov	Views, strange geology
99.	Cathedral Lakes	Moderate	May–Nov	Views, alpine lakes and meadows, wildflowers
100.	Mount Dana	Very strenuous	May–Nov	Views, wildflowers, alpine meadows
Long day hikes				
12.	Sitton Peak	Strenuous	Nov–May	Views, spring, historic trail
14.	Lost Palms Oasis	Moderate	Nov–Mar	Fan palm oasis, rock formations
20.	Martinez Mountain	Extremely strenuous	Nov–Mar	Stunning desert peak, views
21.	Lion Peak	Moderate	All	Solitude, wide ridgetop vistas
22.	Devils Slide Trail to Tahquitz Peak	Strenuous	May–Nov	Pine forest, views, historic lookout
23.	Fuller Ridge to San Jacinto Peak	Extremely strenuous	May–Nov	Incredible views, lush forest
24.	San Gorgonio Peak via Fish Creek	Extremely strenuous	May–Nov	Alpine scenery, solitude, mountaintop vista
25.	Momyer Creek	Extremely strenuous	May–Nov	Mountain vistas, alpine scenery
26.	Dollar Lake	Very strenuous	May–Nov	Alpine lake, lush creek and forest
27.	San Bernardino Peak	Extremely strenuous	May–Nov	Historic land survey marker, breathtaking views
31.	Bighorn Peak	Extremely strenuous	May–Nov	Lush creek, alpine vistas
32.	Mount Baldy	Extremely strenuous	Mar–Nov	Incredible mountain vista and trail loop
34.	Bridge to Nowhere	Strenuous	Sept–Mar	Scenic river crossings, riparian woodland, interesting structures
46.	Smugglers Cove	Moderate	All	Undeveloped coast views, rugged beach, old ranch house
47.	El Montanon	Strenuous	All	Undeveloped coast views, unique mountain vista
50.	Rancho Nuevo/ Deal Canyon Loop	Strenuous	All	Gorgeous canyon, riparian habitat
51.	Vincent Tumaiiat Trail— Peak to Peak	Strenuous	Mar–Oct	Summit views, forested ridgeline

52.	Painted Rock	Strenuous	All	Native American rock art, views
53.	Manzana Schoolhouse	Strenuous	All	Historic schoolhouse, riparian woodland
75.	Franklin Lakes	Very strenuous	May–Sept	Views, wildlife, alpine lakes, wildflowers
78.	Alta Peak	Extremely strenuous	May–Sept	Incredible views, wildflowers, wildlife
83.	Telescope Peak	Very strenuous	All	Views of lowest and highest point in continental United States
86.	Olancha Peak	Extremely strenuous	May–Nov	Views, meadows, secluded trail
87.	Mount Whitney	Extremely strenuous	June–Nov	Lakes, alpine scenery, highest mountain in California
88.	Kearsarge Pass to Mount Gould	Extremely strenuous	May–Nov	Lakes, alpine scenery
89.	Bishop Pass	Strenuous	May–Nov	Lakes, streams, alpine scenery
91.	White Mountain Peak	Very strenuous	May–Nov	Views, third-highest mountain in California
97.	Half Dome via Glacier Point to Happy Isles	Extremely strenuous	May–Nov	Views, waterfalls, death-defying drops
98.	Clouds Rest	Strenuous	May–Nov	Views, alpine lakes and meadows

Short overnight hikes

35.	Mount Hawkins	Strenuous	All	Pine forest, mountain views
45.	Anacapa Lighthouse Trail	Easy	All	Undeveloped coast views, old lighthouse
49.	Forbush Flat	Easy	All	Views, oak woodland
71.	Manter Meadow	Moderate	Mar–Nov	Meadow, wildlife, wildflowers, secluded
94.	Parker Lake	Easy	All	Beautiful alpine lake, quaking aspens, wildflowers

Long overnight hikes

23.	Fuller Ridge to San Jacinto Peak	Extremely strenuous	May–Nov	Incredible views, lush forest
24.	San Gorgonio Peak via Fish Creek	Extremely strenuous	May–Nov	Alpine scenery, solitude, mountaintop vista
27.	San Bernardino Peak	Extremely strenuous	May–Nov	Historic land survey marker, breathtaking views
47.	El Montanon	Strenuous	All	Undeveloped coast views, unique mountain vista
53.	Manzana Schoolhouse	Strenuous	All	Historic schoolhouse, riparian woodland
75.	Franklin Lakes	Very strenuous	May–Sept	Views, wildlife, alpine lakes, wildflowers
76.	Hamilton Lakes	Strenuous	May–Sept	Views, wildlife, alpine lakes, wildflowers

78.	Alta Peak	Extremely strenuous	May–Sept	Incredible views, wildflowers, wildlife
87.	Mount Whitney	Extremely strenuous	June–Nov	Lakes, alpine scenery, highest mountain in California
88.	Kearsarge Pass to Mount Gould	Extremely strenuous	May–Nov	Lakes, alpine scenery
89.	Bishop Pass	Strenuous	May–Nov	Lakes, streams, alpine scenery
97.	Half Dome via Glacier Point to Happy Isles	Extremely strenuous	May–Nov	Views, waterfalls, death-defying drops
98.	Clouds Rest	Strenuous	May–Nov	Views, alpine lakes and meadows
99.	Cathedral Lakes	Moderate	May–Nov	Views, alpine lakes and meadows, wildflowers

KEY TO MAP SYMBOLS

═══════ freeway	○ ○ city or town	🛡76 🛡276 interstate highway
────── major highway	■ building	⬡6 ⬡206 U.S. highway
────── other paved road	★ point of interest	⬡94 state highway
============ graded or dirt road	▲ peak or summit	⬡S2 county road
------------ featured trail	)(pass	21505 National Forest road
············ other trail	⚌ bridge	river or stream
·—·—·— park or wilderness boundary	⅄ picnic area	waterfall
—··—··— state boundary	⛰ campground	lake, bay, or ocean
ⓟ parking	🕯 lighthouse	lake and dam
ⓣ trailhead	⚔ mine	spring

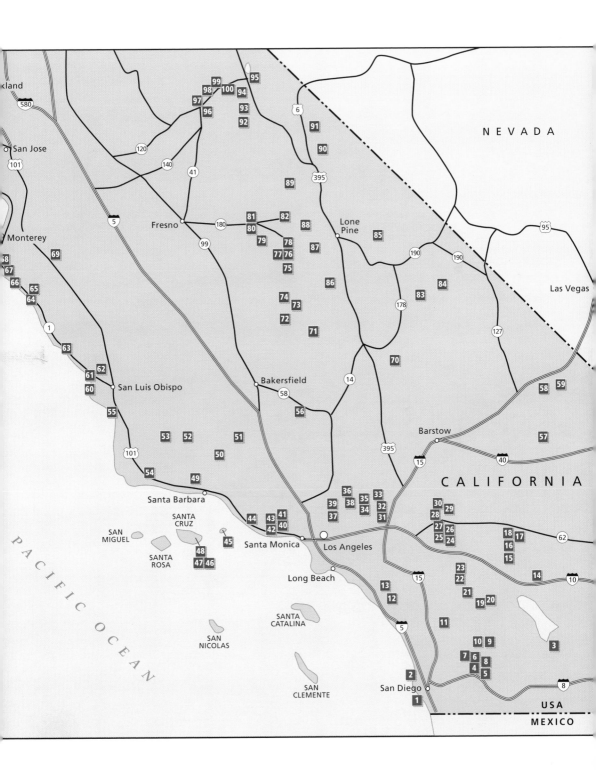

INTRODUCTION

Southern California is a land of extremes, from arid deserts and coastal beaches to soaring peaks that tower high above some of the world's most cosmopolitan cities. Forests and public lands coexist with some of the most expensive real estate in the world, while the region's national and state parks are unmatched in sheer beauty, size, magnitude, and wildness in the lower forty-eight states. The beauty is unquestionable. What is surprising, however, is that so much unspoiled splendor exists within just a short distance of the growing sprawl of the region's urban centers. A simple thirty-to-sixty-minute drive can take most Southern Californians into the heart of the wild.

Geographically speaking, the 37th parallel north divides California almost directly in half, and all but twelve of the hikes described in this book are south of this line. Most—more than sixty—are south of San Luis Obispo. Most people in Southern California are travelers, however, and certain regions like Mammoth Lakes and Yosemite National Park were included here too, simply because of their popular "getaway" status for Southern Californians. Nearly half of the hikes are specifically in the southland counties of Los Angeles, Orange, Riverside, San Bernardino, Imperial, and San Diego, with more than a third within easy driving access of the Los Angeles area. The idea was to provide a sampling of the greatest, most "classic" hikes the area has to offer. Some of these hikes are perfect for a weekend retreat, while others await nearby in the urban areas' proverbial backyards.

Selecting a hundred "classic" hikes obviously involved subjective taste, but several factors influenced a hike's inclusion in this book. Scenery was always first and foremost, whether a turnaround mountain vista or cascading brook. Uniqueness was also a critical factor. Southern California has many things to offer that appear nowhere else in the world. Water, wildlife, geology, and even history played important roles in determining which hikes were selected.

All in all, included in this book are a great variety of hikes, from leisurely strolls to epic adventures. Some are suited for pets and children, while others are only for the hardiest souls ready for adventure. Most hikes in this book are accessible to passenger vehicles; only eight require high-clearance and/or four-wheel-drive vehicles, and those hikes are suitably marked. Some of the roads may be unpaved, slow-going, and bumpy, but most hikes are accessed via pavement. Nearly all of the hikes listed are on maintained trail, though ten of the hikes utilize some off-trail scrambling and/or mountaineer-use trails. Those, too, are marked within the text.

Note: Fees and/or permits may be required for day or overnight use of public lands. Make sure you contact the appropriate agencies for up-to-date information about fees and permits before you depart for your hike. (Contact information is included for each hike in this book.)

GETTING STARTED

The best way to start hiking is to just do it. Set aside time in your monthly calendar and get out on the trails. Ask friends to join you, and explain that it is good for them and their health. If you have difficulty locating a partner, check websites or local hiking clubs, or just venture forth on your own. Hiking is relatively safe as long as good common sense is used.

Hiking is an activity that almost anyone can engage in. People at varying stages of fitness and ability can take pleasure in different trails and experience nature on an intrinsic level, sharing and exploring their own inner selves while enjoying the natural world. In fact, most people forget that hiking is also a great way to exercise; doing it consistently not only helps to keep you

Opposite: The coast is never far away in the Santa Monica Mountains, where secluded beaches still exist.

A safe and steady hip-deep stream crossing

in shape but also conditions your body for longer and harder hikes, assuring you a life of health and fitness.

Make certain not to overdo it, though. Start out slowly and head for the more popular trails. Talk to people you meet and learn about the activity of hiking itself, along with the plant life, fauna, and other features of the natural world.

HIKING

Always stay on the trail. Please follow specific guidelines for each trail. If there is an informational kiosk at the trailhead, make certain that you read all of the data on it. Pack out all your trash, plus any you find on the trail. You will be sharing the trail with other hikers, equestrians, and in some areas mountain bikes. Large animals have the right of way, so step aside and let them pass. Purify all water with a filter, iodine, or boiling before drinking.

CAMPING

Pack out what you pack in. Pay fees before using any campsite. Wilderness camping is fine in many areas as long as "Leave No Trace" practices are used and camping takes place at least a mile from roads and other campgrounds, and 200 feet from streams and water sources.

WHAT TO TAKE

Almost every experienced hiker has a horror story about something that went wrong while hiking, from spending a night (or at least a few hours) lost on the trail, to sustaining an injury, or just plain being a little unsure of what was going to happen. Some of the stories are quite a bit more interesting, i.e., scarier, than others, while many are simply tales of taking the wrong turn at a trail marker and having to spend a few extra miles without the luxury of food or water.

What a person puts into a backpack certainly varies from hiker to hiker, but there are specific lifesaving items that should be carried every time you leave the house. The items you take in your backpack will ultimately decide what type of "horror" stories you will end up telling. Better to have along something that may keep you safe than to leave it at home. While this book is not a how-to-hike manual, the Ten Essentials of hiking are a vital necessity. Truly, when one ventures forth into the wild, there is no guarantee of safety, and the better prepared one is for any eventuality, the better chance there is of surviving any occurrence from the mundane to the life-threatening. The Ten Essentials are basically a small survival kit designed to be the minimal amount of items that could successfully save a life, whether your own or a companion's. These items should be taken along on every hike:

1. **Navigational materials (maps and compass).** While compass skills are not essential on most trails, having a detailed topographic map is a necessity, unless you are already familiar with the trails and landmarks in the area. A portable Global Positioning System (GPS) unit is a good idea for off-trail and cross-country navigation, and is an easy way to keep track of where you are and where your car is parked.

2. **Sun protection (sunglasses, wide-brimmed hat, and sunscreen).** At higher elevations, the sun's rays are very damaging. There is more ultraviolet radiation and less atmosphere. The risk of burning is exponentially greater the higher you go. Spend a summer day at the beach without sunblock and you'll get a bad sunburn. Spend all day in the mountains and you could end up in the hospital with third-degree burns. Sun protection is a must for all complexions.

3. **Insulation (extra clothing).** Clothing should be layered when hiking, so that you can take layers off or add them as needed. Avoid cotton. Cotton does not retain its warmth when wet, and clothing should be your foremost protection against hypothermia and heat exhaustion. Neoprene, wool, or polyester shirts retain their insulating properties even when wet. A number of manufacturers make underapparel that works wonders for keeping you cool or warm depending on the need. Fleece is a superb second

layer. Fleece retains its ability to insulate when wet. Hikers in the know understand that vigorously swinging a fleece sweater above your head will force the water molecules from the fabric, giving you a dry layer in seconds. Rain protection is not a necessity on most hikes in Southern California, though it is advisable for backpacking trips. A little water never hurt anyone, but the first time you hike in torrential rain without raingear, you'll gain a better understanding of its value. Luckily, most days in Southern California are sunny, even in wintertime. The mountains do harbor their own climates, however, and storms can appear rapidly, so it is a good idea to carry at least some sort of rudimentary rain protection. Gloves and thermal head protection are also a good bet. Peaks can be chilly and windswept even in summer.

4. **Illumination (headlamp or flashlight).** After water and fire, light is the next most important thing on this list. It can mean the difference between having to spend the night underprepared on a cold mountain trail, or stumbling out after dark and hopping in your car and driving home. Of course, you should always set turnaround times and never push the time factor, but there are reasons why this list is called "essential."

5. **First-aid supplies.** You should always carry some type of first-aid kit, with a minimum such as bandages (both adhesive and cloth), antibiotic ointment, alcohol wipes, a multitool pocketknife, and first-aid tape (duct tape works as a fine substitute for repairing all sorts of things, not just body parts).

6. **Fire (firestarter and matches/lighter).** Being able to keep warm in a life-threatening emergency is the most important factor to staying alive. If you hike for enough years, chances are that you will eventually spend a night under the stars that you hadn't planned on. It happens at least once even to the best of us. However, fire is never to be taken lightly. In recent years, several boneheads have accidentally destroyed many of Southern California's forests without using the proper precautions that one would use to start a barbecue. Please understand that Southern California is an arid region that has used fire suppression as a forest-management tool for over a century. Thoughtless fires can be deadly to you and others. Starting a fire should be your last resort, and even then, proper precautions should be taken. Clear the area in a ten-foot radius and build an enclosure so that your fire will not escape its bounds. The smaller the better for both fire and enclosure. Before you leave make sure that your fire is completely extinguished. And again, fire should only be used in the direst of life-and-death emergencies.

7. **Repair kit and tools (including knife).** A multitool pocketknife and duct tape can serve both as part of your first-aid kit and a basic repair kit. For long trips fishing line and a needle are a good idea and superglue can work miracles for many items including boots.

8. **Nutrition (extra food).** Always take enough food so that if you should have to spend an unexpected night out-of-doors, you can at least do so with a full belly and still have enough to last you on the hike out the next day.

9. **Hydration (extra water).** A quick rule of thumb is for every hour spent hiking, you should drink between sixteen and twenty-four ounces of water. More liquid should be ingested as temperatures rise. Sipping along the way is a good way to stay hydrated, with occasional stops for longer drinks. Make certain to take more water than you will need. It is also advisable to carry a water filter or iodine tablets for water purification should the need arise.

10. **Emergency shelter.** Most day hikers do not carry tents to the top of local mountains, although the cautious may want to do just that. It is a bit of overkill, but a

Summits like Mount Whitney can produce an ethereal glow after a summer thundershower.

lightweight tarp tent is an option for those who desire to be prudent. A space blanket is a much more modest and adequate substitute for a heavy tent. While it may not provide the most effective cover, it will supply sufficient warmth and protection to keep you alive should disaster strike.

PERMITS AND FEES

California has more national forest land, wilderness, and parks than any state except Alaska, which means that there is ample room to stretch your legs and wander. However, before you set out on your adventures it is important to understand the rules and regulations of the area you plan to hike in. Wilderness areas have their own guidelines, districts under the Bureau of Land Management have different rules than do national forests, so make sure you comprehend the laws and necessary permits before undertaking any outdoor hiking.

Many of the hikes in this book are located in Southern California's national forests. In 2002, the Recreation Fee Program made it mandatory to purchase an Adventure Pass for the Angeles, San Bernardino, Cleveland, and Los Padres national forests. Passes are required for parking your vehicle in most areas in the forest, and at the time this book went to press cost $5 daily, or $30 for an annual pass. A second vehicle pass is an additional $5. (**Note:** Before you depart for your hike, make sure to call the appropriate agency listed in this book for up-to-date information about permit and fee requirements.) Fee revenues have been used for clean-up, maintenance, improvements, and building new facilities within the forests. Many people oppose the passes based upon our right as citizens and taxpayers to free use of public lands. There are positive arguments on both sides of the issue, but regardless of how you feel about it, you will be cited if you do not display the pass from your rearview mirror when you park at a trailhead.

United States Forest Service (USFS)

The USFS manages the Inyo, Los Padres, Angeles, San Bernardino, and Cleveland national forests, which cover many of the hikes in this book. It has jurisdiction over all wilderness and recreation areas within national forest lands, and these areas have stricter regulations that must be heeded as well.

Wilderness Areas

The national Wilderness Act of 1964 defined wilderness as "an area where the earth and its community of life are untrammeled by man, where man himself is a visitor who does not remain." This principle governs the regulations that surround wilderness, and the general guidelines are as follows:

Visitors must have a permit to enter national wilderness areas. This goes for the majority of wilderness areas in Southern California. Normally, the permits are easy to get; all you have to do is stop by the visitor center and talk to a ranger, or self-register at a kiosk. The San Gorgonio area in Southern California is the only wilderness area that has quotas on hiking trails. Campsites can be more difficult to secure as they are in limited supply. If you get your permit in advance or very early in the morning, you should not have any trouble, unless you plan to visit on crowded weekends. Campfires are prohibited entirely in many wilderness areas, except in specifically designated yellow-post campsites. Check before you go.

Groups should be no larger than twelve persons and possess no more than eight stock animals. Camping is only permitted in designated areas. Stock animals cannot be camped within 200 feet of meadows, streams, or trails. It is illegal to dispose of garbage, debris, and other waste materials. Using substances that may pollute bodies of water is also illegal.

Visitors to the wilderness need to carry a hand trowel or shovel for the disposal of human waste in a "cat hole" at least six inches deep and 200 feet away from both trails and water. Please pack out all toilet paper in locking plastic baggies. It is illegal to operate machinery of any kind, including any type of bicycle or wheeled cart. Wheelchair use is permitted, however, under the Americans with Disabilities Act. Small battery-powered devices such as flashlights, GPS units, cell phones, and cameras are allowed. Smoking is only permitted in a seated area that has been cleared of all flammable material at least three feet in all directions.

Lastly, all pets are required to be on a leash or otherwise confined.

National Park Service (NPS)

National parks are protected areas set aside to preserve, protect, and share the natural, cultural, and recreational legacies of the United States. Several national parks are covered in this book, including Mojave National Preserve; Santa Monica Mountains National Recreation Area; Cabrillo and Pinnacles national monuments and Joshua Tree, Channel Islands, Death Valley, Yosemite, Kings Canyon, and Sequoia national parks. Fees range from free to $20 for a seven-day pass. Annual passes to all of America's national parks can be purchased for $80 and are good for entrance to every unit managed under the National Park Service.

State Parks, Preserves, and Beaches

State parks are also protected areas that are set aside to protect, preserve, and share the cultural, natural, and recreational legacies of their state. These areas are sometimes just as beautiful as national parks, but perhaps on a smaller scale, or simply not as significant in the national spectrum. California's state park system is perhaps the greatest in the nation. Several of the state parks in this book expose beauty beyond compare.

Fees for state parks range from free to $10 for some of the more popular state beaches. An annual pass is available that grants entrance to every state park for $125.

Other Lands

Some areas in this book are managed by the United States Department of Fish and Game, the federal Bureau of Land Management, or various city or county agencies, among others. Most of these agencies have their own rules, but are generally much less stringent than regulations for some of the more popular national park and state park regions and trails. Be sure to check with the appropriate management agencies before departing on a hike if you have questions about land usage.

HOW TO USE THIS BOOK

This book is an introduction to the best that Southern California has to offer in many different areas. Further exploration will lead you to find your own favorites and some hidden gems, but the trails covered here are meant to give you a good sampling of the most beautiful and interesting places in Southern California. Seasonal variations may close some of the trails at times or make them impassable. At other times, entire forests can shut down due to fire season. Trails can be washed out or compromised during winter storms. It is best to contact the agency that manages the area you want to hike in, before your trip. You can get up-to-date information and be informed of any hazards.

Phone numbers and website *information* for each hike are given with the hike description. *Distances* are measured in miles by GPS units. GPS provides remarkable accuracy; sometimes the measurements will differ slightly than that on maps or trail signs. Still, trail measurements are never exact, and a little variation should be expected when hiking. Elevation and steepness of trail can impact how long a trail seems, so it is not an exact science anyway. Hike *difficulty* is given as a figure that represents a hiker of average ability and fitness. *Hiking time* is based upon a mile for every thirty minutes of hiking. This is a rough estimate and some people will walk slower, others faster. The trails at a glance chart can also help to quickly locate suitable hikes for your fitness level and desired trip length. The overall map can quickly help you to locate hikes in your area.

Difficulty of a hike is not an exact science, either; many factors come into play in deciding the rigor of a hike. The baseline guide used in this book, however, is as follows. "Easy" hikes are always less than 5 miles, and do not gain more than 1000 feet of elevation. "Moderate" hikes are usually between 5–8 miles and climb 1000–2000

Varieties of purple penstemon and other wildflowers grow throughout Southern California.

feet in overall elevation gain. "Strenuous" hikes are usually more than 5 miles in length and can ascend anywhere between 2000–3000 feet. "Very strenuous" hikes are all more than 5 miles in length and rise between 3000–4000 feet in altitude from start to finish. "Extremely strenuous" hikes gain severe amounts of elevation and travel distances of 10 miles and more. Any trip that gains more than 4000 feet of elevation and 10 miles distance requires you to be in excellent health. These trips should not be attempted until you have mastered several easier hikes. Other factors that influence the difficulty rating of a hike can include steep gains and losses, scrambling over loose rock, or traveling off-trail. Additional considerations may also apply. Make sure the hikes you take are within your ability range. The smartest way to avoid mistakes in the wilderness is in the planning stages.

Elevation gain can be a little misleading. This is the amount of elevation gained between the lowest point on the hike and the highest point reached, so some hikes that undulate up and down multiple times over ridges, mountains, and hills will gain much more elevation than what is listed in the information block. Be sure to look at the elevation profile to get a better idea of what is expected from each hike. A 1000-foot elevation gain at the very end of a long day on the trail can be a real pain if it is unexpected.

High points are listed for peaks and to note where the trail tops out in elevation. Higher elevations are much more subject to adverse weather conditions and lower temperatures. Hikes with tall high points are good to take in summertime, while those at lower elevations are better suited for the wintertime.

Seasons are listed on hikes because access can be limited due to snow, rain, heat, and fire conditions. These are general guidelines; sometimes hikes can be taken at other times throughout the year, with additional planning and caution.

TRAIL ETIQUETTE

While there are no established rules for how to behave on a trail, there are a few guidelines that should be followed. Courtesy is always appreciated: that is the basic mantra that governs how one should behave while partaking in activities in the great outdoors.

When recreating in wild areas, it is important to refrain from boisterous activities. People go hiking to escape the noise of everyday life and the city; no one trying to enjoy the outdoors wants to hear a group of people shouting to one another. Talking is fine; yelling, however, is not. Group size should be limited, too. Wilderness regulations stipulate no more than twelve people to a group, but even that is a pretty large group. Try to keep the number of people below seven or eight, or for large parties split up into different groups and meet up along the trail at a specific location. The local trail is not really the place for a large-scale expedition.

If you take a cell phone, and it gets reception, only use it in case of emergency. Be aware of others and try to keep phone calls to a minimum. It is the outdoors, after all.

On trails, horses and pack animals always have the right of way. Step aside downhill and let them pass. It is courteous to step aside and let other hikers pass as well, especially when they are ascending up an incline; it takes more energy for them to get going again.

It is a good rule of thumb to at least say hello to passing hikers. Who knows, sometimes greeting others will garner you valuable information about vista points or hidden treasures, or possibly even grow into a valuable friendship. Sometimes, the easiest way to find a hiking partner is to meet one on the trail.

Although mountain bikes do not have the right of way and pedestrians do, it is generally easier, and always courteous, to step aside when cyclists approach. Mountain biking is becoming more popular and, as a rule, cyclists are obeying the rules and the guidelines of common courtesy as well.

If you bring pets, keep them on a leash, especially if they are not under voice command. In some areas it is illegal to bring dogs, and in others it is illegal to have them off-leash. If dogs are unruly or vicious, leave them at home; there simply is no place in the wild for a mean dog. Also, make sure to keep doggie bags on hand to clean up after them. The areas that allow dogs are becoming fewer and farther between due to the

The island scrub jay is native to Santa Cruz Island.

thoughtlessness of a few bad pet owners. Being responsible is the key.

LEAVE NO TRACE

"Leave No Trace" is a national (and now international) movement designed to protect the outdoors and our wild heritage. From 1965 to 1984, the number of annual backcountry visits increased from four million to over fifteen million. That number has easily doubled or even quadrupled with the coming of age of Generations X and Y. Urbanization and suburban sprawl are impinging upon the wilderness and forest areas more than ever. These impacts are seriously threatening the integrity of our forests and wild places. Leave No Trace is more of an ethical paradigm than a set of strict rules or harsh guidelines. The basic principle of Leave No Trace is that all visitors to the outdoors should aim to leave no harmful impacts on the land. This ethic should be encouraged and taught to anyone who uses the outdoors, especially the young and those new to hiking and other outdoor activities. Everyone has to pitch in if we wish to keep these lands intact for shared future usage. It is up to all of us to keep our wild places unspoiled.

Even people who love the outdoors are prone to neglectful mistakes. Take, for instance, sunflower seeds. They are wonderful to eat, make for great high-sodium trail food , but their discarded husks are unsightly when covering a trail. Many people do not understand that in an arid environment, it may take over ten years for the shell of a sunflower seed to decompose. Likewise, one irresponsible campfire might not pose a significant risk, but if millions of visitors irresponsibly built campfires in the backcountry, there wouldn't be much of a backcountry left. Please, encourage the use of Leave No Trace ethics to everyone you know, everywhere you go.

There are seven guiding principles behind the Leave No Trace movement:

1. Plan Ahead and Prepare

- Learn the rules and special conditions of the places you plan to visit.
- Be prepared for exceptional circumstances, such as hazards, drastic changes in weather, and emergencies.
- Go during off-times; schedule your trips for times when areas are less crowded.
- Go with small groups of people. For larger outings, split into groups of four to six.
- Reduce waste by taking only the food and packaging you will need.
- Use a Global Positioning System (GPS), or map and compass. Do not build cairns or mark a trail in any way with paint or flags.

2. Travel and Camp on Durable Surfaces

- Durable surfaces are previously established trails and campsites, rock, gravel, dry grasses, snow, and dirt.
- Keep wetland and riparian areas protected by camping at least 200 feet away from water sources.
- Campsites are found, not made. Do not alter campsites.

If you travel in heavy-use areas:
- Stay on the trail and camp only in designated campsites.

- Always stay in the middle of the trail, single file, even if the trail is muddy or wet.
- Make your campsites as compact as possible. Stay in areas where there is no vegetation.

In pristine or wilderness areas:
- Spread out to avoid the creation of new campsites and trails.
- Do not camp or walk in areas showing signs of impact.

3. Dispose of Waste Properly

- Whatever you pack in, pack it out. Always try to carry out more refuse than you took in. Always check your campsite and carry out all trash, leftover food, and litter.
- Keep all solid human waste in a "cat hole." These should be dug six to eight inches deep in the ground, and always at least 200 feet from water, campgrounds, and trails. Always cover and disguise the cat hole.
- Do not bury toilet paper. It does not degrade, and animals will dig it up. Pack it out in locking plastic bags.
- If you must wash dishes, carry all water at least 200 feet away from the water source. Only use small amounts of biodegradable soap. Spread strained dishwater around on the ground.

4. Leave What You Find

- Protect and preserve history. You may look, but do not touch cultural or historic structures, artifacts, or other objects.
- Do not disturb rocks, plants, or anything else you might find on the trail. Leave things the way you found them.
- Do not transport or introduce non-native species.
- Do not create structures, dig trenches, or disturb the natural surroundings in any other way.

5. Minimize Campfire Impacts

- Do not build campfires if you can avoid them. Campfires can create lasting impacts in a wild setting. In desert environments, it may take thousands of years for ashes and campsites to degrade. Instead, use a stove for cooking and natural or battery-operated sources for light.

- If you do build a fire, use only established fire rings, and only in areas where campfires are permitted.
- Build small fires. Do not break off branches, or collect large pieces of fallen wood. Instead use only small sticks that can be broken by hand. This not only keeps the fire more maintainable, but also reduces smoke.
- Let fires burn all of their fuel and coals to ash. Make certain that they are entirely extinguished before leaving camp. Scatter and spread cool ashes.

6. Respect Wildlife
- Never approach wildlife; be observant from a distance. Do not try to follow wildlife, or let your dogs give chase.
- Never give food to animals. Animals have sensitive stomachs and diets. Feeding animals can upset the natural balance and change their behavior, endangering not only the animals but possibly humans as well. Feeding wildlife can be detrimental to their health, and expose them to predators.
- Store your food and trash securely. In bear country, use bear canisters and try to keep food scents off of you, your clothing, and your tent.
- Make certain to control pets at all times, either on voice command or on leash.
- Do not make contact with wildlife during critical and sensitive times such as rutting, mating, nesting, nursing, raising young, hibernation, or winter.

7. Be Considerate of Other Visitors
- Be thoughtful and courteous. People hiking uphill have the right of way, because it is harder for them to get started again. When hiking with dogs, it is always the courteous thing to leash your pets and step aside, allowing all other hikers to pass.
- Horses and other pack animals always have the right of way. Step off the trail to the downhill side to allow them room to pass. Always leash your pets when encountering large pack animals.

- Do not yell or sing loudly. Let wild sounds ring out, so that others may enjoy the silence and solitude that an outdoor experience should bring.

SAFETY

Being prepared is the best way to remain safe while walking in nature. Taking along the right equipment, especially properly fitting lightweight hiking boots and safety supplies (see What to Take) can make hiking a safer activity than sitting at home in front of the television. Planning ahead of time is the best way to remain safe. Get to know the area before hiking by studying maps and calling the ranger station. Watch the weather and get updates before setting out on an adventure. Let at least one person know the trail you are taking, where you are parking, and what time you expect to be arriving home. Give instructions to call the proper authorities should you not report by a specific time, in case something goes awry.

Hiking alone can be a therapeutic and incredibly enjoyable pastime, but it should only be done by those who are properly experienced and prepared. The greatest danger to a solo hiker is

Insects, arachnids, and arthropods are fascinating close up.

injury, and for this reason alone, it is imperative to always let at least one person know where you will be traveling. This point cannot be stressed enough. When traveling alone, always be alert for wildlife. Even though attacks are rare and generally victims are unaware they are being stalked, it is wise to keep your eyes and ears open while hiking on your own.

ANIMALS AND INSECTS

Many species of mammal live in Southern California, most of which will rarely be seen, unless you spend an inordinate amount of time in the wilderness and have infrared goggles to watch those that are nocturnal during their nightly work. Raccoon, skunk, black bear, coyote, deer, feral pig, bighorn sheep, mountain lion, and bobcat all prowl the local mountains. Smaller mammals such as squirrels, rodents, and chipmunks abound, but the larger creatures are seldom seen. Even mule deer are a rare sight, unless you know when and where to look.

All wild animals can be dangerous. Do not approach them or feed them. Most animals, even large mammals, are afraid of humans and will flee at the first sign of encounter. In fact, animals probably watch you a lot more than you watch them. Recently, highly publicized attacks by mountain lions in Southern California have dominated the news media. The reality is that these attacks are extremely rare, even though the frequency has increased due to human encroachment upon the animals' territory. Chances are that you will never come into contact with these majestic beasts.

If you should encounter a mountain lion, make noises and try to make yourself appear larger by raising your arms. *Never crouch.* Keep small children nearby at all times. Slowly stop and move away. Do not run, as this will trigger a chase response in the creature and make it think you are game. If you are attacked, fight back with all means at your disposal.

Bears will most likely flee when they notice you. It is a good idea to make noises as you hike so that you will never surprise a wild animal, since this is when they are the most dangerous. A publicized attack in the Angeles National Forest came a few years ago when a careless camper left his full pack out and unattended. The bear was later destroyed for having contact with humans. Never leave food items out in the open, always secure them in a bear canister or hang them properly from a tree.

Bighorn sheep are becoming increasingly rare in the southern part of the state. They are nearing extinction due to human encroachment upon their territory and increased predation by mountain lions. Bighorn sheep also have a limited amount of energy reserves due to the heat and extreme environment. Do not approach or harass the animals; undue stress can make it difficult for them to survive when drought conditions have undermined their food and water supplies.

A variety of reptiles live in Southern California, the most common being the common bluebelly lizard. Snakes are also common, though rarely seen. Rattlesnakes are the only reptiles in this region dangerous to you, but encounters can be greatly reduced if you monitor where you sit and place your hands. The telltale rattle is also a dead giveaway and a sign to back away from the slithering creature. Bites are venomous, but not immediately life-threatening. If you are bitten, wrap the affected area tightly and seek medical attention immediately.

There are a number of birds and bird migration routes in Southern California. Opportunities abound for bird watchers in national forests and public areas. Hawks, owls, turkey vultures, and other birds of prey are brilliant to watch. Many other species are fun to notice due to their striking color or appearance. Woodpeckers can be heard rattling trees in many forest areas, and roadrunners—running as fast as if Wile E. Coyote were after them—make the chase look exciting.

When it comes to insects and spiders, ticks are the biggest concern when hiking in low-lying regions and coastal areas of Southern California. Higher elevations do not harbor ticks, but ticks are abundant in lower regions especially after heavy rainfall. Use tweezers to get the bloodsuckers out of your skin. Make certain to remove all of the head and body parts, as infection can set in if these are not removed properly. Lyme disease is a threat in Southern California, though it is not nearly as prevalent here as in other regions

Mule deer are frequent visitors on many trails, especially early morning and just before dusk.

of America. Ticks also carry other diseases, so check yourself daily after hikes and remove them promptly. There are a variety of good topical preventative measures out there for ticks.

Mosquitoes have carried the West Nile virus to Southern California. DEET-based solutions can effectively keep mosquitoes away.

Black widow spiders are dangerous and potentially deadly to humans, but the bite is very rare. Black widows usually keep hidden. Tarantulas look imposing and their bites can hurt, but their venom is not poisonous to humans, and is considered nontoxic though the bite can produce swelling and stinging. The chances of a bite are slim even when handling the creature.

WEATHER

Southern California weather is usually warm and mild. However, mountain weather is entirely different and can change on a moment's notice. A pleasant day in the flatland can be windy, chilly, and wintry at 10,000 feet. Conversely, a wet day can create cloud cover below 6000 feet, while higher elevations allow you to look down on the storm from sun-filled heights.

It is very important to be prepared for all sorts of weather, and layer your clothing. It is always better to have items you may not need than to need them and not have them. Summer rainstorms can occur at any time in the higher elevations, and a winter excursion can turn deadly when you are not properly prepared. On the opposite end, the summer sun can cause blistering sunburn if you hike without sun protection, and high and dry temperatures can lead to heat ailments.

Lightning is a specific danger at high altitudes. Storms gather and build in mid- to late afternoon; tall mountain ranges can generate their own meteorological patterns. If clouds are building, keep a watchful eye on the weather. Always descend at the first sign of a storm. It is better to return another day than to press on and not make it back. As a mountain adage explains, the mountain will always be there tomorrow.

Every year, hikers are lured to the high mountains of Southern California in the wintertime. This can be a rewarding experience if you are properly prepared and outfitted and have knowledge of how to use the right equipment. However, the quick and easy access afforded by roads gives some a fool's hope of achieving beyond their ability level. Roads lead all the way up to the base of Mount Baldy, San Gorgonio, San Jacinto, and even some Sierran summits. The mountains are unforgiving, and the mild coastal winters do not translate well into alpine climates. Every year, people die in the mountains because of tragic mistakes and hubris. Never overestimate your own ability, and be ready to turn back if you encounter any situation you are not prepared for.

OTHER HAZARDS

Poison oak is ubiquitous in elevations below 5000 feet in coastal canyons and along streams. This noxious plant can grow anywhere, though it prefers shady areas along waterways. The oil from the plant enters your pores and spreads to everything you touch until it is washed off. Some soaps can further spread the oil instead of dissipating it. The plant is harmful even in winter, when the leftover twigs still secrete the oil. If you touch poison oak, wash all exposed skin vigorously in cold water with oil-dispersing agents that can be bought at any drugstore.

Flash floods, mudslides, and avalanches are uncommon occurrences that can affect you if you are in the wrong place at the wrong time. Avoid hiking in canyons during or directly after heavy rainfall. Also avoid hiking in avalanche paths. Keep an eye on your surroundings, and always be aware of what is going on around you. Keep abreast of changes in the weather, and always err on the side of caution.

GET INVOLVED

Increasingly, America's wild and public lands are at risk because of developers, mining interests, overpopulation, poor planning, pollution, and a host of other detrimental factors. Southern California's forests need your voice. There are many ways to become active: voting, word of mouth, volunteering, joining a hiking group of like-minded individuals, or donating money to groups whose ideals you support. There are a number of good nonprofit organizations that vigorously defend America's last remaining wild spaces. Use your voice, and let your views be heard.

A NOTE ABOUT SAFETY

Safety is an important concern in all outdoor activities. No guidebook can alert you to every hazard or anticipate the limitations of every reader. Therefore, the descriptions of roads, trails, routes, and natural features in this book are not representations that a particular place or excursion will be safe for your party. When you follow any of the routes described in this book, you assume responsibility for your own safety. Under normal conditions, such excursions require the usual attention to traffic, road and trail conditions, weather, terrain, the capabilities of your party, and other factors. Keeping informed on current conditions and exercising common sense are the keys to a safe, enjoyable outing.

The Mountaineers Books

Opposite: The Cuyamacas and Laguna Mountains offer amazing views, such as this one from Stonewall Peak.

SAN DIEGO, IMPERIAL, AND ORANGE COUNTIES

CABRILLO NATIONAL MONUMENT

The Cabrillo National Monument is a small but quaint piece of Americana that is deserving of a visit. The park commemorates the landing of Portuguese explorer Juan Rodriguez Cabrillo at San Diego Bay in 1542. A short hike leads to a startling overview of the city of San Diego and its natural harbor. A historic lighthouse stands sentinel over the tiny reserve, and the high prominent plateau serves as a wonderful spot from which to look for migrating whales in the winter.

1 BAYSIDE TRAIL

Distance: 2.1 miles round-trip
Hiking time: 1 hour
Difficulty: Easy
Elevation gain: 350 feet
High point: 415 feet
Season: All
Water: None, bring your own
Fees and permits: Required
Map: USGS Point Loma
Information: Cabrillo National Monument, (619) 557-5450, *www.nps.gov/cabr/*

Getting there: From Hotel Circle in San Diego, take Interstate 8 west to its end and veer left onto Nimitz Boulevard. A little over half a mile down the road, take the overpass to your right to get onto Catalina Boulevard. It is signed for Cabrillo National Monument. Follow Catalina all the way to the entrance kiosk for the monument.

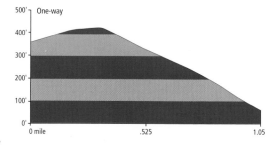

Cabrillo National Monument doesn't have very many hikes, and this really isn't much of a traditional hike either. The entire trip takes place on a paved road that descends for 1 mile along the San Diego Bay coastline. Eventually, it drops very close to the ocean and comes to a fence that separates the national monument from the adjoining military reservation and national cemetery.

Despite the fact that there isn't a "real" trail, an escape from civilization, or even seclusion, there is something quite magical about Cabrillo that gives this hike a classic appeal. The jutting edge of Point Loma sticks out so far and has been such

a danger to mariners that not one but two light-houses were built upon this spot. The historic one that sits on top of the point is the first stop made on this hike. The lighthouse, completed in 1855, is open year-round but the vantage point from the lantern room is only open two days out of the year: November 15 and August 25, the anniversary of the first lighting of the lamp and the date of the inception of the National Park Service, respectively.

The lighthouse, at 462 feet above sea level, is the highest in the nation. When it was operating, its light could be seen for many miles on the sea, but only on clear days. Often, the fog made the lighthouse useless, so a new one was built at the base of the point.

From the lighthouse continue down the main road toward the point. The Bayside Trail is closed to vehicle traffic, and clearly marked. Turn left onto the trail and begin the descent toward the ocean. The road wraps around, providing tremendous views of San Diego, the open ocean, and all of the military, maritime, and air traffic of this bustling port. It is easy to get a sense of why this bay was so important to early navigators, due to its size and geography.

This is a great trail for children. One, it isn't very long. Two, it has sights and sounds that children will enjoy. Three, combined with a trip to the museum, it makes an outing that the entire family can enjoy. Not very many people take this hike, so there is an element of getting away from it all. Watching the planes, ships, and hustle and bustle of San Diego makes it all worthwhile, and gives the Bayside Trail a worthy destination all its own.

A bumblebee adorns a coastal sunflower.

TORREY PINES STATE BEACH AND RESERVE

The Torrey Pines State Reserve, containing 8 miles of trail, is one of the wildest and last large open spaces along the Southern California coastline. It is located entirely within the city of San Diego, but is completely undeveloped. The reserve protects a rare species of pine that grows only here and on Santa Rosa Island. Hiking trails lead along bluffs throughout the reserve, down to beautiful unspoiled beaches and a lagoon that is important in the Pacific Flyway migratory bird route.

The park contains over two thousand acres of open space and is a fairly popular recreational outing for San Diegans, especially university students. Many people run along the trails and beaches.

2 RAZOR TRAIL

Distance: 1.25 miles round-trip
Hiking time: 1 hour
Difficulty: Easy
Elevation gain: 225 feet
High point: 360 feet
Season: All
Water: None, bring your own
Fees and permits: Required
Map: USGS Del Mar OE W
Information: Torrey Pines State Beach and Reserve, (858) 755-2063,
www.parks.ca.gov/default.asp?page_id=657

Getting there: From La Jolla, take Interstate 5 north for about 3.5 miles, then take the Genesee exit, traveling west toward the ocean. Make a right onto Torrey Pines Road. You will drive past a golf course. When you see the slough and wetlands to your right, turn left into the Torrey Pines State Beach and Reserve.

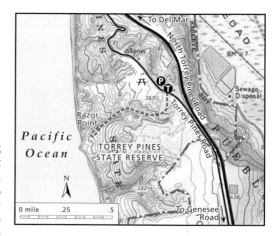

The trail begins at the south end of the parking lot behind the bathrooms. A bit of elevation is lost as the trail winds its way toward the ocean and panoramic Razor Point. There is plenty to look at along the way, from the wonderfully picturesque and rare trees that give the reserve its namesake, to the wide chasm that is Razor Gorge, the eroded red earthen badlands near the point, and the stunning ocean views from the point itself.

To access the point, make a right turn at

0.5 mile. The way is well-signed and particularly easy to follow. There are plenty of beautiful wildflowers and an abundance of coastal sage; the chaparral along the coastline is stunning. In

Badlands erode into the sea at Razor Point.

spring the blossoms are plentiful, but moisture from the ocean provides enough sustenance for many species to bloom all year.

The reserve is a great place for bird-watching; most surveys turn up nearly one hundred avian species common to the region. There are smaller mammals, lizards, and insects to watch out for as well. During the winter months, whales can be spotted along their yearly migration routes, and the point is a perfect place to watch for them.

The point is also a great spot to catch sunsets, which can be sublime and magical. From the point, the trail can be retraced by turning left and heading back to the parking lot, or an extended

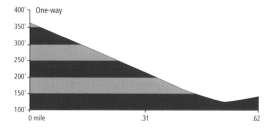

loop can be made by turning right and combining the Beach and Broken Hill Trails with a walk down Torrey Pines Park Road. A shorter loop can also be created using the Yucca Point and Beach Trail, which leads back to the trailhead.

SALTON SEA NATIONAL WILDLIFE REFUGE

The Salton Sea is only around due to an engineering disaster, an oddity, a tale from the early 1900s when water overflowed irrigation canals and broke dikes, plunging hundreds of thousands of cubic feet per second into a deep depression in the desert floor known as the Salton Sink. It took two years and scads of money to finally get the Colorado River back into its proper channels, although scientists worried that it might permanently be diverted from its banks, inundating not only the Imperial Valley, but also the town of Yuma, Arizona.

A shallow but very large inland sea was left over, measuring fifteen miles wide and thirty-five miles long. It remains today due mostly to agricultural runoff, though it is currently endangered by the ever-growing needs of a thirsty and sprawling Southern California. Several plans for "saving" the sea are currently being looked at, and in the near future a protection project will be in place.

3 SALTON SEA—ROCK HILL TRAIL

Distance: 2 miles round-trip
Hiking time: 1 hour
Difficulty: Easy
Elevation gain: 50 feet
High point: -170 feet
Season: Late fall to early spring, very hot in summer
Water: None, bring your own
Fees and permits: None
Map: USGS Niland
Information: Sonny Bono Salton Sea National Wildlife Refuge,
    (760) 348-5278, *www.fws.gov/saltonsea/recreation.html#VisitorCenter*

Getting there: From Interstate 10 in Indio, drive south on State Route 111 for 50 miles. Turn right on Sinclair Road just 4 miles past the town of Niland. Drive for 6 miles to the Salton Sea National Wildlife Refuge visitor center.

On the surface, the sea appears to be little more than a lifeless, greenish-brown pond lined with dead barnacles and the bones of other creatures—a misleading impression, as the sea actually supports a great deal of life. Its vastness is impressive, and the stark beauty of the surrounding mountains makes it a picturesque locale. For birds, however, the sea is a mecca, a wonderland of microorganisms that feed not only insects but over four hundred bird species migrating along

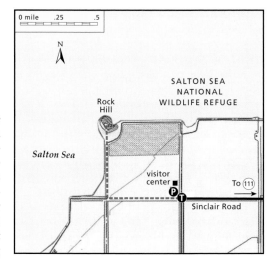

the Pacific Flyway. It is a critical spot, whose future is instrumental in the survival of many avian creatures.

From the observation platform just behind the visitor center, the trail starts along a levee where it begins a short climb to the top of a formation known as Rock Hill. It is the one trail in the refuge, and the top is a fantastic spot to marvel at the many different birds that flock here and the majesty of what has come to be known as one of the great mistakes in California history. The sea itself is beautiful, with the Chocolate Mountains to the east and the San Jacintos and Santa Rosas nestled to the west. It is a great spot to idle away some time or catch a sunrise or a sunset.

Though not much of a hike in the proper sense of the word, it is a one-of-a-kind classic experience not to be missed; the Salton Sea is uniquely Californian.

The Salton Sea extends from horizon to horizon.

CUYAMACA RANCHO STATE PARK AND LAGUNA MOUNTAIN RECREATION AREA

The Cuyamaca and Laguna Mountains are two beautiful ranges that sit high above the desert and coastal regions of the southernmost portion of California. Near to San Diego and the Inland Empire, this secluded and remote area is loaded with vibrant and wonderful forest scenery that straddles Anza Borrego Desert State Park and the California coastal plain. The Laguna Mountains lie within Cleveland National Forest. Views from many of the peaks in the region are astounding and take in hundreds of miles of scenery in all directions on clear days. Rising from the arid lower reaches, the parks are made up of desert shrubs, oak woodlands, and even high-altitude pine forests. Both parks offer an escape from the heat, great hiking, and blue-sky vistas that rival any region in the state.

4 COTTONWOOD CREEK FALLS

Distance: 2 miles round-trip
Hiking time: 1 hour
Difficulty: Easy
Elevation gain: 450 feet
High point: 4450 feet
Season: Late fall to early summer
Water: Cottonwood Creek
Fees and permits: Adventure Pass
Map: USGS Descanso
Information: Cleveland National Forest, (619) 445-6235,
  www.fs.fed.us/r5/cleveland/

Getting there: From Highway 79, turn east onto Interstate 8 and drive 5 miles. Exit onto the Sunrise Highway (County Route S1) and turn left. Drive for 1.8 miles north and park in the large gravel turnout just south of the 15.5 mile marker.

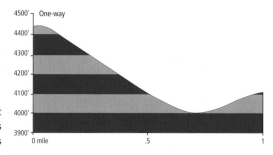

The path begins on the east side of the road just above the northern end of the guardrail. This is not a maintained trail, and there are no signs marking its presence. It goes very steeply downhill for the first half-mile section. In the first 0.25 mile, there is some overgrowth as the route follows the track of the powerlines next to the highway. The trail continues to drop sharply through chaparral until, in about 0.25 mile, it becomes an old dirt road that splits near the creek. Turn left and follow the creek upward into the canyon.

Upon entering the canyon, the creek assumes a splendid mantle. A lovely wooded arbor sits streamside in the open lower reaches. As the trail progresses upward into an eroded desert chasm, pools appear like oases in this parched and arid landscape. Reeds and other wetland plants grow in and around the larger basins. Gentle cascades

The water cascades freely down Cottonwood Canyon.

have formed all along the stream as it trickles down from the higher elevations of the Laguna Mountains. Some of the falls reach heights of 10 feet or higher.

Cottonwood Creek Falls are just beyond the first few cascades. They are almost effortless to reach with only a tiny bit of scrambling; children should easily be able to make the trip. Beneath the falls is a deep pool that always creates an occasion for very enjoyable wading in the spring, when the air is hot and the water is cool. The place is quite idyllic and enchanting. The canyon is open to further exploration, though extensive scrambling and some climbing are required to do so. Enjoy the waters and return to the parking area via the same trail, which is sun-exposed and may be extremely hot during the daytime.

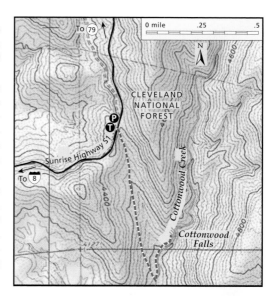

5 BIG LAGUNA TRAIL

Distance: 5 miles round-trip
Hiking time: 2.5 hours
Difficulty: Easy
Elevation gain: 175 feet
High point: 5600 feet
Season: All
Water: Big Laguna Lake
Fees and permits: Adventure Pass
Map: USGS Monument Peak
Information: Cleveland National Forest, (619) 445-6235,
     www.fs.fed.us/r5/cleveland/

Getting there: From the town of Julian, head south on State Route 79 for nearly 6 miles. Turn left onto Sunrise Highway (County Route S1) and drive south for 10 miles to the Penny Pines parking area just past mile marker 27.5. Alternately, heading east from San Diego on Interstate 8 take the Sunrise Highway north for 13.5 miles.

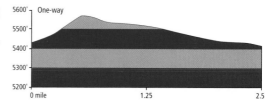

Head west on the Noble Canyon Trail for a few hundred feet as the path winds its way through the southerly reaches of the Cedar Fire that cut a devastating swath across San Diego County in fall 2003. Turn left (south) onto the Big Laguna Trail and follow the well-trodden byway as it contours around a hillside and enters Laguna Meadow. From the first few footfalls into Laguna

Taking in the spacious Laguna Mountain views

Meadow, the region has a majestic beauty superbly outlined by towering lodgepole and Coulter pines, which grow to prodigious heights in the basin. The valley hinges beneath an azure sky that resembles something out of the mountains of Montana rather than Southern California. Clouds float by as if painted on a postcard backdrop, and the lovely lakes lining the forest are a rare sight in these arid climes.

Upon entering the meadow, continue south at the junction with the Sunset Trail, and eventually veer right onto the short use trail that goes down to the edge of Big Laguna Lake at 2.5 miles. This is a perfect spot for a picnic, or simply to take a breather and enjoy the wondrous sights. Birds use the ponds for food and serenely float on the water. Arrive early enough, and there is a good possibility of sighting creatures not normally seen in the daylight hours. No matter what time of day, resting alongside a tranquil mountain lake, taking in the clouds, and simply enjoying the sunshine is a perfect way to while away the hours and fashion memories that will last a lifetime. The hike is perfect for smaller children, as there is very little elevation gain or distance, and giant rewards for everyone involved.

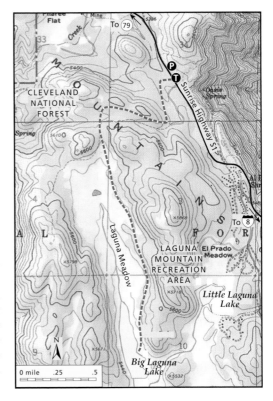

The hike can be made into a 7-mile point-to-point trek by parking another vehicle between the 25 and 25.5 mile markers on Sunrise Highway, so that there is no backtracking involved. Or those wishing to spend a day and wanting to take in all that Laguna Mountain Recreation Area has to offer can turn the trail into a much longer 10-mile loop by following the Big Laguna Trail to its junction with the Pacific Crest Trail (PCT) and continuing north along the PCT back to the Penny Pines parking lot. This section of the PCT has stunning and expansive views that extend three thousand feet below into the Anza-Borrego Desert and across to the Salton Sea.

6 GARNET PEAK

Distance: 4 miles round-trip
Hiking time: 2 hours
Difficulty: Easy
Elevation gain: 400 feet
High point: 5835 feet
Season: All, hot in summer
Water: None, bring your own
Fees and permits: Adventure Pass
Map: USGS Monument Peak
Information: Cleveland National Forest, (619) 445-6235,
www.fs.fed.us/r5/cleveland/

Getting there: From Julian, drive south on State Route 79 for 6 miles to the turnoff for Sunrise Highway (County Route S1). Veer left onto the Sunrise Highway and drive for 9.5 miles just past mile marker 27.5 to the turnout on both sides of the road for Penny Pines.

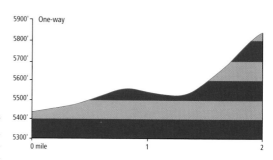

Garnet Peak is named for the red gemstones that were once mined in the area; there are still some remaining outcroppings and an occasional loose stone, though most were carted away by the old miners who once inhabited Julian. The hike begins on the east side of the road and travels through a partially burnt forest along an old roadway. After a short distance, turn left onto the Pacific Crest Trail (PCT) and follow it as it climbs gently and intermittently levels off for nearly a mile to the junction with the Garnet Peak Trail.

Turn right and head up to the mountaintop. The way is rocky and steep. The starkness of the region is highlighted by the transition between the forest to the west and the desert of Anza-Borrego thousands of feet below. Much of the forest bordering to the west was burned in the Julian Fire of 2002 and then again during the Cedar Fire of 2003. Even with the fires, the area has retained a natural beauty that is astounding.

This is one of the most picturesque and beautiful regions in Southern California. The austere scenery is stark and desolate to be certain, but there is an underlying elegance to its openness and the vast immeasurable distances that spread out below the peak. Nothing but the wind touches this thick chaparral-filled plateau. The silence coupled with the song of the currents creates a natural lucidity that engages the spirit and forges

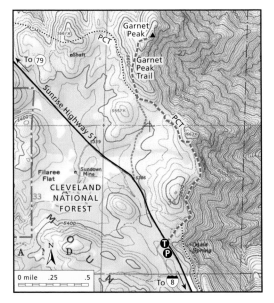

a connection with the barren landscape. From the apex, the view is staggering: an entire swath of Southern California can be seen, from the Salton Sea to the Herculean summits of San Gorgonio and San Jacinto. The dome of the Palomar Observatory is conspicuous to the north; to the west and south, the entire Cuyamaca and Laguna Mountain Recreation Area appear. This may be the best view in all of San Diego County.

In the wintertime, a small amount of snow can fall on the summit, but it does not normally stay for very long. Still, from fall to spring the temperature can vary from chilly to hot. There is no shade to speak of for the entire route, which is exposed the entire way, with vertical exposure in spots. There are rocks to scramble on near the summit, for those who wish to do a bit of climbing. A shorter route to the top exists, but the scenery is so beautiful, it is best to spend at least half a day enjoying the hike.

The vast Anza-Borrego Desert State Park sits below the summit of Garnet Peak.

7 STONEWALL PEAK TRAIL

Distance: 4 miles round-trip
Hiking time: 2 hours
Difficulty: Easy
Elevation gain: 850 feet
High point: 5730 feet
Season: All, hot in summer
Water: None, bring your own
Fees and permits: Required
Map: USGS Cuyamaca Peak
Information: Cuyamaca Rancho State Park, (760) 765-0755,
   www.parks.ca.gov/default.asp?page_id=667

Getting there: From Julian, drive 11 miles south on State Route 79. Turn right into the headquarters for Cuyamaca Rancho State Park and the parking area for Paso Picacho Campground. There is a fee for day use. Park in the day-use area.

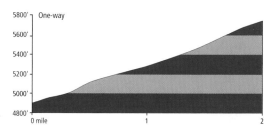

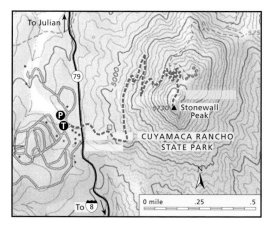

The Stonewall Peak Trail is a popular outing in Cuyamaca Rancho State Park, and for good reason. The peak offers a nice workout and exceptional clear-day views of well over a hundred peaks in the Southern California region, not to mention the immediate beauty of Cuyamaca Lake and the surrounding state park. The climb can be made by almost anyone, including small children, as the gradient is easy and a goodly number of switchbacks keep the steepness to a minimum.

The Cedar Fire of 2003 burned up large sections of the park, and most of the shade has been lost, but both the trail and the region have retained their beauty. Fire is a natural process, and the area is simply altered from what it was a few years ago. Many people think of a burned forest as an ugly one, but that really is not the case. Cuyamaca is the perfect place to visit for viewing and interacting with the forest after a large conflagration. A century of fire suppression led to the huge fires of 2003. Walking through Cuyamaca Rancho shows the devastation caused by fire-suppression policies that led to the buildup of too much flammable material in the forest. However, the natural ecosystem itself is quite the show-off

as it begins the rebirth process. Like the phoenix rising from the ashes, Stonewall Peak and its parent park have made a glowing comeback.

The trail starts across the highway from the park entrance. It immediately begins climbing gentle switchbacks that undulate back and forth up the mountain in long arcing sweeps. The undergrowth has returned to the slopes, but the views, which begin immediately, are completely

Lake Cuyamaca sits below North Peak on the Stonewall Peak Trail.

unobstructed. In about 1.5 miles the top becomes readily discernable; a little farther on, the way opens up to rock and steeper climbing. A guardrail and steps cut into the stone have been put into place to make the ascent easier. On top, there is plenty of room to enjoy the pastoral and picturesque views. The two miles to the parking lot are considerably easier on the way down, so if children begin to complain near the top, there won't be any problems on the trip out.

ANZA-BORREGO DESERT STATE PARK

Anza-Borrego Desert State Park, located in San Diego, Imperial, and Riverside counties, is the largest state park in California. It is named after the overland explorer Juan Bautista de Anza and the Spanish word for bighorn sheep, *borrego,* which used to be abundant in the region.

The park has more than 100 miles of hiking trails, many of which lead to wonderful canyons, oases, Native sites, and beautiful, stark vistas. The park features desert washes, slot canyons, palm groves, cactus, wildlife, and a wildflower show in early spring that can be astounding and spectacular when the rainfall is just right. The horseshoe-shaped park is bounded by tall mountains on almost every side. It is the only park in California where open camping—that is, car camping with no fires, anywhere along the road—is allowed.

8 PACIFIC CREST TRAIL—LAGUNA MOUNTAIN RIDGE

Distance: 5 miles round-trip
Hiking time: 2.5 hours
Difficulty: Easy
Elevation gain: 300 feet
High point: 5500 feet
Season: All, hot in summer
Water: None, bring your own
Fees and permits: Required
Map: USGS Monument Peak
Information: Anza-Borrego Desert State Park, (760) 767-5311,
   www.parks.ca.gov/default.asp?page_id=638

Getting there: From Julian, drive south on State Route 79 for 6 miles to the turnoff for Sunrise Highway (County Route S1). Veer left onto the Sunrise Highway and drive for 5 miles, then turn left onto the unmarked road. Park at the end by the overlook.

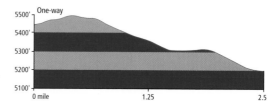

Head north along this section of the Pacific Crest Trail (PCT) and follow a wonderful path that perfectly hugs the northerly vestiges of the Laguna Mountains. The route enters Anza-Borrego Desert State Park almost immediately, as noted by signs directing hikers to follow all rules and regulations of the state park system. From very near the trail's outset, spectacular views of the region open up. The way follows along the mountainside close to the roadway, though separated by enough distance and a hillside as to make the sounds of automobiles inaudible. For the entire length of the trip, the contour of the mountain slides down to the east into the lower reaches of the Anza-Borrego Desert. "Beautiful" is an understatement for this area's raw aesthetic simplicity. Indeed, this is a perfect place to take someone unfamiliar with the higher reaches of the desert and share its immaculate allure.

The Pines Fire of 2002 and the Cedar Fire of 2003 swept through this area and devastated much of the vegetation, but hardy desert chaparral grows back quickly, especially with the record amounts of rainfall that struck the region in the following three years. The area has rebounded completely, though some blackened branches

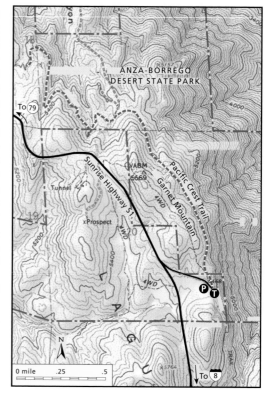

remain along with soot in the soil. The added nutrients have given regional wildflowers a boost, although the window for seeing the full array is a very short span of a few weeks in early spring.

The hike is mostly level, though it does lose a minimal amount of elevation throughout the trip which must be regained on the way out. The trail is well used and easy to follow as it traverses along both Garnet and Oriflamme mountains. Basically, hikers can take as long as they wish and go as far as they like along the trail, as it stretches all the way from Mexico into Canada. The scenery is stunning in this section, and there are a number of rocky outcroppings and vista points where lunch breaks and/or turnaround points can be made. This hike is a classic in the truest sense of the word; anyone able to walk can enjoy it, and the memory of the surroundings will last for a lifetime. The area is fantastic for photography, especially in the low light of mornings and evenings, and both sunsets and sunrises can be especially ethereal.

The PCT traverses an awesome ridgeline through the Laguna Mountains.

9 PICTOGRAPH TRAIL

Distance: 2.5 miles round-trip
Hiking time: 1.5 hours
Difficulty: Easy
Elevation gain: 200 feet
High point: 3325 feet
Season: Late fall to early spring
Water: None, bring your own
Fees and permits: Required
Map: USGS Earthquake Valley
Information: Anza-Borrego Desert State Park, (760) 767-5311,
   www.parks.ca.gov/default.asp?page_id=638

Getting there: From the town of Julian, head east for 10 miles on State Route 78. From there take County Route S2 south for 5 miles. Follow it to the dirt road (Blair Valley Road) marked for Ghost Mountain, Portreros, and Pictographs. Turn left and follow the signs on the dirt road to the parking area.

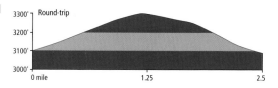

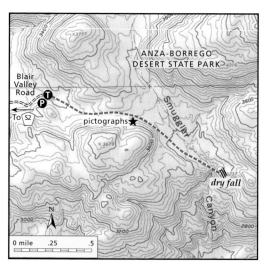

This is a nice short, easy trail that even a three-year-old should be able to handle, except for maybe a few rough and difficult spots. The trail is a bit steep at first, but the gain only lasts for a short while as the route climbs and eventually arrives at a beautiful plateau at about 0.5 mile. From there the trail is level all the way to the boulder outcropping, about 0.5 mile farther, that contains the pictographs.

The rock and pictographs are easy to spot, and virtually impossible to miss, but pay careful attention to the right side of the trail, as there are several smaller offshoots that lead around the rock and to other sites indicative of the earlier Native American Kumeyaay inhabitants. The pictographs are typical of the San Luis Rey style of the Luiseno Indians characterized by red rectangular geometric designs— zigzags, diamonds, diamond chains, dot patterns, and straight lines—often placed in vertical series. These markings were most likely made for female puberty initiation ceremonies, and are representative of the rattlesnake spirit guide.

From the pictographs continue southeast on the trail, which from here is quite a bit less traveled,

as the majority of visitors come to see the pictographs and then return to their cars. There is considerably more to see on this trip, though, and to turn around at the pictographs is to miss a good part of the fun. At 1.25 miles, the path ends at a wonderfully scenic dry waterfall overlooking Smuggler Canyon and the Sawtooth Mountains. This is a charming vista, but there is no way to

continue without climbing gear, so this is a good spot for a picnic and a turnaround.

On the way out, watch for archaeological signs of prehistoric life in the region. There are *mortreros*, or mortar rocks, everywhere, deeply gouged into the boulders in the area. There are remnants of pottery that show signs of long-term inhabitation. Please remember to tread lightly; removing objects of any kind is illegal, and disturbs the natural history for others. Places like this are protected for a reason, so the children of our grandchildren can one day come and enjoy the same natural beauty and history that is the heritage of all of us.

Pictographs in the Kumeyaay tradition

10   GHOST MOUNTAIN

Distance: 2 miles round-trip
Hiking time: 1 hour
Difficulty: Easy
Elevation gain: 600 feet
High point: 3388 feet
Season: Late fall to early spring
Water: None, bring your own
Fees and permits: Required
Map: USGS Earthquake Valley
Information: Anza-Borrego Desert State Park, (760) 767-5311,
    www.parks.ca.gov/default.asp?page_id=638

Getting there: From the town of Julian, head east for 10 miles on State Route 78. From there you will take County Route S2 south for 5 miles. Follow it to the dirt road (Blair Valley Road) marked for Ghost Mountain, Portreros, and Pictographs. Turn left and follow the signs on the dirt road to the parking area.

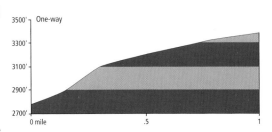

Ghost Mountain is the home of a unique piece of Southern California history. Halfway up the spine of the mountain find the remnants of Yaquitepec, a one-of-a-kind desert experiment concocted by Marshal and Tanya South, an author and his artist wife. The couple left civilization in 1930 to raise their three children amongst the harsh desert environs, unspoiled by what they saw as the callousness of society. There, they felt freed from the confines and pressures of modern life. Ultimately, the couple split after their seventeen-year undertaking, and the children do not talk of their life there to this day. The remnants of their adobe homestead, including a foundation, cistern, a few standing walls, and some bedsprings, are available for exploration,

The views from Ghost Mountain are truly stunning.

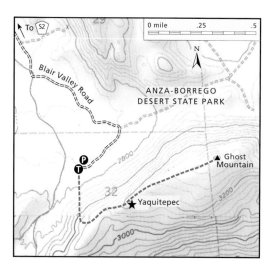

and quite a few people come to check out the oddity, especially on the weekends. During the week, there is considerably less foot traffic.

Hike half a mile to the dwelling, which is quite accessible on a well-traveled trail. The view from the homestead is magnificent, but the additional half-mile climb to the actual summit is more than worthwhile. First, not many people continue beyond the ruins. Most are content to explore and

ponder the strange existence of the South family and the difficulty that must have surrounded the intimacies of their everyday existence. Secondly, the 360-degree summit vista is superb. The entire Blair Valley, the Great Southern Overland Route of 1849, and the Vallecito Valley and Mountains are all visible, as are the high Laguna Mountains rising toward the west and Julian.

The second half of the trail is not as defined. There are many paths to the top, and all are rocky and unmarked. Take care, as the rough terrain makes it easy to twist an ankle. Also, it is best to avoid the fragile plant life in the area. Expect normal desert flora and fauna, such as lizards, cacti, mesquite, and rattlesnakes. The South family did not denude the hillside of their mountain home; instead they spent hours foraging and gathering in many locations, spreading out their impact upon the land and leaving this region pristine and untarnished. The natural beauty of the region attests to this. It is impossible to visit here and not be touched by the surreal circumstances and the transcendental nature of this place. Sunrise from the top of Ghost Mountain is a preternatural experience, as the desert conjures majestic colors and shadows from its inexhaustible palette.

CLEVELAND NATIONAL FOREST

Cleveland National Forest, the southernmost national forest in California, is located in the counties of Orange, Riverside, and San Diego. It is mostly a sun-scorched, chaparral-covered land with a few oak woodlands, pine-topped peaks, and some riparian habitat. The Santa Ana, Palomar, Laguna, and Cuyamaca Mountain chains appear here. From high atop peaks such as Palomar, Cuyamaca, and Sitton, a hiker can see wide-ranging vistas of Southern California. Lovely seasonal streams flow through colorful canyons, and in some places vibrant waterfalls cascade into wading pools. The forest is a haven for wildlife, with much of it still covered in shrubbery the way Southern California used to look before the onset of civilization.

11 PALOMAR MOUNTAIN OBSERVATORY TRAIL

Distance: 4 miles round-trip
Hiking time: 2 hours
Difficulty: Easy
Elevation gain: 700 feet
High point: 5571 feet
Season: All
Water: Observatory Campground, Museum
Fees and permits: Adventure Pass
Map: USGS Palomar Observatory
Information: Cleveland National Forest, (760) 788-0250,
www.fs.fed.us/r5/cleveland/

Getting there: From Interstate 15 near Fallbrook, drive east on State Route 76 for 21 miles. Turn north on County Route S6, continue 6.5 miles to the junction with County Route S7, then continue 3 miles north along CR S6 to the Observatory Campground. Parking for the trailhead is in the back of the campground.

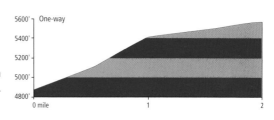

The hike to Palomar Observatory along the trail from Observatory Campground is best taken in the spring when wildflowers are in full bloom. The Palomars are one of the highest mountain ranges in the region, and the tops are covered in lovely Coulter and Jeffrey pine. The hike traverses a charming oak forest interspersed with the conifers. The views and floral displays can be quite stunning if the visit correlates with the highest percentage of spring blossoms.

The trail mostly stays within hearing distance of the road, and cars can actually be seen along the hike in spots, though there is generally not much traffic. The trail itself is lovely, peaceful, and not very long. At just 2 miles to the top, it is an up-and-down jaunt that almost anyone can accomplish. The trail is well constructed with an easy vertical gradient. Wonderful views open up as early as half a mile into the hike, where an overlook grants a wide vista of Mendenhall Valley, a lovely plateau that sits high up on the mountain. From there the trail continues through

Palomar Observatory

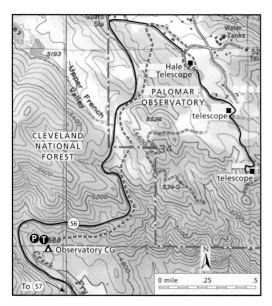

the forest the rest of the way to the top, where even more expansive views can be had.

Near the end of the hike, the trail intersects the road just beside the parking lot. Turn right and follow the path to the observatory, a splendid white dome that stands starkly against the cobalt blue skies frequent in this region. It is open to the public from 9:00 AM to 4:00 PM daily, except December 24 and 25. The 200-inch telescope opened in 1948 and has taken many photographs, including a catalog of the northern sky that was digitized as a reference map inside the Hubble Space Telescope. Currently, the telescope is being used in the Near Earth Asteroid Tracking Program in conjunction with other sites around the world. There is a picnic area near the top that is a good stopping place, a welcome rest before beginning the turnaround.

12 SITTON PEAK

Distance: 9.8 miles round-trip
Hiking time: 5 hours
Difficulty: Moderate to strenuous
Elevation gain: 1300 feet
High point: 3273 feet
Season: Late fall to spring, can be very hot in summer
Water: Pigeon Springs (seasonal), bring your own
Fees and permits: Adventure Pass
Map: USGS Sitton Peak
Information: Cleveland National Forest, (951) 736-1811,
 www.fs.fed.us/r5/cleveland/

Getting there: From Interstate 5 in Orange County, take State Route 74 east for 19.5 miles. (Alternately, from Interstate 15 in Riverside County, go west on SR 74 for 13 miles.) Park in the large lot on the north side of the highway. The trailhead is on the south side of the highway and west of the legendary Ortega Oaks Candy Store.

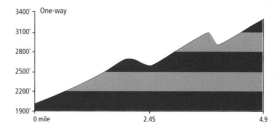

Head up the Bear Canyon Trail which climbs through the San Mateo Wilderness, a mixture of beautiful brush-strewn hillsides, streams, rolling lands nestled between coastal canyons, and

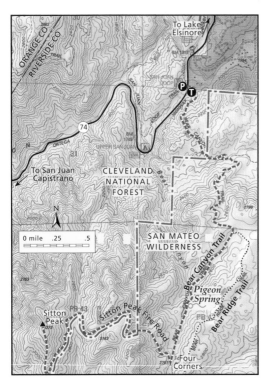

old crisscrossed truck roads. The route ascends through low-lying coastal chaparral and meadows, passes a wonderfully wooded oak glen called Pigeon Springs, and eventually meets up with an intersection of trails called Four Corners before turning to ascend Sitton Peak.

At 1 mile, take a right at the fork and stay on the Bear Canyon Trail. A few steps ahead, cross the road to follow a newer path or take the pedestrian-only road itself; both head to the same point. Pigeon Springs sits a bit under 3 miles into the trail, at almost the halfway point. It makes for a wonderful rest spot: shady, complete with a seasonal stream that can flow quite nicely when the winters are wet. From here, another 0.5 mile brings the hike to the Four Corners junction, a meeting of four major trails that run through the Santa Ana Mountains.

From here, head right (west) onto an old portion of the Sitton Peak Fire Road—the road is unsigned but obvious. Climb and then descend to a saddle at 1.3 miles from the Four Corners junction, where a use trail heads steeply up 0.4 mile to the top of the peak.

Coastal chaparral lines the trail for most of the hike to Sitton Peak.

When the days are clear, the views from the summit are most impressive. The blue Pacific shines like a dazzling gem against cobalt skies. The many cities of Orange County can be seen in the distance as antlike cars inch along Highway 74 below.

This is a perfect hike for wintertime, when the higher summits in the Angeles and San Bernardinos are covered in snow, the temperatures are lower, the bugs are gone, there isn't a hint of smog, and the horizon stretches for miles and miles. It is possible to return via a semi-loop along the road, if you desire to see more of the surroundings, but the way in is just as good on the way out.

Another alternative here is to make a 6.8-mile loop by combining the Bear Ridge Trail with the Bear Canyon Trail, returning from Four Corners via the ridge then reconnecting to the Bear Canyon Trail.

13 HOLY JIM FALLS/TRABUCO CANYON

Distance: 3 miles round-trip
Hiking time: 1.5 hours
Difficulty: Easy
Elevation gain: 675 feet
High point: 2375 feet
Season: Late fall to spring
Water: Holy Jim Creek
Fees and permits: Adventure Pass
Map: USGS Santiago Peak
Information: Cleveland National Forest, (951) 736-1811,
   www.fs.fed.us/r5/cleveland/

Getting there: From southbound Interstate 5 in Lake Forest, exit at El Toro Road, turn left off the exit ramp, and take another left onto El Toro Road. Continue for 6 miles. Turn right onto Live Oak Canyon Road (County Route S19) and drive for 4 miles. Turn left onto Trabuco Creek Road, which is an unsigned dirt road just past Rose Canyon Road. Drive about 4.5 miles to the trailhead parking lot. High-profile vehicles recommended.

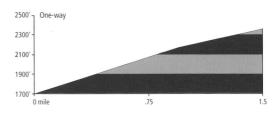

The trail to Holy Jim Falls begins from the north side of the parking lot and climbs a short hill, passing some old cabins before straddling Holy Jim Creek. Before 1900, beekeepers used to eke out a living here, one of whom gave his name to the canyon, trail, and falls. James T. Smith went by the moniker of "Cussin' Jim," apparently due to his prodigious use of colorful adjectives and verbs. Evidently, when cartographers drew up maps of the region they balked at the idea of placing such a name on this lovely sylvan glen, and instead gave the place a kinder, gentler tone.

Proceed for a half mile of hiking. Just beyond the last cabin, the trail reaches a steel gate. Beyond this gate lie seven creek crossings spread out over the next mile. Some are easier to cross than others; depending on the amount of water in the creek, it is a good possibility that even the most careful feet will get wet. The trail can become overgrown and some trees in the canopy hang very low, making several creek crossings more difficult to undertake without wading. It

Buckwheat and other shrubs line the lush shores in Holy Jim Canyon.

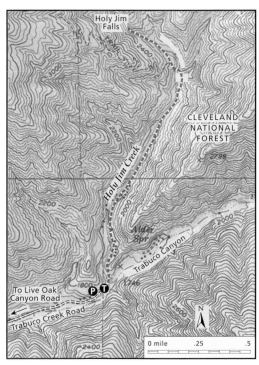

really is just easier to walk through the water; the hike is rather short anyway, and the water shallow. After the final crossing, a highly traveled use trail turns right and leads a short distance to the falls. Follow it and relax in the falls' calming atmosphere.

The trek to Holy Jim Falls serves as a wonderful introduction to one of the nicest spots in the Santa Ana portion of the Cleveland National Forest. There is a spirited creek, an 18-foot cascade, a beautiful riparian canyon, and lovely oak woodlands. The falls may not be the largest, but their beauty is mesmerizing and a true escape from the urban landscape of Orange County.

The canyon is also home to a more somber piece of history: in 1907, the last grizzly bear in the Cleveland National Forest was shot and killed in the canyon, after succumbing to the tantalizing allure of the fresh honey kept by the settlers.

Opposite: Joshua trees were named by Mormon settlers who believed the trees look like the biblical figure with his arms upturned to heaven.

JOSHUA TREE

JOSHUA TREE NATIONAL PARK

Joshua Tree National Park is a charming desert ecosystem at the intersection of the lower Colorado Desert and the higher elevations of the Mojave Desert. The area is a geological treasure, with otherworldly mountains and large boulder fields, one enticingly titled the "Wonderland of Rocks." Besides geology, the major attractions are wildlife—especially birds—and the famous many-limbed Joshua tree. Rock climbing is especially popular among the larger boulder faces.

The region is pockmarked with signs of history, from past mining activity as well as Native American habitation. There are several oases that can be hiked to, and any number of desert peaks, some with trails to the top. Joshua Tree National Park is better as a winter destination, though spring and fall can be cool as well.

14 LOST PALMS OASIS

Distance: 9.5 miles round-trip
Hiking time: 5 hours
Difficulty: Moderate
Elevation gain: 900 feet
High point: 3475 feet
Season: Late fall to early spring
Water: Lost Palms Oasis
Fees and permits: Required
Map: USGS Cottonwood Spring
Information: Joshua Tree National Park, (760) 367-5500, *www.nps.gov/jotr/*

Getting there: Take Interstate 10 east from Palm Springs and head toward the town of Chiriaco Summit. The turn will be a few miles before you reach the town; you will see a sign that says Joshua Tree National Park. This is the park's south entrance. Enter the park and drive for 7 miles until you come to a junction with Cottonwood Springs Road. Turn right and park.

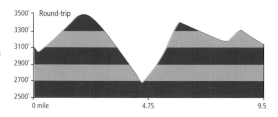

From the Cottonwood Spring Oasis parking lot, head southeast along the nature trail and continue straight for the entire 4 miles to the Lost Palms Oasis. The trail is well signed, with posts marking off each mile traveled. Just before the first mile marker is a branch to Mastodon Peak and the Mastodon Mine, but continue straight and explore this area on the return trip out.

From the outset, the scenery is spectacular; the outcroppings of granite boulders are imposing and beautiful. There is an abundance of rocky washes, ridges, small canyons, and the looming rock formations that line the mesa. The trail stays on a high plateau that descends alongside the ravine and crosses several washes.

Cacti (including hedgehog, California barrel, several species of *Mammillaria,* cholla, and prickly pear), ocotillo, yucca, and springtime desert wildflowers line the sandy reaches of the trail and especially the washes beneath. Overpowering blue skies stretch from horizon to

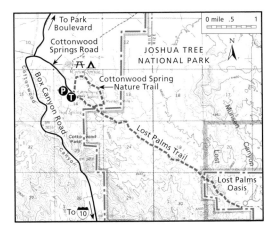

horizon, providing a perfect backdrop for outdoor photography.

The initial mile ascends through a slender ravine, gaining a couple of hundred feet; the next mile continues to add a similar amount of elevation as the trail crosses several dry desert drainages. The trail begins to fluctuate between losing and gaining elevation for the third mile as the rocky tableau begins to open up, presenting views of austere desert. The contrasts between the clear blue skies, the dazzling white rocks, and the harshness of the desert are mind-blowing. As the trail nears the oasis in the fourth mile, it descends rapidly to its conclusion. Views extend in many directions for most of the trip. Considering that the canyon below the oasis was used by General Patton to train desert troops for World War II, this hike holds some historical significance as well.

On the return trip, take the loop past Mastodon Mine and head to the small summit of Mastodon Peak. Some short scrambling is required to attain the apex, but it isn't technical or difficult. The views are incredible and offer a nice survey of the local area.

Continue back toward Cottonwood Spring and enjoy the short nature trail with its many interpretive signs about the flora of the Colorado Desert. At the final junction, take the left branch back toward the parking lot; do not continue on to the campground.

California fan palms flourish from the spring water at the hidden oasis.

15 LOST HORSE MINE

Distance: 4.5 miles round-trip
Hiking time: 2 hours
Difficulty: Easy
Elevation gain: 600 feet
High point: 5278 feet
Season: Late fall to early spring
Water: None, bring your own
Fees and permits: Required
Map: USGS Keys View
Information: Joshua Tree National Park, (760) 367-5500, *www.nps.gov/jotr/*

Getting there: Take Interstate 10 for 10 miles east of Cabazon. Exit on State Route 62 and head north for 26.5 miles to the town of Joshua Tree. Turn right on Park Boulevard and follow it 10 miles to Keys View Road, then turn right (just before Cap Rock) and follow it until you see a sign for Lost Horse Mine. Drive about 1 mile down the dirt road to the parking area.

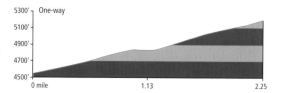

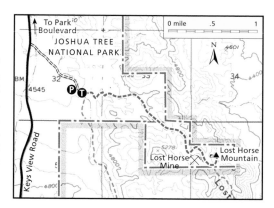

The way to Lost Horse Mine and Mountain is wide and easy to navigate. The entire trail is a well-used wagon road that in its time brought out over $5 million worth of gold and silver from the bowels of the earth. The mine was operated from 1894 to 1931, with the bulk of the bullion mined during the first decade of operations. Lost Horse Mine was the most successful of the more than three hundred mines located in what is now Joshua Tree National Park. The route in follows an easy grade through a picturesque desert tableau lined with yuccas, nolinas, creosote bush, silver cholla, and many other varieties of desert flora. Most Joshua trees in this area are gone, used as firewood for the operation of the mine, but some survivors remain.

The story of the mine reads like a piece of folklore and is most assuredly a tall tale from the Wild West with several circulating versions, each instilled with at least a grain of truth. Most include some version of horse rustlers, a stolen horse, a local legend named Johnny Lang, and a group of tough miners who banded together to stake a claim in the region now known as Lost Horse Valley. Some claim an old prospector named Johnny Lang simply sat down while searching for his lost horse, and found a vein of gold. After he sold the mine, Lang purportedly stayed around working for the new owners while skimming off the top. Tales of his buried treasure also run rampant, though no specific location has ever even been speculated upon or found. With that stated, digging or prospecting is expressly forbidden in national parks, and is punishable by both a fine and jail time.

Whatever the truth is, the hike itself is a gem. It follows a wide old wagon path to the mine, and

The old stamp mill stands proudly in the desert despite its chain-link fence.

most sections parallel a wash that crisscrosses the trail numerous times. The way is relatively flat and easy and follows a steady climbing gradient all the way to the mine. A perfectly preserved ten-stamp mill stands at the base of the mine, protected by a chain-link fence, which is unfortunately needed to preserve this legacy from defacement. There are also many remains of lodgings, wells, cisterns, and outbuildings in the area waiting to be explored. The turnaround panorama from the top of Lost Horse Mountain is a sight not to be missed. The summit itself is an easy five-minute scramble from the stamp mill. The entire park can be surveyed from this lofty perch, and both sunsets and sunrises are sublime.

16 RYAN MOUNTAIN

Distance: 3 miles round-trip
Hiking time: 1.5 hours
Difficulty: Easy
Elevation gain: 1050 feet
High point: 5461 feet
Season: Late fall to early spring, hot in summer
Water: None
Fees and permits: Required
Map: USGS Keys View
Information: Joshua Tree National Park, (760) 367-5500, *www.nps.gov/jotr/*

Getting there: Take Interstate 10 east beyond Cabazon for 10 miles. Exit onto State Route 62 heading north. Follow SR 62 for 26.5 miles into the town of Joshua Tree. Turn right onto Park Boulevard and follow it to the entrance gate. From there continue 12 miles to Sheep Pass Group Campground. A sign says reservations are required, but there is plenty of trailhead parking in the large lot just beyond the campground.

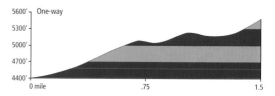

The trailhead begins in the parking area and travels along the roadway, circling up and around the backside of the mountain. Ryan is perhaps the park's most popular mountain to climb. The trail to its summit is incredibly easy to follow and well-used. Many summits in the park do not have maintained trails, so this one is easier to access. It is not so overcrowded as to be considered a "freeway," but there will almost always be someone else on the trail, even on weekdays.

Head west from the parking area for a little more than half a mile. At the trail fork, go left and continue around and up the mountain. The trail ascends steadily through cholla, rocks, and cacti up to the base of a smaller mountain which sits just to the south of the summit of Ryan Mountain. As the trail edges higher and higher, views open up into Lost Horse Valley and toward the Wonderland of Rocks. The trail then continues to move up a ravine between the two peaks and then climbs beyond the saddle up to the top of Ryan Mountain, at about 1.25 miles. There isn't much shade along the way, and only an occasional rock or rock overhang to provide a bit of respite from the sun. Joshua trees do sporadically

The huge boulders in the Wonderland of Rocks look tiny from the trail.

line the lower portion of the trail, but they are not known for their arboreal covering.

From the summit and its wonderful turn-around views, much of Joshua Tree National Park can be seen sprawling below. So can parts of the Salton Sea and the Coachella Valley. Many of the tallest peaks in Southern California are also visible from the top, including San Jacinto and San Gorgonio. The way out is a simple return trip, but it is wise to use care and caution. It is always easier to get injured on a descent, and this extremely rocky trail is particularly hazardous in that respect. This hike is best taken in winter when the peaks of Southern California are capped with snow and the views extend for miles and miles in the crisp, clean air. This trail is also great in spring and fall when the sun isn't too hot. Summer hiking here is best early in the morning.

17 PINE CITY

Distance: 5 miles round-trip
Hiking time: 2.5 hours
Difficulty: Easy
Elevation gain: 350 feet
High point: 4875 feet
Season: Late fall to early spring
Water: None, bring your own
Fees and permits: Required
Maps: USGS Queen Mountain, Keys View
Information: Joshua Tree National Park, (760) 367-5500, *www.nps.gov/jotr/*

Getting there: Take Interstate 10 east beyond Cabazon for 10 miles. Exit onto State Route 62 heading north. Follow SR 62 for 26.5 miles into the town of Joshua Tree. Turn right on Park Boulevard. Follow the road for 5 miles to the entrance gate. Drive for 9 miles, until you see the sign for Barker Dam. Turn left, and then right at the fork in 0.5 mile, and follow this road almost to the parking lot. Here you will see a dirt road on your right, called Queen Valley Road. Follow it for 3.8 miles total. Stay left at the first fork a mile in, and continue straight at the four-way intersection at another 1.4 miles. A high-clearance vehicle is recommended, though four-wheel drive is not required. In 3.8 miles turn left and park in the new parking area.

The trail follows an almost flat wagon road/sandy wash the entire route. It has almost no elevation loss or gain on the way in to Pine City, which is an abandoned settlement with a series of mines and lots of tall pine trees (for a desert). This is a "trail" that is not often frequented; it is not marked on the brochures, plus the one-lane dirt road used to access the hike discourages a large percentage of the tourists who flock to the more popular and easily accessible trails. This area is guaranteed to be quite a bit less traveled.

The trip includes many of the highlights one would expect to see in a desert park such as this. Starting in a forest of Joshua trees, the trail wanders along a wide sandy path that is easy to hike on, and enters a boulder-filled juniper and pinyon pine forest. Many species of cacti grow here, and there are spectacular and abundant wildflowers in the early spring. Some of the pine trees have matured to remarkable heights for such an arid landscape, especially those that flourish in the basins below the main trail.

Negro Hill, a rarely climbed peak that offers tremendous and uncrowded views

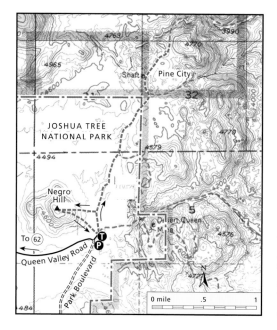

At a little over 2 miles, arrive at Pine City. Here are several remnants of old structures and many old mine shafts and claims that can be found through use of a topographical map of the area. **Note:** For safety, mine shafts should never be entered. After spending some time exploring and boulder-hopping, return the way you came.

The return trip utilizes a bit of off-trail scrambling to reach the top of Negro Hill. Choose any path to head to the top, but be mindful of cholla, spiky succulents, and various other cacti. Loose rocks pose a danger as well. It should only take fifteen to twenty minutes to reach the summit, and the view is awe-inspiring. Enjoy clear-day vistas of the surrounding desert and the high mountains to the west. The Salton Sea is readily visible in the distance, and a beautiful tableau spreads beneath the summit. Return carefully back down the mountain using the ridgelines, and try to avoid loose rock and prickly plants.

18 BARKER DAM

Distance: 1.25-mile loop
Hiking time: 1 hour
Difficulty: Easy
Elevation gain: 100 feet
High point: 4340 feet
Season: Late fall to early spring
Water: None, bring your own
Fees and permits: Required
Map: USGS Indian Cove
Information: Joshua Tree National Park, (760) 367-5500, *www.nps.gov/jotr/*

Getting there: Take Interstate 10 east beyond Cabazon for 10 miles. Exit onto State Route 62 heading north. Follow SR 62 for 26.5 miles into the town of Joshua Tree. Turn right on Park Boulevard. Follow the road for 5 miles to the entrance gate. Drive for another 9 miles until you see the sign for Barker Dam; turn left and follow this road to the parking lot.

The trail begins across sand, on a walkway of wooden posts connected by rope. The way is wide and level as it wanders and enters a boulder-filled paradise known as the Wonderland of Rocks. This hike traverses through a small portion of that beautiful landscape. Here, the arresting majesty of the desert is readily apparent. This hike makes a great introduction to the wonders of Joshua Tree National Park. There is perhaps no better place to discover the austere majesty that is the Mojave Desert.

The route is well traveled, well signed, and suitable for just about anyone ambulatory. Even the elderly and very small children can complete the simple circuit. As the path wanders through

Winter reflections off the water at Barker Dam are often dazzling.

"Disney" pictographs near Barker Dam were made more colorful by a careless film crew in 1961.

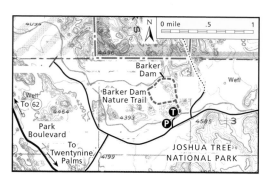

towering boulders, desert flora of all kinds can be seen, including creosote bush, cholla, yucca, cactus, Joshua trees, and several species of lush trees, including pinyon pines and junipers.

After about 0.4 mile, the man-made reservoir at Barker Dam comes into view. It is a beautiful reflecting pool, once used as a livestock watering hole, now a site for migrating birds, bighorn sheep, and a host of other desert critters that call the region home. The contrast of water and rocks makes for memorable photography. Historical markers can be seen in the concrete of the dam,

left behind by the builders, and a few other remnants of mankind's touch survive in the area. Due to the water, wildlife is very common, especially in the morning and early evening. There is also a lot of human traffic, as the trail is quite popular. Crowds tend to scare off wildlife, but there are times when privacy is easier to come by: most people tend to get off the trails around sunset. Generally, most humans do not arise before the sun, either.

From the lake, the trail winds below the dam through the jumbo boulders and a wondrous grove of Joshua trees. It stays level and nears a cave covered with Native American pictographs. Unfortunately, the markings were vandalized during the filming of a Disney special made in 1961 called *Chico, The Misunderstood Coyote*. Evidently, the paint had faded and did not show up on film, so the crew undertook making the symbols brighter and even added some of their own. As a consequence, the markings look nice, but their authenticity has been seriously compromised.

At 1.25 miles, the loop trail returns to the parking lot.

Opposite: Snow blankets the Angeles Forest along the Mount Baldy Ski Hut Trail.

SAN BERNARDINO AND ANGELES NATIONAL FORESTS

SAN BERNARDINO NATIONAL FOREST

The San Bernardino National Forest is comprised of three mountain chains that ring the Southern California Basin: the San Bernardino, San Jacinto, and Santa Rosa Mountains. The national forest and its mountains offer the bulk of hiking opportunities for most people who live within the major outlying regions of Los Angeles, Orange County, and the Inland Empire.

The San Bernardino Mountains include a lower and a higher section. Starting in the Mount Baldy region in the west, the range drops east into Cajon Pass; the mountains gradually extend from a height of 3000 feet into the Big Bear region, which sits just below 7000 feet. The mountains also hold the distinction of being the most heavily populated forested region in the country. The San Gorgonio Wilderness is the largest alpine region south of the Sierra Nevada and one of the loveliest parcels of land anywhere in California, loaded with sylvan streams, snow-fed lakes and fantastic summits.

Many Californians have a special reverence for the San Jacinto Mountains; you will hear many speak of them in tones reminiscent of those used to refer to the Sierra Nevada. The elevation changes, the granite boulders, the rocky peaks and crags, and towering lodgepole pines offer a local alternative for those who can't frequently trek to the Range of Light. The second-highest mountain range in Southern California proper, the San Jacintos are incredible. An impressive but rarely visited section of the range is the Desert Divide. Hot in summertime, it is a perfect place to while away winter afternoons, with its jaw-dropping views of the desert, Salton Sea, and the higher elevations in the range.

The much-overlooked Santa Rosas are primarily a desert range, although Toro Peak tops out at over 8000 feet and is covered in luxurious pines. Some of the peaks in this wilderness region are visited so infrequently that the summit registers date back to the 1960s.

19 ALTA SECA BENCH

Distance: 6.5 miles round-trip
Hiking time: 3 hours
Difficulty: Moderate to difficult, off-trail hiking
Elevation gain: 1000 feet
High point: 8200 feet
Season: All, road is closed in snow and fire seasons
Water: None, bring your own
Fees and permits: Adventure Pass
Map: USGS Toro Peak
Information: San Bernardino National Forest, San Jacinto Ranger District,
   (909) 382-2921, *www.fs.fed.us/r5/sanbernardino*

Getting there: Take State Route 74 east from Hemet for 22 miles. Turn right (south) onto Santa Rosa Road. Follow it for 11.5 miles to the locked gate. Park in the turnout. The road itself is interesting in that it traverses through a variety of ecosystems, from desert to alpine woodlands. This is a bumpy and rutted dirt road, not recommended for low-clearance vehicles, and four-wheel drive is preferable.

Alta Seca Bench—the name means "high" and "dry"—is a beautiful forest island in the sky. Its proximity to big cities belies its calm and serene nature. High above the smog, cars, and people, it is easy to gain a lucid understanding of why this area needs to stay protected.

The trip begins as a hike on the road that takes you to the top of Toro Peak; however, this is an off-trail scramble that loses elevation and climbs out on the return. At nearly a mile, where the road turns upward, head straight off onto the old unsigned trail. The hike follows an old Cahuilla Native American trail, although it is impossible to stay on it. Describing the trail as "faded" is an understatement. This is the perfect place to experiment with off-trail trekking. The vegetation is light, and there are many little peaks to ascend for those who choose to.

Toro Peak is the highest mountain around; since it is always in sight, it is all but impossible to get lost. To top it off, the views are superb from any of the tiny unnamed summits. This is pristine and unspoiled wilderness. There aren't

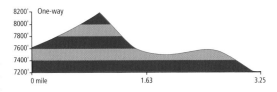

many people out here. Part of this hike passes through the Santa Rosa National Game Refuge, so it is possible to see endangered Peninsular bighorn sheep.

The objective of this hike is to reach unnamed peak 7280, easily recognizable from any of the higher ground along the trail. From the summit, the mountainside drops away on three sides at a rate of more than 2500 feet in less than a mile into Nicholias, Alder, and Black Rabbit canyons. The view is stunning and the sights can bring about a near dose of sensory overload. The mountains

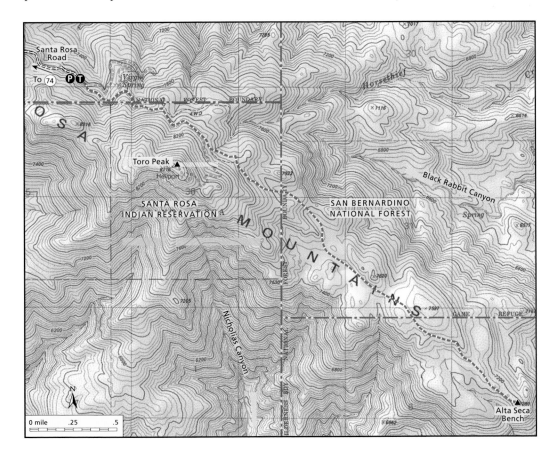

Though Alta Seca means "high and dry" in Spanish, wonderful pines grow atop the plateau.

trail off into Mexico with sentinel-like Rabbit Peak standing as the last bastion before the border. The Cuyamacas and Palomars are easily visible, as is the silver-blue glimmer of the Salton Sea, while all of Anza-Borrego lies 6000 feet beneath your boots.

There is no water here in this "high" and "dry" place, so be sure to bring enough *agua*. Off-trail hiking is strenuous activity; a general rule of thumb is that each mile you spend off a trail equates to the difficulty of 2 to 4 miles spent walking on a maintained trail. The hike in isn't all that difficult, but the return trek will take more energy, so be sure to conserve resources.

20 MARTINEZ MOUNTAIN

Distance: 16 miles round-trip
Hiking time: 8 hours or overnight.
Difficulty: Extremely strenuous
Elevation gain: 3075 feet
High point: 6560 feet
Season: Late fall to early spring, summer is blisteringly hot
Water: Horsethief Creek, Cactus Spring
Fees and permits: Adventure Pass
Maps: USGS Santa Rosa Peak, Martinez Mountain
Information: San Bernardino National Forest, (909) 382-2921,
    www.fs.fed.us/r5/sanbernardino/

Getting there: From Hemet, take State Route 74 east for 17.75 miles. Turn right onto paved Forest Service Road 7S09, and see a sign for the Ribbonwood Equestrian

Park, the Sawmill Trail, and the Cactus Spring Trail. Follow the road to its end and the large parking lot.

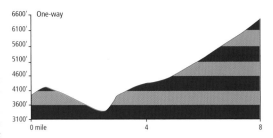

Martinez Mountain is a large, prominent desert mountain recognizable from the top of many peaks in Southern California. Its size, shape, and location make it easily identifiable. It sits at the far eastern terminus of the Peninsular Range of mountains that run from San Jacinto down to the Santa Rosas. While not the largest mountain in the region, it rests far enough away from the other peaks in the area to make it a worthwhile summit, not only for its difficult, remote, and isolated access, but also for its tremendous views.

Follow the Cactus Spring Trail for about half a mile as it passes Dolomite Mine and then begins losing elevation as it drops into Horsethief Canyon. If there has been recent rain, the trail may follow a tiny seasonal creek into the canyon before crossing Horsethief Creek, which generally has at least some water even into summer. From there the trail climbs up toward Cactus Spring, which sits about 20 yards northeast of the trail. Not that easy to find, Cactus Spring is simply a hole in the ground that is an important source of water for the endangered desert bighorn sheep. The trail continues beyond the spring. After 6 miles, the trail meets a use path at a saddle that sits just over 1 mile west of the summit of Martinez Mountain.

Follow the use trail east (left) to the region near the peak, then scramble up the rocks to the summit, which is rated as Class III climbing. The short route to the top is not difficult, but it may be tough for those afraid of heights. Nothing technical is required to reach the actual summit, but there are a few holds where a fall could be dangerous.

Once on top, the views are extraordinary. The entirety of the Coachella Valley is visible, and the desert below is a stunning display. Every bit of the Salton Sea lies within view as it tapers off toward Mexico. The nearby summits of Toro, Santa Rosa, Rabbit, and San Jacinto loom to the north and west. San Gorgonio sits farther off in the distance, but the 360-degree view is breathtaking and well worth the long hike to get there.

Get an early start and bring flashlights and or headlamps, as the trip can stretch into a longer one with bits of exploring or off-trail travel. Some important Cahuilla Native American sites are located within the Cactus Springs

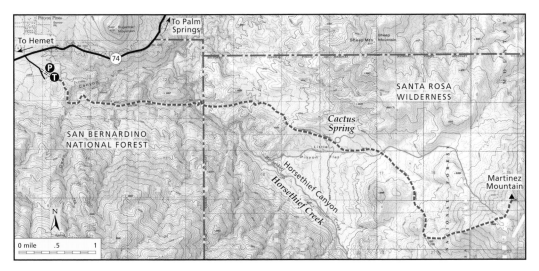

Taking a lunch break after a hearty climb up Martinez Mountain

region including old villages, mortrero sites, petroglyphs, and pictographs. The area contains a crossroads of trails and paths used by the Native people who once lived here. Keep an eye out for bighorn sheep and the least Bell's vireo, an endangered bird. Return the way you came.

21 LION PEAK

Distance: 8.5 miles round-trip
Hiking time: 4.5 hours
Difficulty: Moderate
Elevation gain: 1400 feet
High point: 6868 feet
Season: All, hot in summer
Water: None, bring your own
Fees and permits: Adventure Pass
Map: USGS Palm View Peak
Information: San Bernardino National Forest, (909) 382-2921,
   www.fs.fed.us/r5/sanbernardino/

Getting there: Take State Route 74 east from Hemet to the junction with Highway 243. Continue east on SR 74 for 9 miles. Turn left onto Morris Ranch Road, and drive 3.7 miles to an iron gate on the right signed for Cedar Springs Trail. Park in the pullout just before the gate.

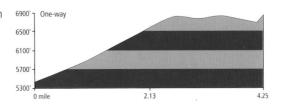

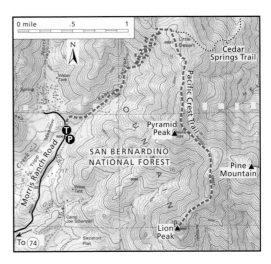

The trip to Lion Peak is an excellent outing along a particularly wild and wonderful section of the San Jacinto Range known as the Desert Divide. Here the mountains separate from the valleys and extend along a prominent ridge that produces some of the most stunning vistas in Southern California. The desert drops away south and east from the San Gorgonio Pass to the farthest reaches of the Salton Sea. The higher peaks in the San Jacintos stretch into the north while Garner Valley nestles between the magnificent Santa Rosas to the south.

From the turnout, head down the road about 50 yards to the trailhead. Go through the gate. Be sure to close all gates on the hike, as there are several near the beginning of the trail. This hike crosses private property, and all of Southern California is fortunate to have access to this hike. Many property owners balk at allowing access to public lands via their own, so please take care to respect their property. Follow the road past a water tank and turn left onto the trail. Go through the next gate, close it behind you, and enter the forest. Walk up the road until it eventually becomes the trail. The final gate is part of a fence designed to keep cattle on the correct side of forest property; close it and continue past a relatively undeveloped picnic area a little over a mile into the journey.

From there, the hike ascends to the beautiful ridgeline via a system of remarkably well-graded switchbacks. At the top of the climb the trail junctions with the Pacific Crest Trail (PCT), which extends south all the way to Mexico and northward into Canada. It also continues 1 mile eastward to lovely and wet Cedar Spring, which generally has water year-round. Since the region is lower in elevation than many of the higher peaks in the San Jacintos, it is not heavily forested. This makes the trip mostly shadeless, very hot in summer and even on wintry afternoons. It is good to get

an early start. The lack of trees, however, is what gives the trail such wonderful views. A lone oak tree does stand at the junction, and offers a great place for a respite and snack break.

Turn right on the PCT and follow it south past Pyramid Peak on the right at 1 mile, then pass Pine Mountain on the left at 1.5 miles. Lion Peak sits 2 miles down the trail only a little ways off the PCT on the right, and is easily recognizable by its woody top, covered with lovely pines. The use trail to its summit is worn and marked by a cairn.

All three summits can easily be bagged in a day, and each is a worthwhile venture based on its own merits. For those who want to make this an overnight trip, primitive (wilderness) camping is available. When you're done exploring here, return to the parking area the same way you came in.

The Desert Divide is lightly visited, despite its outstanding views.

22 DEVILS SLIDE TRAIL TO TAHQUITZ PEAK

Distance: 9 miles round-trip
Hiking time: 4.5 hours
Difficulty: Strenuous
Elevation gain: 2350 feet
High point: 8846 feet
Season: Late spring to late fall
Water: Middle Spring, Tahquitz Meadow
Fees and permits: Adventure Pass
Map: USGS San Jacinto Peak
Information: San Bernardino National Forest, (909) 382-2921,
www.fs.fed.us/r5/sanbernardino/

Getting there: From State Route 243 in Idyllwild, turn east on North Circle Drive. Continue straight for over 1 mile until you reach South Circle Drive. Turn right, and then take the first left onto Fern Valley Road. Follow Fern Valley Road all the way to Humber Park, about 2 miles from downtown.

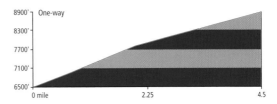

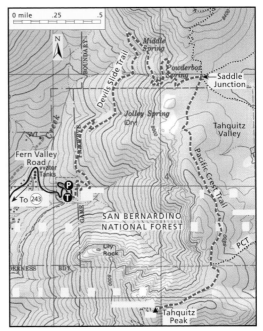

The Devils Slide Trail is the second most popular trail in the San Jacinto Wilderness, with only the Palm Springs Tramway Trail to Round Valley and San Jacinto Peak getting more visitors. This is a well-groomed, nicely graded, and well-shaded hike through beautiful tall yellow pines, with a moderate 2.5-mile climb to Saddle Junction, a meeting place for a number of trails that venture off in five directions.

There are many options from the junction, but most hikers take the trail to Tahquitz Peak and the fire lookout that sits atop its lofty prominence. Tahquitz was named for a demon that haunted local Native American legends, luring away beautiful maidens to devour them whole.

Hikers can take one of two routes from Saddle Junction to reach the lookout. The first right turn follows the Pacific Crest Trail (PCT), which is the shortest way to the top and the one given in the information block for this route. The second right turn leads through Tahquitz Valley and Little Tahquitz Valley, a more scenic section of the forest than the PCT route, but this adds an additional half mile to the trip each way.

Either way, at 1 mile via the PCT or 1.5 miles via Tahquitz Valley, the trip reaches another junction where left and right are the only options;

From the lookout on Tahquitz Peak, early morning clouds cover everything below 7000 feet.

turn right and head to the top of Tahquitz Peak. From this point, the trail makes its final half-mile ascent up a steeper stretch to the last portion of the summit push. Just below the peak sits a steep shady slope that gets extreme ice and snow during the winter; it can be incredibly dangerous without proper mountaineering gear. It is inadvisable to attempt this section in winter unless properly trained.

The fire lookout, built in 1937, is on the National Historic Lookout Register. Since 1998, it has been staffed entirely by volunteers. The lookout affords incredible views of the surrounding mountains and all of Southern California, including the Pacific Ocean and the more southerly of the Channel Islands. The hosts in the lookout have a wealth of information. They staff the lookout primarily to watch for fires, but are also happy to assist visitors with information about the local mountains, flora, and fauna.

23 FULLER RIDGE TO SAN JACINTO PEAK

Distance: 14 miles round-trip
Hiking time: 7 hours or overnight backpack into Little Round Valley
Difficulty: Extremely strenuous
Elevation gain: 3100 feet
High point: 10,834 feet
Season: Late spring to early fall, icy in winter
Water: None, bring your own
Fees and permits: Adventure Pass
Map: USGS San Jacinto Peak
Information: Mount San Jacinto State Park, (951) 659-2607,
    www.parks.ca.gov/default.asp?page_id=636

Getting there: Take State Route 243 south from either Banning or Idyllwild. Turn east onto Black Mountain Road (Forest Service Road 4S01). It is a rutted and rough washboard of a road, but even a low-clearance vehicle should be able to make it. After 8 miles there is a signed turnoff for the Fuller Ridge Trail. Take a right and park in the open lot.

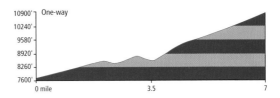

Fuller Ridge skirts the edge of the San Jacinto Wilderness and enters Mount San Jacinto State Park. Almost from the hike's outset, the view across the San Gorgonio Pass is simply outstanding. The north face of the San Jacinto massif juts out of the desert in one of the steepest elevation changes in the continental United States. The escarpment rises over 10,000 feet in 7 miles. San Jacinto is often listed as the second highest peak in Southern California, but this is not true. Both Jepson and Anderson peaks in the San Gorgonio Wilderness are higher.

The Fuller Ridge Trail is a part of the Pacific Crest Trail (PCT), and is often the most challenging and precarious outing for Mexico-to-Canada through-hikers before the Sierra Nevadas. Early in the year, the trail is covered in treacherous snow and packed ice, and there are many exposed sections that could lead to drops from 4000 to 7000 feet straight down to the desert floor. Before hiking here, always call ahead and check road conditions.

The trail is nicely wooded. At the wilderness boundary, signs say that a wilderness permit is needed to continue beyond 1.5 miles ahead. This is an excellent duff-covered trail, shady, secluded, with plenty of jaw-dropping views. All types of wildlife, including mule deer and squirrels, are common along the trail. Pass the aptly

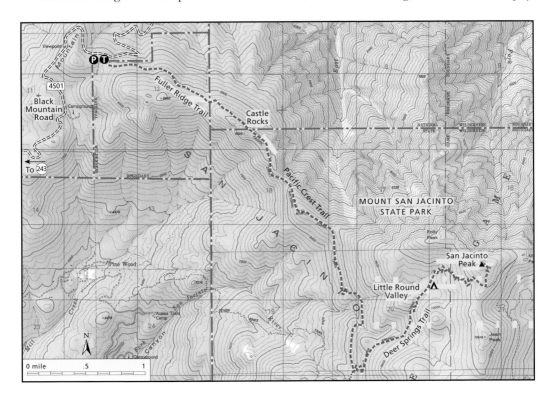

named spires of Castle Rocks as the trail gains and loses elevation. At 4.5 miles, the trail meets a junction with the Deer Springs Trail; turn left and ascend upward into Little Round Valley. As it climbs, there are portions of hot, dry manzanita- and whitethorn-covered slopes, but towering trees remain a frequent sight and offer respite from the sun. About 1 mile below the peak, there is a campground for backpackers. As you near the top of the peak, turn left onto the short summit trail, and clamber on the rocks to the top.

The rocky apex is definitely one of the iconic peaks of Southern California. John Muir reportedly mused that the view from the top was the most sublime he'd ever seen, and there is no doubt that he stood astride many a mountaintop. Of course, his day was before the advent of smog, so one can only imagine a view of the coast from Point Mugu to Cabrillo, with the ring of beautiful mountain ranges encircling the Los Angeles Basin, and into the desert beyond Joshua Tree as far as Mount Charleston in Las Vegas, not to mention the Coachella Valley and the Salton Sea. Even these days, on a clear day one can see the Pacific and the Channel Islands from this peak (though clear days are few and far between in summer).

When you're done enjoying the views, return the way you came.

Surveying the summit of Mount San Jacinto

24 SAN GORGONIO PEAK VIA FISH CREEK

Distance: 22 miles round-trip
Hiking time: 11 hours or overnight
Difficulty: Extremely strenuous
Elevation gain: 3550 feet
High point: 11,500 feet
Season: Late spring to late fall
Water: None, bring your own
Fees and permits: Adventure Pass
Map: USGS San Gorgonio Mountain
Information: San Bernardino National Forest, (909) 382-2881,
   www.fs.fed.us/r5/sanbernardino/

Getting there: Take State Route 38 north and east from Angelus Oaks, Forest Falls, or Mountain Home Village, and follow the highway toward Big Bear. Turn right 6 miles beyond Barton Flats Visitor Center onto Forest Service Road 1N02. Follow the paved road until it forks, then continue right onto Forest Service Road 1N05 and go 7 miles to the trailhead. The road is unpaved and not suitable for low-clearance vehicles.

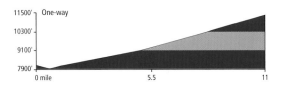

No matter which route is taken to the top of Mount San Gorgonio, the trip is a long all-day climb. The Fish Creek Trail is one of the longest

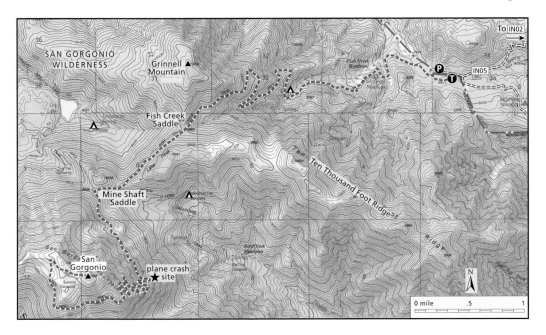

Two hikers make light work of the long route to the top of "Old Greyback."

routes to the top, which paradoxically also makes it one of the easiest. Due to its longer mileage, the trail is not as steep, and the starting elevation is higher, which makes the gradient to the top much less severe. This, however, does not make the hike a proverbial walk in the park; any trail over 20 miles is bound to give even the strongest of hikers a workout. For those who prefer not to tackle it all in one day, primitive (wilderness) camping is available along and off the trail.

The trail begins in the wilderness and its beauty is apparent from the very first steps. Wildflowers blossom and green grasses grow alongside the banks of beautiful Fish Creek. As the path wanders into meadows, wildlife is abundant, especially in the early morning and early evening. The trail drops down for a gentle mile before starting the climb toward the Fish Creek campsite around 2 miles into the trip. From the wilderness camp, the trail climbs for 4 miles to Fish Creek Saddle. It eases up a bit for another mile to Mine Shaft Saddle, where expansive views of the Ten Thousand Foot Ridge open up and the canyon of the North Fork of Whitewater River descends into the desert below.

Turn left onto the Sky High Trail and begin the push to the summit, as the hike begins to switchback in long arcing sweeps up the mountain. The trail passes the wreckage of a military C-47 cargo plane that crashed in November 1952, killing all thirteen crew aboard. A placard and a few laminated pages tell the story of the downed plane and the fateful events that led to the crash. As the trail continues to climb, it eventually wraps its way in a semicircle 180 degrees around the entire summit before connecting with the short half-mile spur to the top.

At the peak, the views are second to none. This is truly the high point of Southern California proper. At 11,500 feet, no taller peak exists within sight, even on the clearest of days. Telescope Peak in Death Valley can be seen from the summit, as can Mount Charleston, which is a bit higher, but it resides solely in Nevada just outside of Las Vegas. Across the pass the sightline to Mount San Jacinto just 20 miles away is perhaps the grandest view available: it seems merely a stone's throw from summit to summit. Enjoy this view of everything in Southern California and return via the same trail.

25 MOMYER CREEK

Distance: 13 miles round-trip
Hiking time: 7 hours
Difficulty: Extremely strenuous
Elevation gain: 5200 feet
High point: 10,691 feet
Season: Late spring to late fall
Water: None, bring your own
Fees and permits: Adventure Pass
Map: USGS Forest Falls
Information: San Bernardino National Forest, (909) 382-2881, *www.fs.fed.us/r5/sanbernardino/*

Getting there: From eastbound Interstate 10 in Redlands, take the University Street exit. Turn right and then immediately left on East Citrus Avenue. Follow Citrus to Judson/Ford Street and turn left. Turn right onto State Route 38 (Lugonia Avenue). Continue east as it becomes Mentone and then Mill Creek Road. When the highway turns sharply right to climb up the mountain, continue straight (east) on Valley of the Falls Road for about a mile. Park at the signed lot for Momyer/Alger Creek Trail.

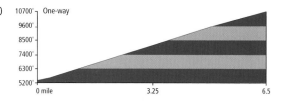

The Momyer Creek Trail is the shortest route to the San Bernardino Ridge from the southern side of the San Gorgonio Wilderness. It is a gorgeous trail that begins along Mill Creek and then scrawls its way through a steep section of oak forest up to the wilderness boundary. Much of the first mile and a half is exposed and can be very hot in the late morning or afternoon, and as such it is better to get an early start. The first half mile crosses the creek in a few places and can sometimes be difficult to follow.

After 2 miles the trail enters the wilderness, and the lodgepole pine forest provides a shady respite for a short mile-long stretch. Watch for the unsigned trail junction less than a quarter mile beyond the sign for the wilderness; turn left. From here, the trail climbs steeply upward for a little more than 2 miles.

The "unmaintained" trail is well taken care of by volunteers, but since it is not a Forest Service trail, it does not make use of switchbacks the way a more popular trail might. As the trail forces its way up the mountain, it does so amidst a bramble of whitethorn and manzanita that can cut, scrape, and puncture the hardiest of ankles

Mount San Jacinto becomes visible above the Yucaipa Ridge as the trail nears the top.

and legs. This is a good trail to wear long pants on, even though the sun can hammer the slope in the afternoon. Eventually the trail hits some welcome switchbacks near the top that ease the steepness of the climb. Finally the trail wraps its way along the southeast face of San Bernardino Peak before reaching the ridgeline.

The view from the ridge is enough of a reward for those who wish to call it a hike and return to their cars. For those who want to go farther, from the saddle there are two directions to choose from, east or west. Either way holds adventure, with peaks above 10,000 feet in elevation. To the east lies Anderson and Shields; to the west, San Bernardino East and San Bernardino Peak. All have expansive and outstanding views, most of which encompass a complete 360 degrees. From any of these peaks' lofty vantage points, nearly all of Southern California can be seen on a clear day. With the summit of San Bernardino East Peak within a half mile and only a couple of hundred feet above, it seems the likeliest target for those with just a little bit more energy and reserves. The vistas are beyond compare.

Yucca blossom among pines as desert transitions into forest on the Momyer Creek Trail.

26 DOLLAR LAKE

Distance: 11 miles round-trip
Hiking time: 6 hours
Difficulty: Very strenuous
Elevation gain: 2600 feet
High point: 9550 feet
Season: Late spring to late fall
Water: Plentiful
Fees and permits: Adventure Pass
Maps: USGS San Gorgonio Mountain, Moonridge
Information: San Bernardino National Forest, (909) 382-2881,
www.fs.fed.us/r5/sanbernardino/

Getting there: From Redlands, take State Route 38 (Lugonia Avenue) as it becomes Mentone Boulevard and then Mill Creek Road. Continue on SR 38 past Mountain Home Village. Follow SR 38 as it makes the hairpin turn left and continues up the mountain to Angelus Oaks, then continue for another 5.5 miles and turn left onto Jenks Lake Road. Follow Jenks Lake Road for 2.5 miles to the parking area for the South Fork trailhead.

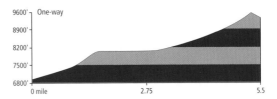

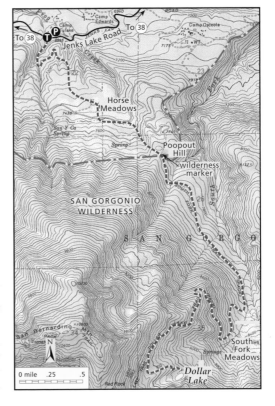

From the parking area, head south across the road to the trail, which is wide and well traveled. This is the most popular trail in the San Gorgonio Wilderness, with good reason. Not only does this region contain beautiful alpine lakes nestled beneath towering peaks where wildflowers grow abundantly and wildlife frolics in the canyon recesses, but water is ever-present even in dryer years, and the snow hangs around later here due to the north-facing slopes and higher elevation. The combination of all of these elements makes the area gorgeous and spectacular. It contains, without a doubt, some of the most stunning forest scenery in all of Southern California.

The trip begins through a mixed forest of shady pine and oak that eventually opens up into shadeless manzanita- and chaparral-covered slopes after exiting the lovely and historic Horse Meadows. At 2 miles, the trail enters the wilderness. A short spur marked by a sign with a camera

The South Fork of the Santa Ana River rushes by the trail junction to Dry Lake.

on it leads to the top of Poopout Hill, where a large plaque commemorates the wilderness and provides information about the area set in a stunningly scenic backdrop with a grand view of San Gorgonio Mountain. Here the pine forest returns in majestic splendor.

From the overlook, the trail begins to follow the creek drainage as it gently climbs for another 1.5 miles to South Fork Meadows. At this point, the path splits; take the right fork to Dollar Lake. The trail gains another 1000 feet in 2 miles, switchbacking up the mountainside until it meets the short offshoot that heads down to Dollar Lake. Turn left at the junction (heading straight would lead to Dollar Lake Saddle and the San Bernardino Mountain ridgeline).

Dollar Lake itself is rather small, but it is quaint and pretty and nearly circular, which is how it derived its name, due to its resemblance to a silver dollar. The lake itself is not as popular as Dry Lake, which is larger, lower in elevation, and slightly easier to reach, but still, here are ample opportunities to relax, enjoy the scenery, take photographs, and take a dip in the cool, refreshing waters. In the spring, stay on the lookout for lovely wild irises of varied colors and beautifully symmetrical columbine that grow in the rich soil along the trail.

27 SAN BERNARDINO PEAK

Distance: 15 miles round-trip
Hiking time: 8 hours or overnight
Difficulty: Extremely strenuous
Elevation gain: 4650 feet
High point: 10,649 feet
Season: Late spring to late fall
Water: None, bring your own
Fees and permits: Adventure Pass
Maps: USGS Big Bear Lake, Forest Falls
Information: San Bernardino National Forest, (909) 382-2881,
www.fs.fed.us/r5/sanbernardino/

Getting there: Take State Route 38 north and east from Mountain Home Village, and follow the highway toward Big Bear. Drive up the mountain for 5 miles to the town of Angelus Oaks. Turn right onto Manzanita Street and follow Forest Service Road 1N07 0.25 mile to the trailhead.

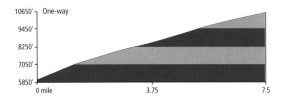

Colonel Washington's initial survey was made at this very site.

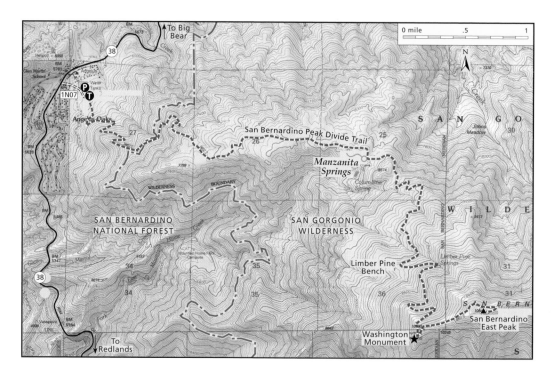

San Bernardino Peak is the westernmost high point along the San Bernardino Peak Divide in the San Gorgonio Wilderness, the farthest west of the nine named summits above 10,000 feet in the wilderness area. The trail to the summit is a no-nonsense elevation gainer, climbing a steady 800 feet per mile through shady pine forest until reaching a plateau 3 miles into the hike at about 8200 feet at Manzanita Springs. The respite from climbing lasts for about a mile, passing through scrub mountain chaparral and manzanita. Viewpoints abound from this location and the high country scenery is splendid.

The trail begins climbing upward again after passing the trail junction for Columbine Springs and Johns Meadow. Continue straight and follow the signs for San Bernardino Peak and Limber Pine Bench. As the trail heads upward again, it enters into lovely pine forest. The trail skirts the contours of the mountain and passes several canyons and spring-fed creeks coming off the mountainside.

Just below the summit lies an important piece of Southern California history. Colonel Henry Washington and his team of thirteen surveyors built a tower 24 feet high and began a land survey line stretching all the way from Mexico to the Tehachapi Mountains. To this day, every piece of land in Southern California is tangibly but invisibly tied to this baseline. Interestingly enough, the crew originally sought to assess the land during the day, but the heat from the valley floor made it impossible to do so. Instead the crew lit a fire and made the measurements at night. The monument still stands, albeit in a slightly different form. The original rocks that were used to support the tower are still there, but the rocks have been restacked over the years.

Half a mile from the initial survey point, the trail splits; follow the summit trail to the right as it curves around the peak's backside to the top. There is a summit marker and a trail register atop the peak. Those with more energy can choose to summit San Bernardino East Peak as well, which sits less than a mile away on the trail.

Return the way you came, or break the hike into two days by camping in a primitive (wilderness) site along the way.

28 CASTLE ROCK AND CHAMPION LODGEPOLE PINE

Distance: 4 miles round-trip
Hiking time: 2 hours
Difficulty: Easy
Elevation gain: 800 feet
High point: 7640 feet
Season: All
Water: None, bring your own
Fees and permits: Adventure Pass
Map: USGS Big Bear Lake
Information: San Bernardino National Forest, (909) 382-2790,
    www.fs.fed.us/r5/sanbernardino/

Getting there: From Interstate 10 in Redlands, take State Route 30 north to the connection with State Route 330 north. At Running Springs, take Rim of the World Highway (State Route 18) east across the dam to the south side of Big Bear Lake. Go a little over a mile past the bridge and you will see the signed trail on your right and a small turnout on your left 20–40 yards beyond the turn.

From the parking area, walk down the road to the trailhead. Follow the trail as it climbs rather steeply over 600 feet in around half a mile. The steepness is sure to provide a workout, though the short distance makes getting to the top fairly simple. The trail is generally easy to follow, though in spots where it is particularly rocky painted arrows help guide the way. Since a lot of people have used this trail, many have lost their way and there are a lot of tiny offshoots that lead nowhere. Most of the time, it is easy to tell where the trail is going; when it isn't, it does not take very long to get back on the right path. The length of the route is shady and the entire trip is peaceful and cool due to the high density of tree growth in the area.

There are several spots to scramble atop the formation known as Castle Rock, which is easy to make out from the trail at about 0.75 mile, because it truly towers above the forest below like the hardened battlements of a fortress. A spectacular view of the lake makes Castle Rock a nice rest stop. Continue southbound on the trail

and stay straight at the junction with Forest Road 2N85. The way climbs and strays through some lovely stands of lodgepole and Jeffrey pine along with nice-looking boulder formations. Since this is the south side of Big Bear Lake, the area retains a higher amount of precipitation, which makes it quite a bit greener than the north side.

When the trail junctions with Forest Road 2N86,

The Champion Lodgepole Pine stands out as a giant among trees.

turn right and follow the road for nearly half a mile. The trail picks up again after passing some private property, and heads left and south again toward the Champion Lodgepole Pine. This massive pine tree, standing on the edge of a verdant meadow, is truly a monster at 110 feet. Most pines, especially lodgepoles, do not grow so tall, but for some reason the perfect conditions came together at this spot to make this the tallest lodgepole pine in the world.

If the region seems somehow strangely familiar, it could be childhood memories of television programs like *Bonanza*, which filmed many episodes here.

29 COUGAR CREST

Distance: 5 miles round-trip
Hiking time: 2.5 hours
Difficulty: Moderate
Elevation gain: 1370 feet
High point: 8201 feet
Season: All
Water: None, bring your own
Fees and permits: Adventure Pass
Map: USGS Fawnskin
Information: San Bernardino National Forest, (909) 382-2790,
    www.fs.fed.us/r5/sanbernardino/

Getting there: From Interstate 10 in Redlands, take State Route 30 north to the connection with State Route 330 north. At Running Springs, take Rim of the World Highway (State Route 18) east toward Big Bear City for 13 miles. At the dam, veer left onto State Route 38. At 6.5 miles, park in the large parking area on your left.

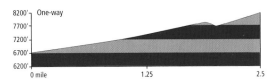

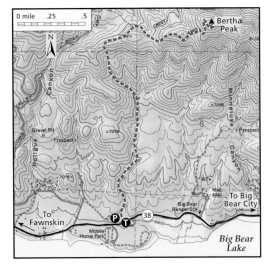

Cougar Crest is a wonderful trail for beginners. It doesn't need to be completed to be enjoyed, and the area has enough scenic beauty to make it a fantastic place to get in touch with nature. Many people use this trail for running and exercise; there are almost always hikers, too, as this is perhaps the most popular trail in the Big Bear area.

The trail traverses forest filled with towering lodgepole and Jeffrey pine. Some rather large western junipers, with their distinctive twisted and gnarled red bark, also thrive on this trail. There is not much water on the north side of the lake. The snow melts quickly due to the direct sunlight and the streams dry up much earlier as a result. There is plenty of shade, however, and the trail is mostly duff-covered with only a few rocky areas.

The Cougar Crest Trail dead-ends after 2 miles at the Pacific Crest Trail (PCT) atop a ridgeline. The first mile is a nearly level easy walk on an old fire road, gaining only minimal elevation until reaching the end of the road. From there the trail climbs steadily to the top of the ridgeline. In another half-mile an expansive view of Big Bear

Lake and the San Gorgonio Wilderness emerges. This is a good stopping and turnaround point for those who are only looking for a short hike and just want to enjoy the benefits of the natural world. From there, the trail continues to climb up to the PCT.

At the PCT, options such as Bertha Peak and Delamar Mountain (Hike 30) present themselves

Western wallflowers on Bertha Peak overlook the San Gorgonio Wilderness and Big Bear Lake.

to those who want to extend their hike. Turn right at the junction and follow the PCT until it intersects with the service road that goes to the top of Bertha Peak; or turn left and take the longer route to Delamar Mountain. Either peak offers sizeable rewards, though the views of the lake are much less unobstructed from Bertha. Delamar is a considerably longer hike and not as frequently visited. People looking for solitude and isolation, and/or an all-day outing, should opt for this choice, while those looking for a shorter hike should choose Bertha Peak.

30 DELAMAR MOUNTAIN

Distance: 8 miles round-trip
Hiking time: 4 hours
Difficulty: Moderate to strenuous
Elevation gain: 1800 feet
High point: 8398 feet
Season: All, road may be closed for winter snows
Water: None, bring your own
Fees and permits: Adventure Pass
Map: USGS Fawnskin
Information: San Bernardino National Forest, Big Bear Ranger Station, (909) 382-2790, *www.fs.fed.us/r5/sanbernardino*

Getting there: From Interstate 10 in Redlands, take State Route 30 north to the connection with State Route 330 north. At Running Springs, take Rim of the World Highway (State Route 18) east toward Big Bear City for 13 miles. At the dam, veer left to follow

State Route 38 to the north side of Big Bear Lake and the community of Fawnskin. Turn left (north) onto Rim of the World Drive. After about 1.5 miles, Rim of the World becomes Coxey Truck Trail; stay on Coxey and park just before Holcomb Creek Road. The Pacific Crest Trail (PCT) crosses the road on the south side of the creek bed. Park and start your hike.

Another option is to approach Delamar Mountain via the Cougar Crest Trail (Hike 29) from Fawnskin. The elevation gain on that hike is the same, but the distance is 12 miles round-trip instead of 7. If Coxey Truck Trail is closed in the winter, Cougar Crest is the only way to reach this peak.

This is a perfect trail to take in low-snow winters. The trail begins at around 6000 feet elevation, and snow rarely sticks around very long at that level. The higher you go, the more you will see, but you won't need an ice ax or crampons to traverse this section of the Pacific Crest Trail (PCT). The final summit push up an old jeep road is steep, so if you do go during the snow and ice, take crampons if you have them. In all probability, you will not need them; still, it is always better to be safe rather than sorry.

Even though this trail presents winter recreational activities, that does not mean it is devoid of fall, summer, and springtime fun. On the

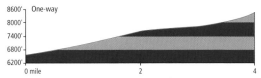

contrary, this makes a fine hike at any time of the year. You are a lot less likely to see other people on this hike than on other trails in the area. The Cougar Crest Trail (Hike 29) is very popular, so if you take that option, there will be a plethora of people; but after the saddle and junction with the PCT, most day hikers opt to go on to Bertha Peak rather than Delamar Mountain. By driving on a dirt road, even for just 2 miles, you exponentially decrease the numbers of people who will be joining you on this trail.

This is Big Bear at its finest, with enormous ponderosa pine trees, large flats, and meadows. You will be hiking through San Bernardino mining country, and there are old mines and prospects all over the area (though none directly by the trail). Delamar Mountain is named after a miner who worked several of the mines in the area. Many of the nearby campgrounds used to be mining encampments. The Greenlead Mine is still clearly visible to the north from the peak and the trail.

Finding the actual summit of Delamar Mountain is a bit tricky. The best way to do it is with a Global Positioning System (GPS) because of a

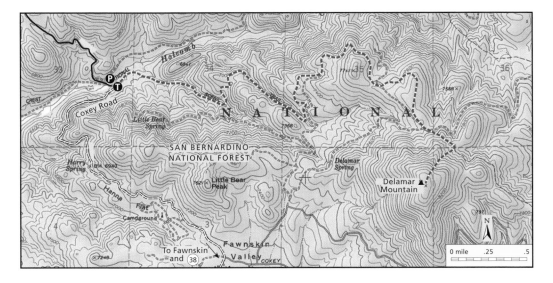

The final push to the summit of Delamar Mountain is an old and steep road.

preponderance of roads in the area. Once you cross Delamar Mountain Road, which is un-signed, in less than 0.25 mile you will come to a rarely used jeep road heading very steeply uphill to the south (your right). Use your instinct, and ascend this road to the summit.

ANGELES NATIONAL FOREST

The San Gabriel Mountains include a front range and a back range running almost parallel to one another. The front range is lower, hotter, and drier, and is covered in thick chaparral. The mountains rise steeply from the floor of the basin up rugged canyons that run with seasonal streams. The back range is considerably higher, topping out with Mount Baldy. At over 10,000 feet, Baldy is one of the most picturesque mountains in the state, its snow-capped summit frequently seen on postcards of Los Angeles. The mountains contain acres of wilderness, lush canyons, rivers, waterfalls, rocky crags, and alpine summits.

Several wilderness areas within Angeles National Forest offer rugged appeal, and the Angeles Crest Highway makes them readily accessible. They range from granite-topped peaks that amass enough snow to make for true alpine conditions in winter, to hardy and isolated desert summits that can only be attempted as the temperatures begin to drop. From the San Gabriel Valley, the mountains rise to a precipitous height. Camping, backpacking, and hiking are available for all to enjoy.

The Angeles National Forest, along with San Bernardino National Forest, provide an outdoor playground for twenty-five million people. They are some of the most heavily utilized and, in places, overused outdoor areas in the world. With urban encroachment, global warming, and bark beetle infestations, they are also some of the most threatened.

31 BIGHORN PEAK

Distance: 11.5 miles round-trip
Hiking time: 6 hours
Difficulty: Extremely strenuous
Elevation gain: 3500 feet
High point: 8441 feet
Season: Late spring to late fall
Water: Columbine Spring, Icehouse Creek
Fees and permits: Adventure Pass
Maps: USGS Cucamonga Peak, Mount Baldy
Information: Angeles National Forest, (909) 982-2829, *www.fs.fed.us/r5/angeles/*

Getting there: From Pasadena, take Interstate 210 east to Claremont. Exit and turn left on Baseline Road. Turn right onto Padua Avenue and continue 1.8 miles. Then turn right onto Mount Baldy Road. Continue for 9.5 miles through Baldy Village to the fork at Icehouse Canyon; turn right into the parking lot.

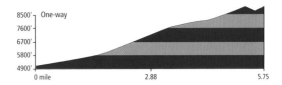

Bighorn Peak is a prominent summit in the southeastern section of the San Gabriel Mountains. Along with Etiwanda, Cucamonga, and Ontario, the dominating south face of these peaks is a stalwart bastion looming over a large portion of Southern California. From the Inland Empire, the mountains' south face is steep and ominous. Another thing these summits share in

common is that the most popular approach to each of them begins in Icehouse Canyon.

The walk through Icehouse Canyon wanders and climbs through a lovely wooded glen filled with sparkling cascades, vernal pools, lush vegetation, towering pines, ruined structures from near the turn of the century, and even getaway cabins that require a short hike for the occupants. There are numerous places to play in the water and enjoy an outing in this beautiful forest. The year-round water in Icehouse Creek can be a dangerous raging torrent during high runoff season, or a gentle stream during warmer months.

The trail up Icehouse Canyon begins at the gated road on the north end of the parking lot. Walk up the road until it becomes a large path passing cabins and foundations of the historic lodge that was destroyed by a flash flood in 1938. In just under a mile the trail junctions with the Chapman Trail, which is a longer, flatter, and less crowded alternative to the main trail. Taking it adds a couple of miles each way to the overall distance. The trail enters the Cucamonga Wilderness at about 1.5 miles and continues on toward Columbine Spring, which has fresh

Leaving the wide-open summit of Bighorn Peak

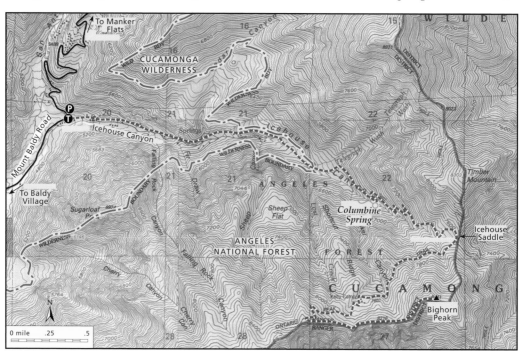

running water year-round. The trail switchbacks and climbs, meeting the second junction with the Chapman Trail at just over 3 miles, below Icehouse Saddle. Most of the route is shaded by large sugar pines.

Several trails converge at this point. From the notch, take the first trail on the right. Follow it for 1 mile to Kelly Camp, and head uphill to the left

toward another saddle. Turn left and ascend to the top of Bighorn Peak (a right turn leads to Ontario Peak). Return the way you came, or make a semiloop with the Chapman Trail.

The summit can also be reached via an off-trail scramble directly up the side of the mountain from Icehouse Saddle. Though this is the most direct way, it is steep, thorny, and difficult.

32 MOUNT BALDY

Distance: 10.5 miles round-trip
Hiking time: 5 hours
Difficulty: Extremely strenuous
Elevation gain: 3900 feet
High point: 10,064 feet
Season: Spring to late fall
Water: San Antonio Creek
Fees and permits: Adventure Pass
Maps: USGS Mount San Antonio, Mount Baldy
Information: Angeles National Forest, (909) 982-2829, *www.fs.fed.us/r5/angeles/*

Getting there: Take Interstate 10 to Mountain Avenue in Upland. Exit and travel north (toward the mountains—you can't miss them). Follow Mountain Avenue all the way up, veering left as it merges with Euclid Avenue. At the road's end, turn right onto Mount Baldy Road. Park where the road splits just beyond Manker Flats Campground.

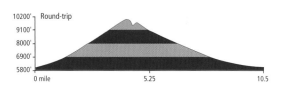

Mount Baldy is the preeminent mountain in the Angeles National Forest. Although its real name is Mount San Antonio, no one calls it that; to everyone, it is simply Mount Baldy. Once on top, it should be obvious as to why it has been given this moniker. Though there are no trees on top, the trail itself is lush and filled with vegetation. In fact, there aren't many trails in the entire forest that are much nicer.

From the parking area, head toward the road with a locked gate near the portable toilets and walk up San Antonio Falls Road. In a little less than half a mile, the roar of the falls will become evident. A short use trail winds to the base of the falls, and is a recommended side venture.

From the falls viewpoint, the road hairpins and continues up the mountain. Just after another 0.25 mile, beyond the next turn in the road, the trail junctions almost immediately. Watch carefully for the trail on the left side. It is unmarked, though obvious, but many people walk right on by, which is easy to do because the views begin to open up at this spot and they might cause a distraction.

This is now the Baldy Ski Hut Trail, maintained by the Sierra Club. It follows the contours of the mountain as it steadily climbs to the ski hut. The trail passes an old mine along the way, and a little exploring leads to some foundations and ruins of outbuildings. At about 2 miles, the halfway point of the Ski Hut Trail, cross lovely San Antonio Creek and the Baldy Bowl and

Traversing an awe-inspiring section of the Devils Backbone

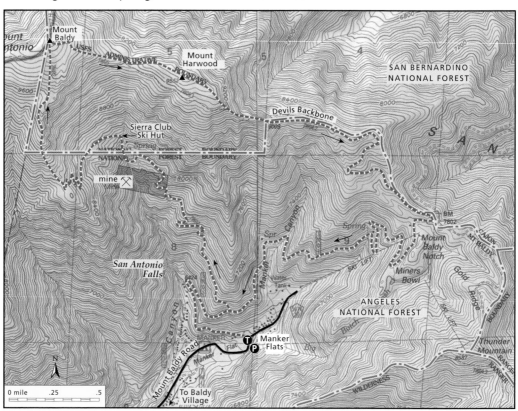

continue a steep climb to the summit. As you reach a plateau and the rocky spires above the bowl, keep an eye out for wreckage from two Hellcat fighter planes that crashed near the trail in 1949. Head on upward to the summit, marked with an iron placard.

From the top, the views are absolutely breathtaking, even on a smoggy day. All of Southern California is visible: from the High Desert to San Diego, every mountain and every valley is within sight.

The Baldy summit is huge, and there is a confluence of trails, so be watchful of the signs. There have been instances of people getting lost and stranded by taking the wrong trail. Head east and take the Devils Backbone Trail directly down the summit toward the ski lifts. Another

side trip that is mapped out is the trek to the top of Mount Harwood—a short 200-foot elevation gain, but well worth the additional effort. The view is almost as nice as that of Baldy, but there are no people and it adds a two-summits-for-one value to the hike.

The Devils Backbone Trail is notoriously icy and not recommended in the wintertime; many have lost their lives on Baldy. Maybe it is due to its closeness to a major metropolitan area, but this is a mountain that should never be underestimated; weather changes can be severe even in summer.

From the ski area, follow the road back down to Manker Flats, or if the ski lifts are operating, buy a ticket and ride most of the way down, eliminating 2 miles of walking on the road.

33 PINE MOUNTAIN

Distance: 6.5 miles round-trip
Hiking time: 3 hours
Difficulty: Strenuous
Elevation gain: 1600 feet
High point: 9648 feet
Season: Late spring to late fall
Water: None, bring your own
Fees and permits: Adventure Pass
Map: USGS Mount San Antonio
Information: Angeles National Forest, (909) 982-2829, *www.fs.fed.us/r5/angeles/*

Getting there: From Interstate 15 at Cajon Junction, take State Route 138 west for 8.5 miles. Turn left onto Angeles Crest Highway (State Route 2). Pass the town of Wrightwood and then continue another 10.6 miles. Turn left onto signed Blue Ridge Road. Drive 5 miles to Guffy Campground and park by the locked gate. There is room for only a couple of cars. Do not block the gate. At times the gate is unlocked and drivers can proceed all the way to the trailhead for Pine Mountain.

The backside of the Devils Backbone Trail from Pine Mountain to Mount Baldy is obvious all along this hike. Pine Mountain is the largest peak

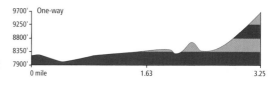

in the vicinity. From the locked gate proceed up to Guffy Campground, then drop down behind the restrooms to the Pacific Crest Trail (PCT). Follow the PCT east for 1.25 mile to an intersection with a road near the north ridge; turn right and take the road. Stay on the road until Pine Mountain looms into view straight ahead and just off the trail to the right. At about 2 miles the ridge meets up with the road just after an old sign that says "Burn Area." Take the use trail to the right, which is easy to make out and well traveled for a nonmaintained trail.

Look for the wilderness sign just a few hundred feet down the trail, and then begin the scramble upward that gains almost all 1600 feet in a little more than 1 mile. The trail contains not one switchback, but follows the rocky, sheer ridgeline straight up the mountainside. One can look at this trip as more of a "climb" than a hike, though technically it only involves some Class II scrambling; the altitude, the exposure, and the steepness make it a wonderful adventure. The trail does get away from precipitous drops about halfway up the mountain, but it retains a sharply vertical gradient for the entire trip up to the summit. From the top, there is no 360-degree view; the summit block is large and round, and part of the view is obscured no matter which way you

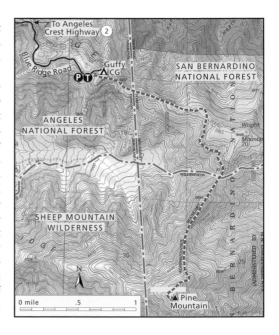

A hardy stalwart clings to the mountainside along the steep ridgeline to Pine Mountain.

The sap of sugar pine cones can be chewed like gum, although it tastes a bit like turpentine.

look. But nonetheless, the views are impressive. Mount Baldy sits like an overlord above the Los Angeles Basin, and the entire Inland Empire and High Desert are strewn beneath the lofty summit. On clear days, the Pacific Ocean can be seen glimmering behind downtown Los Angeles, and the entire San Gabriel Range is visible trailing off into the west toward the Santa Monicas and the Los Padres National Forest.

Those wishing for a longer adventure can continue on from Pine Mountain along the Devils Backbone Trail to Dawson or even to Mount Baldy (Hike 32). Return on the same trail and be careful when descending.

34 BRIDGE TO NOWHERE

Distance: 10 miles round-trip
Hiking time: 6 hours
Difficulty: Strenuous
Elevation gain: 900 feet
High point: 2900 feet
Season: Fall to spring
Water: San Gabriel River
Fees and permits: Adventure Pass
Map: USGS Mount San Antonio
Information: Angeles National Forest, (626) 574-5200, *www.fs.fed.us/r5/angeles/*

Getting there: From Interstate 210 in Azusa, exit on Azusa Avenue (State Route 39) and drive north for 10 miles. Turn right on East Fork Road and continue 8 more miles to the East Fork Ranger Station.

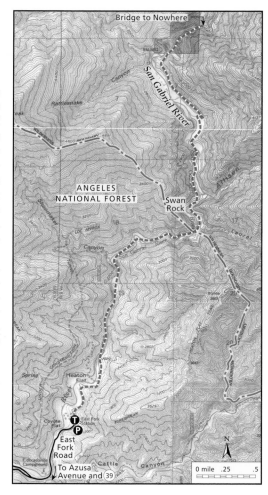

This hike leads along the vibrant and wild East Fork of the San Gabriel River. With many of the region's tallest mountains nearby, and lots of high-altitude runoff, this section of the river is one of the lushest unbridled flows of water in the southernmost reaches of California. There is normally enough water that some crossings involve getting wet up to the knees. **Note:** During spring in wet years, or just after a very rainy period, it is inadvisable to set out on this hike; the torrential waters can be dangerous and even fatal. Always check with the ranger station.

The Bridge to Nowhere is a spectacular and bizarre piece of architecture, in that no road connects to either side. It was engineered in the 1930s along with a highway that was set to be a route out of the Los Angeles Basin up into the High Desert. In 1938, torrential flooding obliterated the highway, and the bridge is all that remains of a once-grand scheme.

Begin hiking just beyond the yellow gate near the parking area, and follow the roadway along the river and the remnants of the old highway through adumbral thickets of alder and oak. After descending into the canyon, at 0.5 mile the trail meets the junction with the Heaton Flats Trail, and begins a series of river crossings. Fourteen crossings await those with nimble feet and those without—all of whom will be getting wet. Enjoy the crossings by just wading on through to the other side, and the experience will be a much more pleasant adventure. Since much of the trail is not shaded, the crisp water serves as a relief even on cooler days.

The trail is overgrown in spots, difficult to follow in places, and rocky in others. It is highly traveled, though, so watch for signs of heaviest usage, and when in doubt ask others hikers, fishermen, and the occasional panning prospector.

At just over 2 miles look ahead to the canyon walls for the formation of grey rock aptly named Swan Rock, and continue, crossing the river. At 3.5 miles the trail turns abruptly right and climbs sharply to the old road. After the short climb,

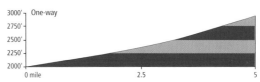

turn left again and head north up the canyon. An old white tub serves as the 4-mile marker, and shortly thereafter the trail meets the bridge.

Views are spectacular from the bridge. While it is a worthwhile destination all by itself, a steep and vertical gorge, known as the Narrows, awaits those who would hike just a half mile farther up and into the canyon.

Bungee America owns the bridge and surrounding property; jumps can be arranged by calling (310) 322-8892.

The Bridge to Nowhere is an engineering oddity. (Photo ©Bruno Lucidarme)

35 MOUNT HAWKINS

Distance: 7.5 miles round-trip
Hiking time: 4 hours or overnight
Difficulty: Strenuous
Elevation gain: 2200 feet
High point: 8850 feet
Season: All
Water: Little Jimmy Spring
Fees and permits: Adventure Pass
Map: USGS Crystal Lake
Information: Angeles National Forest, (626) 574-5200, *www.fs.fed.us/r5/angeles/*

Getting there: From Interstate 210 in La Cañada, take the Angeles Crest Highway (State Route 2) north and east for 39.5 miles to the parking area at Islip Saddle.

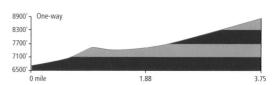

Mount Hawkins was named for a popular waitress, Nellie Hawkins, who worked at the Squirrel Inn near what is now Coldbrook Campground at the turn of the last century. She is immortalized in three peaks: Mount Hawkins, Middle Hawkins, and South Mount Hawkins. This trail takes you up to the summit of Mount Hawkins.

Cross the highway and head south on the Pacific Crest Trail (PCT) as it crosses and switchbacks across an open, manzanita-filled hillside. The trail is shadeless, rocky, and hot for the first ten to fifteen minutes, but eventually it climbs and enters into beautiful pine woodlands with

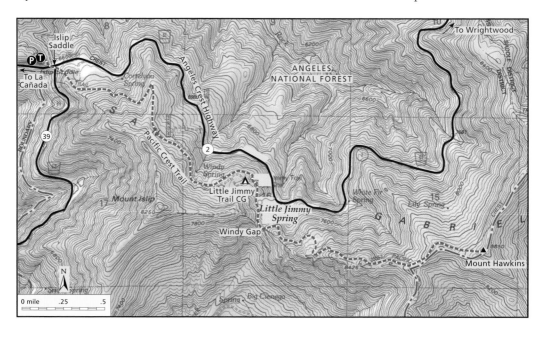

Mountain views in the Angeles National Forest are more than rewarding.

dirt and duff covering the majority of the trail. The rest of the way from here is incredibly shady and cool.

In close to 2 miles into the trail comes Little Jimmy Camp, Little Jimmy Spring, and eventually a spot called Windy Gap. Little Jimmy Camp is an excellent place to spend a night or a short weekend of backpacking. It is easy to get to, set in a nice woodland with easy access to fresh spring water as well as relatively comfortable, clean restrooms. Boy Scouts and PCT through-hikers regularly use the camp as well. The camp was named for a famous cartoonist who spent a lot of time here in the early 1900s; he drew pictures for hikers and campers traveling through.

This camp was the site of a bear incident a few years back, when a camper did not properly store his food. As a result of this human negligence, the bear was destroyed by officials. Please keep wildlife wild, and be sensitive to the needs of the animals that call the forest home. Humans are merely visitors.

From Little Jimmy, the Windy Gap—so named

because wind often whizzes through it from the desert to the San Gabriel Valley, or vice versa—is just a short jaunt away. Mount Hawkins sits directly in front of you as you follow the PCT almost the entire way to the summit. Passing a few trail crossings, the PCT heads to a saddle at about 8800 feet. From there, turn right and ascend the short distance to the summit. Since Mount Hawkins is one of the tallest peaks in this section of the Angeles Crest, and isolated from the other tall mountains, the view on top is astounding. Mount Baldy is clear and open, the similarly sized Mounts Islip and Williamson sit off to the north and west, while the ridge to Mount Baden Powell leads off to the east. On clear days, downtown Los Angeles and the ocean are visible.

Looking to the south, Middle Hawkins and South Mount Hawkins are visible. The entire remnants of the Curve Fire of 2002 can be clearly seen, as most of the damage was done in the area between this peak, the San Gabriel Wilderness, and Crystal Lake sitting below.

36 WATERMAN MOUNTAIN

Distance: 4.5 miles round-trip
Hiking time: 2.5 hours
Difficulty: Moderate
Elevation gain: 1300 feet
High point: 8038 feet
Season: All, snow in winter
Water: Streams are dry by early summer most years
Fees and permits: Adventure Pass
Map: USGS Waterman Mountain
Information: Angeles National Forest, (626) 574-5200, *www.fs.fed.us/r5/angeles*

Getting there: From the Interstate 210 split in La Cañada, take the Angeles Crest Highway (State Route 2) east for 34 miles to just past the Waterman ski lift. (If you reach Buckhorn Campground, you've gone too far.) There is a big rounded shoulder off the westbound lane; this is the parking area. Park and cross the highway, where you'll find a trail sign for the Waterman Trail. (There is a confusing number of pullouts, side roads, and trail-like areas here, and Forest Road 3N03 runs close to the trailhead. If you can't find the trailhead, take the forest road. In less than 0.25 mile, the road intersects the trail; turn right.)

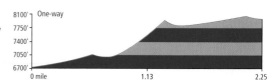

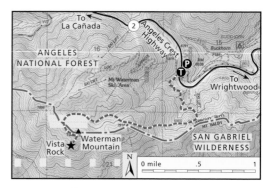

This is a pleasant hike. The area is wonderfully wooded, and streams guard the lower reaches of the mountain. The trip is fairly short, not too rocky, and at least some of the way is soft and duff-covered. Much of the trail is shaded. Wildlife, including bighorn sheep, can be seen in the region. If any peak can be described as a beginner's hike, then this is it: less than 5 miles round-trip, and 1300 feet in elevation gain.

The trail itself skirts and then enters the San Gabriel Wilderness as it quickly ascends away from the highway. Since there is no true assigned parking for this hike, it is a little less traveled than some of the other peaks in the forest. On weekends it is fairly busy, but if you go during the week you might have it to yourself.

Look for enormous Jeffrey and ponderosa pines, along with incense cedar trees all along the route. There are fantastic granite boulder out-

croppings almost the entire trip, and the area has a very Sierra-esque feel to it, unlike most places in the Angeles. The trail affords views for the entire hike. Although there are roads and ski lifts close by, it feels a long ways away from the city.

The first mile gently climbs at a steady pace, but the majority of the ascent is to be had in the second mile. The top of Waterman Mountain is a large, flat plateau. The trail is very well maintained until you reach the summit area, where it disappears into a confusing mix of possibilities. At this point you should look for the tallest rocks to the south in the broad expanse around you; that is the peak.

Although this hike's actual high point of 8038 feet is a bit anticlimactic— there is barely a view

A rocky outcropping just a few hundred feet south of the peak provides an impressive vista of Twin Peaks.

because of the trees and the flat-plateau nature of the summit—there is a shelf 150 feet below to the south, off-trail, that affords incredible views of the San Gabriel Wilderness including Twin Peaks, Bear Creek, Devils Canyon, and the entire high country. The old State Route 39 cuts a line across the horizon as you gaze in turn at Mounts Islip, all three Hawkinses, Baden-Powell, Baldy, Pine, Dawson, Burnham, Ross, the Three Tees, Cucamonga, and Ontario Peak. The vista is awesome, to say the least. If the day is clear, you can gaze all the way to San Jacinto.

37 EATON CANYON FALLS

Distance: 3.75 miles round-trip
Hiking time: 2 hours
Difficulty: Easy
Elevation gain: 550 feet
High point: 1525 feet
Season: Late fall to spring
Water: Eaton Wash
Fees and permits: Adventure Pass
Map: USGS Mount Wilson
Information: Angeles National Forest, (626) 574-5200, *www.fs.fed.us/r5/angeles/*

Getting there: From Interstate 210, exit at Altadena Drive and turn north toward the mountains. One block past New York Drive is the entrance to the Eaton Canyon Nature Center on the right.

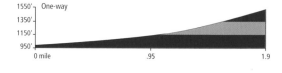

Eaton Canyon is a lovely and peaceful wooded escape not far from the confines of the city center of Pasadena. The nature center contains some very useful information, a hands-on exhibit for children, and friendly, well-informed rangers. The culmination of this trip is a lovely pool and a 40-foot waterfall that drops over a sharp precipice. Both the trail and the parking area are busy on weekends, but during weekdays both can appear nearly abandoned.

Almost anyone can make the journey to the falls, although some of the boulder-hopping on the way might be a little much for the very young and the very old. In dry years the creek bed holds just a trickle until reaching the falls, which flow year-round, albeit with greater ferocity during the rainy season. It is not advisable to hike in the canyon during heavy rainfall or runoff.

From the large parking area, head up the canyon. Follow the path for a few minutes and then veer right across to the creek bed. The trail continues on a shelf above the creek. There are small patches of shade from some of the taller oaks and sycamores, but a majority of the way is sun-scorched and arid. It can be very hot in the summertime.

At a junction, there is a sign for the falls.

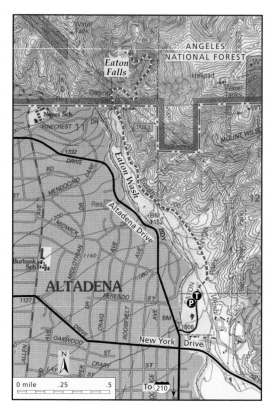

A prickly pear cactus blossoms near the start of Eaton Canyon Trail.

Head left. After a mile's worth of hiking, the trail passes under a bridge. Continue straight to get to the falls. The trail here is a scramble along rocks in the creek. There are at least ten crossings en route to the falls, which are reached in less than a half-mile of creek scrambling.

The falls are some of the most spectacular in Southern California. Here are plenty of places to relax, enjoy lunch, take a dip, or get an impromptu shower in the cataract. Unfortunately, since the area is so close to the Los Angeles major metropolitan area, it gets a fair share of people who do not understand the aesthetics of unspoiled beauty: sadly, the area is marked with graffiti and litter. Do a good deed and help keep this wonder of the southland clean—take along a bag, and pack out what others have carelessly left behind.

38 SAN GABRIEL PEAK

Distance: 4 miles round-trip
Hiking time: 1.5 hours
Difficulty: Easy
Elevation gain: 1050 feet
High point: 6161 feet
Season: All, hot in summer
Water: None, bring your own
Fees and permits: Adventure Pass
Map: USGS Mount Wilson
Information: Angeles National Forest, (626) 574-5200, *www.fs.fed.us/r5/angeles/*

Getting there: From Interstate 210, take the Angeles Crest Highway (State Route 2) north for 13 miles to Red Box Junction. Turn right onto Mount Wilson Road. Drive 2.3 miles to Eaton Saddle and park on the right side of the road; avoid blocking the gate.

San Gabriel Peak, like many other geographical features in Southern California, was named for the mission in the valley below, founded by the Spanish padres, which also carries the same appellation. The mountain has had other designations throughout historic and prehistoric times, but this is the one that has stuck. Carrying the distinction of being the second-highest peak in the front range of the Angeles National Forest, its pointy prominence is visible and recognizable from almost anywhere in Los Angeles.

The trail is covered in manzanita and chaparral, but it is well maintained and gently ascends the entire distance to the peak. Start hiking west beyond the gate on Mount Lowe Fire Road. In about 0.5 mile the trail passes through Mueller Tunnel, which was built by the U.S. Forest Service in 1942. The tunnel is narrow and about 100 feet long, with room for one car to drive through back when it was used for auto traffic. Just a few minutes walk ahead is the trail junction at Markham Saddle; when you reach it, turn right. Views begin to open up immediately of Bear Canyon and the beautiful San Gabriel Wilderness.

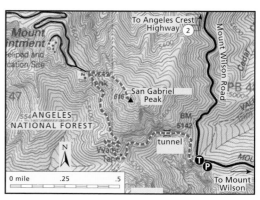

Head north up the gently switchbacking Jet Propulsion Laboratory (JPL)–engineered trail to the saddle between Mount Disappointment and San Gabriel Peak. Just before the saddle, at over 1.5 miles, turn right again and continue toward

The summits of Mount Disappointment and San Gabriel Peak sit above the Los Angeles Basin.

the summit. Some sections of the trail are shady and covered with oak and fir, but others are sun-scorched, and this trail can be very hot in the summertime as it crosses the west slope of the mountain.

The summit contains foundation remnants of a fire lookout tower that stood from 1927 to 1938. A makeshift bench has been placed between two of the support anchors. The view from the summit is heavenly. Although some oak trees partially obscure the vista, it is generally a 360-degree panorama that includes the peaks and the craggy, eroded canyons of the front range of the San Gabriel Mountains; the entire Los Angeles Basin, including the Los Angeles skyline; Mount San Jacinto; and, on clear days, the Pacific Ocean and Catalina Island. It is best to hike here on clear, smog-free days. Winter is optimal.

39 SWITZER FALLS

Distance: 3.5 miles round-trip
Hiking time: 2 hours
Difficulty: Easy
Elevation gain: 450 feet
High point: 3250 feet
Season: Late fall to early spring
Water: Arroyo Seco
Fees and permits: Adventure Pass
Map: USGS Condor Peak
Information: Angeles National Forest, (626) 574-5200, *www.fs.fed.us/r5/angeles/*

Getting there: From Interstate 210 in La Cañada, take the Angeles Crest Highway (State Route 2) north and drive 10 miles to Switzer Picnic Area. Turn right and drive 0.25 mile to the parking area.

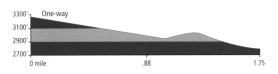

Switzer Picnic Area is a heavily utilized section of the Angeles National Forest, and the Gabrielino Trail to Switzer Falls gets a large amount of traffic, especially on weekends and holidays. There is good reason for its popularity, as this slice of the front range contains some of the loveliest and most idyllic scenery in the Angeles range, complete with a relatively easy yet arresting hike leading to a 50-foot waterfall. Be certain to arrive early to enjoy the most solitude (and the best chance of finding a parking spot).

This area also has historic significance and usage, delighting Hollywood luminaries and dignitaries alike. The Switzer family once ran a wilderness camp here which was quite arduous to reach before the Angeles Crest Highway was built. To get here required a tough climb up Arroyo Seco Canyon. By the 1940s the camp had lost its wilderness value due to ease of access; it was closed and destroyed shortly thereafter.

Beyond the picnic tables at the drive-up camp lies a footbridge that leads across Arroyo Seco to the trailhead. The trail descends for 1 mile beneath an awning of alder, willow, oak, and maple to the remnant foundations of the old Switzer Camp. During springtime, these woods boast a floral display without parallel.

Cross the stream and follow the trail along the western bank. Do not attempt to walk downstream; the creek drops precipitously at the edge of the falls. Soon, grand views of the falls appear along the trail, and remnants of the stone chapel that once held Sunday services above the falls can be seen. Turn left at the signed junction and

A pale swallowtail alights on a wildflower near Switzer Falls.

descend again to the creek bed. At the creek, leave the trail and follow the use trail back upstream toward the falls. A lesser cascade sits above a gorgeous pool that serves as an excellent spot for a snack or a swim. Signs warn against climbing the slick and dangerous rock by the falls, as many people have been injured in and around this lovely place.

It is hard to imagine that the center of the sprawling megalopolis of Los Angeles sits less than 15 miles away from this placid vale. Cool waters rush down the mountain and gather in mirrorlike basins that offer many chances for contemplation, or recreational dipping. Even on busy weekends, the area rarely feels overcrowded, and the canyon is so lovely that visitors, too, often have an air of friendliness and wonder.

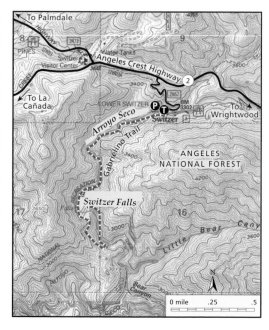

Opposite: The Channel Islands hint at how the Central Coast must have looked hundreds of years ago.

SANTA MONICA MOUNTAINS AND CHANNEL ISLANDS

SANTA MONICA MOUNTAINS NATIONAL RECREATION AREA

anta Monica Mountains National Recreation Area is the largest urban national park in the United States. It is comprised of state, county, city, and federal parklands, as well as privately owned lands. The Santa Monica Mountains, which are part of the Transverse Ranges, run west to east across Ventura and Los Angeles counties. The park and mountain range actually divide the city of Los Angeles in two, the only major city in the world to be split in such a manner.

The mountains provide numerous recreational activities as well as scenic beauty and historical significance. From rolling canyons to coastal overlooks and high-mountain views, the park has it all. It is an easy getaway with multiple choices of destinations. Parts of the park are well touristed, but others are secluded and isolated without much visitation at all. The coastal chaparral-covered hillsides produce abundant flowers year-round. Wildlife, insects such as butterflies and bees, and amazing geology all play a part in the park's allure. Its closeness to Los Angeles belies its wilderness appeal.

40 SOLSTICE CANYON

Distance: 3.25 miles round-trip
Hiking time: 1.5 hours
Difficulty: Easy
Elevation gain: 700 feet
High point: 800 feet
Season: All
Water: None, bring your own
Fees and permits: None
Map: USGS Malibu Beach
Information: Santa Monica Mountains National Recreation Area, (805) 370-2301, *www.nps.gov/samo/*

Getting there: From Malibu Canyon Road, drive northwest on the Pacific Coast Highway (Highway 1) for 2 miles to Corral Canyon Road. Turn right and drive less than 0.25 mile to the entrance of Solstice Canyon Park. Turn left and continue another 0.25 mile to the parking lot.

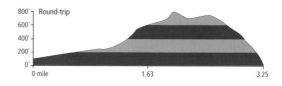

Solstice Canyon, formerly known as Roberts Ranch, is a lovely piece of the Santa Monica Mountains National Recreation Area (NRA). It was opened in 1988, and has been delighting visitors ever since with a variety of trails for different uses. The loop hike described here utilizes two of these trails. Solstice Canyon, home to a year-round stream, is shaded by a thick canopy of sycamore, alder, bay, and live oak; some of the trees are large and ancient.

The first half of the route travels along an old road (which means strollers, wheelchairs, and bicycles are all allowed). Kids, mountain bikes, and dogs on leash are also welcome, though only 1.5 miles of trail—the paved portion—are open to bikes. The entire passage to the Roberts' mansion is sheltered from the sun, which makes this hike

to follow, shadows the perennially green creek. Less than 1 mile into the hike, an old stone cabin, believed to have been built sometime after 1900, emerges alongside the pavement.

Continue along the road to the ruins of the beautiful Roberts Ranch house, which was partially destroyed by a fire in 1982. It is now known as Tropical Terrace. The remnants are enchanting enough alongside the pastoral creek. Behind the far side of the foundations of the ruined dwelling is a dazzling thirty-foot waterfall. Explore the pools, exotic plants, and remnant statuary before continuing on. At this point, the trail becomes dirt single-track and is not useable by those in wheelchairs, bikes, or strollers. Hikers with small children may wish to return down the road, the way they came.

Adventurers continuing on should cross the creek and follow the signed Rising Sun Trail as it climbs away from the canyon and up to a coastal ridge offering fantastic views of the Pacific Ocean. The loop follows a highly frequented trail, which is nicely maintained and also very easy to follow. It returns to the parking area close to the start of the pavement.

a perfect outing for any time of year. Birds and squirrels intermingle in the treetops while the trickle of the creek water creates an impermeable sense of serenity.

The hike begins by following the Solstice International Trail along old Sostomo Road. The road, well traveled, well marked, and easy

Still waters pool in many areas of Solstice Canyon.

41 MALIBU CREEK

Distance: 5.25 miles round-trip
Hiking time: 2.5 hours
Difficulty: Easy
Elevation gain: 200 feet
High point: 750 feet
Season: All, hot in summer
Water: Malibu Creek
Fees and permits: Required
Map: USGS Malibu Beach
Information: Malibu Creek State Park, (818) 880-0367,
   www.parks.ca.gov/default.asp?page_id=614

Getting there: From US 101 in Calabasas, exit at Las Virgenes/Malibu Canyon Road and drive south for 3.5 miles to Malibu Creek State Park. Pass through the entrance and drive to the second parking lot.

Malibu Creek State Park has been used as a background for many movies and television shows, most notably *Planet of the Apes* and *M.A.S.H.* The park, once owned and operated as a movie ranch by Twentieth Century Fox, was eventually bought by the State of California in 1974. Movie and television aficionados will instantly recognize the scenery as familiar. The truly devoted may be able to pick out exact filming locations.

Walk to the trailhead that leads south and west from the parking lot. It is very obvious where the trail goes; follow the people. The entire route is on a wide dirt path. For the first mile the trail is an old dirt road that is smooth and well traveled. The California State Parks service also utilizes the road for maintenance and other tasks, but it is closed to all other vehicle access. Still, it is not unusual to see a docent's or state patrol vehicle or two on this hike.

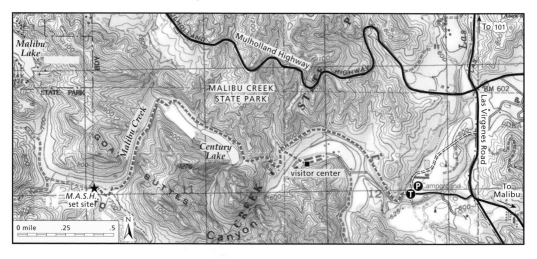

Malibu Creek State Park's scenery has been the background for many movies and television shows.

A little ways into the hike, a junction with the Grassland Trail leads off to the right; stay on the trail signed for Century Lake and the M.A.S.H. Trail, the widest and most frequently walked in the park. Just a few hundred steps farther, Malibu Creek comes into view on the left and the roadway is lined with old stately oaks.

Beyond the oak trees, a short trip to the visitor center (open only on weekends, noon to 4:00 PM) is the way to learn about the park's natural history. From there head back to the main trail and begin an easy climb, then descend to idyllic Century Lake at about 2 miles. From there continue west and south to the site of the former *M.A.S.H.* set. Passing the Goat Buttes and some distinctive rock formations, it is easy to pick out the famous television show's familiar opening shot. The rocks themselves are very interesting and strange to look at. All that remains of the set is an old rusted-out army jeep and remnants of an ambulance from the show. A picnic table has been installed at the site, and is a great place for a meal.

There are many options to take from this point, though most people will opt to turn around and return the way they came. The trail continues in many different directions and several short out-and-back trips can be made, including nice jaunts to Reagan Ranch, Malibu Lake, and Castro Crest, adding anywhere from 2 to 5 miles to the total day's hike.

42 ZUMA DUME TRAIL

Distance: 2.5 miles round-trip
Hiking time: 1.5 hours
Difficulty: Easy
Elevation gain: 160 feet
High point: 160 feet
Season: All
Water: None, bring your own
Fees and permits: None
Map: USGS Point Dume
Information: Point Dume Natural Preserve, (805) 488-1827 or (818) 880-0350

Getting there: From Malibu, take Highway 1 west past the intersection with Kanan-Dume Road, then take the second left onto Heathercliff Road. Make another left onto Dume Drive. Folow Dume Drive until it comes to a Y intersection; veer left. At the T intersection with Cliffside Drive, turn right. Park on the left.

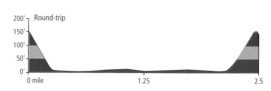

Below the point, the ocean scenery is picturesque and idyllic.

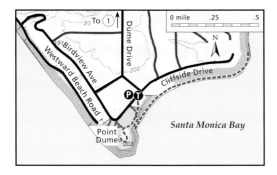

Most people heading to the beach at Point Dume go to Zuma Beach County Park. They fight for parking spaces and cram together on crowded, though ample, coastline. At the county park there are volleyball nets, lifeguard towers, sunbathers, surfers, and the usual beach fare. Few realize that heading up the hill and around the point leads to a nearly unspoiled and secluded section of beach that is primarily the haunt of local residents. No stores, rental shops, bathrooms, or volleyball nets line this waterfront, but natural beauty abounds; and while the park is not very big, it makes up for its lack of size with elegance and ambience.

There is not much parking near the state beach, but generally a space will open up rather quickly. It is a short hike to the beach but it involves descending a hundred steps, which might be another reason the average beachgoer is not inclined to visit this wonderful little spot.

There are many minor trails that all go to the beach, so taking any trail will eventually lead to either the beach or Point Dume. The point is rather small but amazing nonetheless, with expansive views of the Pacific Ocean and the Malibu region all the way down to Santa Monica. Enjoy the views and then take the walk toward the beach and the stairs that lead there.

Once on the beach, one can imagine the Malibu of yesteryear, without houses, unspoiled, and pristine. There are beautiful rocks here, and geographic points compete with small tide pools for your attention. This isolated beach rests in a natural bay that makes for flawless, rolling waves. Head from promontory to promontory to explore all that this wonderful section of Southern California beach has to offer.

43 BACKBONE TRAIL—ZUMA CANYON

Distance: 5 miles round-trip
Hiking time: 2.5 hours
Difficulty: Easy
Elevation gain: 500 feet
High point: 1800 feet
Season: All, hot in summer
Water: None, bring your own
Fees and permits: None
Map: USGS Point Dume
Information: National Park Service, (805) 370-2301, *www.nps.gov/samo/*

Getting there: From Highway 1 in Malibu, turn north onto Kanan-Dume Road and drive for nearly 3.5 miles, passing through the first tunnel, labeled T-1. Look for the large parking area, bus stop, and display on the left for Newton Canyon.

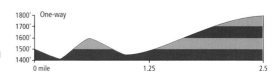

The Backbone Trail provides many opportunities to admire the Santa Monica mountain chain.

The Backbone Trail has been a dream of hikers, naturalists, conservationists, and recreation enthusiasts for nearly half a century. As it finally nears completion, the trail will connect the entire chain of parks, preserves, and recreation lands within the Santa Monica Mountains National

right of the bulletin board and descends west into a lovely oak-filled canyon that provides shade even on the hottest of days. There are several offshoots of the main trail near the beginning of the hike, but as long as careful attention is paid, it remains relatively easy to keep on the main path. (Eventually, the shorter spurs reconnect up with the trail.) The trail follows Kanan-Dume Road for a little over half a mile and then continues along the edge of the canyon until it dips down into riparian woodland, crossing a small bridge and a perennial stream that eventually empties into Zuma Creek.

The oak gives way to mostly chaparral as the hike enters into a hotter, drier section at a little over 1 mile. The trail climbs upward to connect with the Zuma Ridge Trail; stay on the Backbone Trail, where views soon open toward the ocean, far and wide. An overlook of Upper Zuma Falls at 2.5 miles is quite lovely just after a rain, and can make for an excellent turnaround point for this hike. Those with energy for a short uphill stretch can continue right on the Zuma Ridge Trail and follow it until it connects with Encinal Canyon Road in a very short distance, enabling this hike to be turned into a point-to-point with relative ease. Watch for the lichen on the rocks, as it is quite distinctive in this region.

Park Unit. It crosses ridgelines, canyons, chaparral-covered hillsides, woodlands, and valleys forming a 65-mile long chain that will one day traverse from Point Mugu through Will Rogers State Historic Park. As of the time of writing this book, 60 of the 65 miles of trail have been completed. This hike covers a 2.5-mile portion of the larger trail.

From the parking area, the trail begins to the

44 MUGU PEAK

Distance: 2.2 miles round-trip
Hiking time: 1 hour
Difficulty: Moderate to strenuous
Elevation gain: 1250 feet
High point: 1250 feet
Season: All
Water: None, bring your own
Fees and permits: Required
Map: USGS Point Mugu
Information: Point Mugu State Park, (805) 488-1827,
    www.parks.ca.gov/default.asp?page_id=630

Getting there: From the Kanan-Dume Road in Malibu, drive 17 miles northwest on Highway 1 to just beyond Point Mugu and Mugu Rock. Park at the turnout on the right, northbound side of the highway just across from the naval gunnery range.

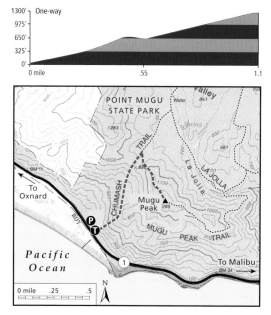

briefly, turn right at the unsigned trail leading up the mountain. Climb for nearly 0.25 mile until you reach the top. The views from the summit are invigorating: jagged coastline, and a myriad of canyons eroding into the ocean. Often, fog obscures the view, but the ruggedness and steepness of the coastline is apparent to all who stand on Mugu Peak. To the north, the view of the Camarillo Valley and the Point Mugu Naval Base is unobstructed; to the east lie the ominous spires of the Boney Mountain Ridge, a sacred mountain to the Chumash tribe. If the day is clear, the Pacific Ocean's royal blue splendor extends into infinity. Enjoy the summit views, and then return the way you came. Or, for those so inclined, a much longer 9-mile loop can be made by traveling straight through lovely La Jolla Canyon and then arcing back around to rejoin the Mugu Peak Trail.

Ladybugs having a meal

The Chumash Trail ascends steeply and directly up a Santa Monica Mountains cliffside through coastal scrub and chaparral. It is best to get an early morning start, as the sun can truly cook even this close to the ocean. Unless there is a low-lying fog, the coastal breezes don't seem to register until the trail reaches the plateau.

Park and begin to hike up the steep hillside on the Chumash Trail. The trail starts its nononsense climb and never really lets up until the final steps leading to the American flag unfurled on the flagpole at the Mugu Peak summit. This hike's short distance and high elevation gain make this a great workout, and an excellent elevation trainer for those who live nearby or can get to the trailhead daily.

The beauty of the area lies in its abundant wildflowers. Since the state park is directly on the coast, there is moisture aplenty here, which accounts for the flora blooming nearly year-round. Spring to early summer is the best time to see blossoms, but many can be found regardless of season. Also prevalent are desert plants such as yucca and prickly pear cactus, which bloom but can also be a danger to unprotected skin.

Follow the trail as it winds upward for an aerobic 0.9 mile. After the way levels off very

CHANNEL ISLANDS NATIONAL PARK

The Channel Islands are a shining gem of the National Park Service and Southern California itself. Retaining much of the character of Southern California of old, these islands act as a gentle reminder of what life was once like here when there were no freeways, or urban sprawl. The flowing hillsides have unspoiled beauty that will be protected for posterity. Although non-native vegetation has long since compromised all of California's coastal regions, Channel Islands included, the National Park Service is doing what it can to eradicate invasive species and reintroduce the native plants of Southern California. The Channel Islands are a wonderful palette of color and beauty complete with coastal views, cliffs, sea caves, wildlife, wildflowers, and endemic species.

The tranquility of the islands is magical. Many visitors return time and time again to experience the peace and serenity that pervade the atmosphere. The islands are not highly visited, and are a wonderful place for camping. Solitude can be found on just about any hike; staying midweek can mean having an island and its campground all to yourself.

45 ANACAPA LIGHTHOUSE TRAIL

Distance: 2 miles round-trip
Hiking time: 2 hours or overnight
Difficulty: Easy
Elevation gain: 250 feet
High point: 250 feet
Season: All
Water: None, bring your own
Fees and permits: No entrance fee, but camping is $15 per night
Map: USGS Anacapa Island
Information: Channel Islands National Park, (805) 658-5730, *www.nps.gov/chis/*

Getting there: To get to Anacapa Island from Ventura, contact Island Packers, (805) 642-1393. From Santa Barbara, call Truth Aquatics at Sea Landing, (805) 963-3564.

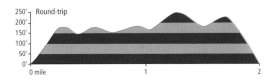

Like all Channel Island adventures, this loop hike on East Anacapa Island begins with a spectacular boat ride. While not part of the hike, it is definitely an entertaining element of the adventure. The boat may pass dolphins, seals, whales, and numerous aquatic birds, including the endangered California brown pelican. As the boat nears the island dock, the iconic formation of East Anacapa Arch is visible. After debarking, all hikers must climb 153 stairs to reach the top of the island. The remaining portion of the trip follows the gentle, easy, and flat contours of the island plateau.

In about 0.25 mile, the trail leads to the ranger station where visitors can pick up a brochure for the self-guided interactive nature trail. The brochure describes the plants, animals, and other features of the island. The island itself is actually a series of three islands, creatively named East, West, and Middle Anacapa. Middle and West are not open to hiking.

Endangered California brown pelicans fly over Anacapa in a V formation.

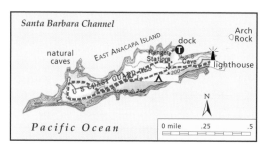

Rangers provide a guided walk on the nature trail throughout the day, although the figure-eight loop is relatively easy to follow, well signed and heavily traveled. Visitors can go about their own way and follow the trail however they like. Anacapa Island receives more visitors than any of the other islands due to its easy, family-friendly access. This island is certainly the most readily accessible of the Channel Islands for the novice hiker, or the visitor seeking a short outing. The scenery here is stunning and impressive; the entire trip is filled with majestic overlooks, vantage points, and breathtaking scenery. In the spring, western gulls breed, their nests lining the trail with pretty little chicks chirping, and vibrant wildflowers blossom.

The trail sets out westward from the museum toward a glorious overlook at Cathedral Cove, where visitors can look at sea life and the natural caves in the beautiful coves. From here continue west to Inspiration Point and then back to the middle of the island, where there is a campground. The final leg of the trail leads past Pinniped Point, where sea lions frolic and bark on the rocks below, and on to the historic lighthouse, the last one built in California.

Anywhere along the trail, pick a spot to have a picnic. To camp, reserve a campground before booking the boat trip to Anacapa. Since this is the most heavily visited of all the islands, please be especially mindful of your impact on the place. Stay on the maintained trails, and keep behind the wooden barriers where they are placed for safety purposes.

46 SMUGGLERS COVE

Distance: 8.25 miles round-trip
Hiking time: 4.5 hours
Difficulty: Moderate
Elevation gain: 700 feet
High point: 700 feet
Season: All
Water: None, bring your own
Fees and permits: No entrance fee, but camping is $15 per night
Map: USGS Santa Cruz Island D
Information: Channel Islands National Park, (805) 658-5730, *www.nps.gov/chis/*

Getting there: To get to Santa Cruz Island from Ventura, contact Island Packers (805) 642-1393. From Santa Barbara, call Truth Aquatics at Sea Landing (805) 963-3564.

Smugglers Cove is a beautiful sandy bay on the eastern edge of Santa Cruz Island, away from the ocean winds and tumult of the open Pacific Ocean. Originally the inlet was named for a group of "pirates" who used the natural shelter of the cove to protect their merchandise. In the late 1800s it seemed a perfect place for a ranch, complete with self-sustaining agricultural pursuits, an extensive sheep operation, and a winery. The olive grove still stands, along with some fruit and

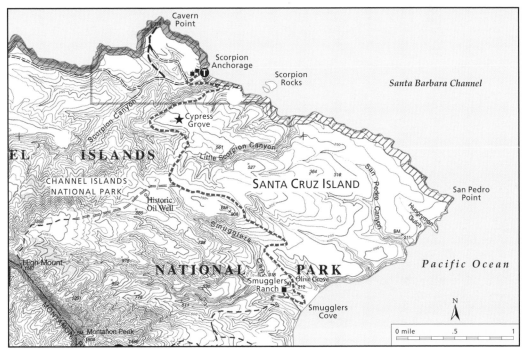

The beach at Smugglers Cove is secluded and pristine.

nut trees by the old ranch house, but the ranch's isolation proved to be its undoing. The owners eventually left the island for the mainland, and the next set of owners ultimately transferred stewardship and control of the island to the Nature Conservancy and National Park Service.

This hike is moderately sized, relatively easy and quite scenic. It may be the perfect Santa Cruz Island outing for anyone with only a half-day to spend before the boat sets sail back to Ventura. While not a difficult hike, the 700-foot climb out of the cove can be strenuous if one is hurrying to make a scheduled departure.

This hike, like almost all of the trails on Santa Cruz Island, follows an old ranch road for the entire journey. Start at Scorpion Anchorage and turn left in just under 0.25 mile at the trail junction for Smugglers Road; it is well signed. The trail climbs and eventually gains incredible

views of Anacapa Island, passing by a lovely grove of non-native European cypress. At just over 1.5 miles, continue straight when the trail branches. Follow it as it descends toward the obvious olive grove and beautiful sandy beach at Smugglers Cove. If time allows, play in the water, walk along the sand, or take a short side trip to the old ranch house, built in 1889. Oranges grow on one of the trees in the front yard, and are deliciously edible. Watch for island scrub jays which have grown larger than their mainland cousins due to the absence of natural predators in their ecosystem.

If this is a day hike, return to Scorpion Anchorage via the same route. Those camping on the island may wish to make this an 11-mile journey to the top of El Montanon (Hike 47). An old road continues partway up the mountain, but bushwhacking is required nearer to the top.

47 EL MONTANON

Distance: 8.5 miles round-trip
Hiking time: 4.5 hours
Difficulty: Strenuous
Elevation gain: 1800 feet
High point: 1808 feet
Season: All
Water: None, bring your own
Fees and permits: No entrance fee, but camping is $15 per night
Map: USGS Santa Cruz Island D
Information: Channel Islands National Park, (805) 658-5730, *www.nps.gov/chis/*

Getting there: To get to Santa Cruz Island from Ventura, contact Island Packers (805) 642-1393. From Santa Barbara, call Truth Aquatics at Sea Landing (805) 963-3564.

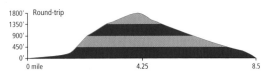

El Montanon is the highest mountain on Santa Cruz Island that is open to the public. Mount Diablo, 12 miles to the west, is 650 feet higher, but is situated solely on Nature Conservancy property and off-limits to hiking for the foreseeable future. No matter; the views from El Montanon are striking, spectacular, and arguably some of the most inspiring in all of Southern California.

Some people will go so far as to argue that the views from this mountain's crest are the best that California has to offer, period. From the summit, all six other islands in the Santa Barbara Channel can be surveyed, as well as the coastline of Southern California north from Point Conception in Santa Barbara County south to Palos Verdes in Los Angeles County.

Santa Cruz Island is truly a hiker's paradise, cut off from civilization by an hour-long boat ride, undeveloped, and nearly pristine. The flora has been compromised by non-native vegetation, as in the rest of the state; but while hiking, one cannot help but think that this is how California must have been hundreds of years ago. Looking across the channel provides a glimpse into the past. The island's windswept beauty will have even the most pragmatic person dreaming of days of yore and life among the island's natives.

The trail begins at Scorpion Anchorage and actually comprises several trails on the island. Hike up the road for 0.75 mile to Upper Scorpion Campground, then continue straight ahead into Scorpion Canyon. At 1.5 miles, the trail begins to climb and doesn't really let up until the summit. In just under 2 miles the trail forks; turn right and continue climbing up to Montanon Ridge and High Mount. After High Mount, the trail becomes a use path along the ridgeline to the summit, which is obvious due to the installation towers situated on and around the peak. While not the most aesthetically pleasing, the towers do

A use trail leads east from El Montanon toward Smugglers Cove and can turn the trip into an epic loop adventure.

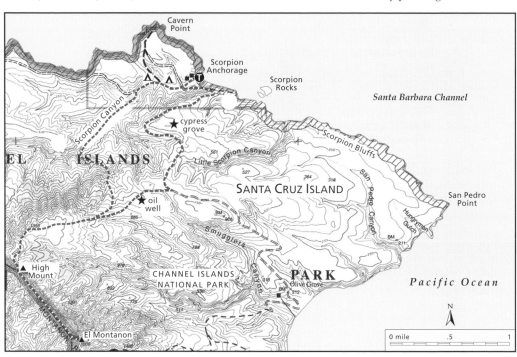

not really detract from the awe-inspiring nature of the peak, though they do slightly obstruct the 360-degree view. There is something satisfyingly surreal about looking around at water surrounding the land while being located in Southern California.

From the summit, there are several options. The map and mileage listed return the same way until the trail fork, at which point the hike becomes a loop passing an historic oil well and the cypress grove, all the while taking in a stunning in-your-face view of Anacapa Island. The trail then dips back to a split near Scorpion Anchorage, and can be completed as a day hike by those hardy and fast enough to do so within the time constraints of the boat schedule.

Those camping on the island and off-trail hikers may want to scramble down the entire ridge and return via the old road into and out of Smugglers Cove (Hike 46). The opposite ridge to Potato Harbor is also a nice off-trail scramble and loop (Hike 48).

48 POTATO HARBOR

Distance: 4.8 miles round-trip
Hiking time: 2.5 hours
Difficulty: Easy
Elevation gain: 350 feet
High point: 400 feet
Season: All
Water: None, bring your own
Fees and permits: No entrance fee, but camping is $15 per night
Map: USGS Santa Cruz Island D
Information: Channel Islands National Park, (805) 658-5730, *www.nps.gov/chis/*

Getting there: To get to Santa Cruz Island from Ventura, contact Island Packers (805) 642-1393. From Santa Barbara, call Truth Aquatics at Sea Landing (805) 963-3564.

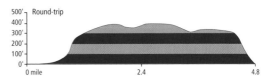

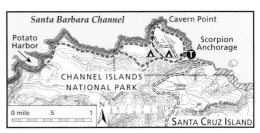

The trip to Potato Harbor is perhaps the easiest and best-suited outing for those on half-day excursions to Santa Cruz Island. The way is easily marked, the elevation gain is rather minimal, and the best the island has to offer is highlighted along the trail. From Scorpion Anchorage, follow the main road past the old farmhouses and equipment beyond the first campground to Upper Scorpion Camp. The trail branches to the right and continues along an old road that climbs to a plateau 350 feet above the ocean. The road/trail continues on to Potato Harbor, which is rather obviously named for its shape.

The views here of the Central Coast are staggering. The flora is abundant and verdant; even in summer the island gets a constant barrage of coastal moisture and fog, making it a wonderland for growth. California poppies, wallflowers, and a mix of low-lying coastal flowers make for an interesting display. There are not as many visible animal species as there once might have been. Bird-watching is wonderful here, however,

Hiking amongst clouds on the wide trail to Potato Harbor.

as many species can be spotted on the island, including the scrub jay which is endemic only to Santa Cruz Island. Look for it in canyons and in the campgrounds. Also keep an eye out for endangered California brown pelicans soaring through the skies above the sea.

Unfortunately, there is no beach access at Potato Harbor, but the views along the way are more than worth the effort. If getting sand between one's toes is the desired outcome of hiking on Santa Cruz Island, Smugglers Cove (Hike 46) is the only destination on the park side of the island, besides the initial landing.

The return trip can be made into an interesting loop via Cavern Point. The map and distance shown here include this loop, which travels cliffside for a little more than 1 mile. The trail itself is unmarked but the split is obvious, as is the point which can clearly be made out with its upturned, angled cliff. From the point, which provides a good vantage, the trail can be seen; it wanders through a large grassy area which may be closed in the future, due to hundreds of Chumash middens located along the raised plateau. The path winds down toward the old buildings and back to the main trail.

Opposite: The Central Coast contains a vast wealth of untapped and isolated wilderness.

SANTA YNEZ, SIERRA MADRE, AND SAN RAFAEL MOUNTAINS

The Santa Ynez, Sierra Madre, and San Rafael mountains belong to the Transverse Ranges that run west-to-east across much of Southern California. These three mountain ranges stretch from San Luis Obispo to Ventura County, and vary from coastal chaparral-covered mountains to high pine-covered peaks more than 7000 feet in elevation.

Created by fault lines that pushed the coastal plates into the continental plates, the mountains correspond with a bend in the San Andreas Fault. Ranging from beautiful grass-covered slopes to oak woodlands, these mountains contain a vast arrangement of beauty, including natural and historic oddities, along with fantastic scenery. Due to their orientation and the Mediterranean climate, the mountains are extremely susceptible to fires. Some of the higher peaks get snow in the wintertime, though in general they get very little precipitation.

The mountains were home to the Chumash Indians, who left traces of their existence all over the region. Pictographs and petroglyphs can be found in many places.

49 FORBUSH FLAT

Distance: 3 miles round-trip
Hiking time: 1.5 hours, or overnight backpack
Difficulty: Easy, but moderately steep elevation gain and loss
Elevation gain: 1000 feet
High point: 3400 feet
Season: All, very hot in summer
Water: Forbush Camp has filterable water year-round in wet years
Fees and permits: Adventure Pass
Map: USGS Santa Barbara
Information: Los Padres National Forest, Santa Barbara Ranger District, (805) 968-6640, *www.fs.fed.us/r5/lospadres*

Getting there: Take US 101 north to Santa Barbara. Exit at State Street/State Route 154, and take SR 154 (San Marcos Pass) 8 miles to the top of the crest. Make a right onto El Camino Cielo. Follow East Camino Cielo as it winds along the upper ridge of the Santa Ynez Mountains for 14.5 miles to Cold Springs Saddle. Park here.

From the parking area, trails lead down both sides of the crown. The Cold Springs Trail leads south to Montecito, and north to Forbush Flat and beyond. This area is secluded; you are not likely to see many people on your hike, if any at all.

Forbush Flat is an inverted hike. Dropping 1000 feet in elevation in 1.5 miles means the climb out will be fairly steep. Keep this in mind if taking this hike on a hot day. This hike is short enough not to be dangerous, but it can be very uncomfortable in the heat. The good thing is that the sun will drop below the crest and keep the trail in the shade during late afternoon. If it is too hot, stay awhile down in the Flat and hike back

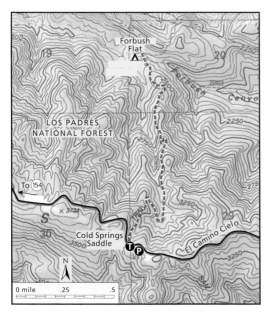

unexpected and surprisingly beautiful sylvan glen a couple of hundred feet below the trailhead. The secluded dale is encircled by pine trees and a trickling stream. Since this is coastal low country, the area is also replete with poison oak, sometimes spreading onto the trail—this is definitely a long-pants hiking area, especially in winter. Ticks can be abundant here just after rains.

It is perfectly reasonable to stop here if you are only looking for a short walk to stretch your legs. However, to get to the campsite at Forbush Flat you will need to continue down. The trail maintains a steady downward pace, which makes going in very easy. The trail winds around a ridge and drops into the wooded flats at 1.5 miles. You'll find a quaint and isolated primitive campground, complete with a fire ring and a picnic table, nestled within a grassy grove of oaks. There is year-round water that collects in a pool behind the camp. As the year and heat progress, the water level will get lower, but there should be water available for filtering no matter when you arrive.

out just before sundown. Small microclimates along the trail are quite refreshing, cooler by up to 10 degrees Fahrenheit. The views into Santa Ynez Canyon and the San Rafael Wilderness make this short trek breathtaking.

A short half-mile walk leads you down to an

The way out is the same way you came in. There are also options for making this a longer trek or a short backpack with a car shuttle to either Gibraltar Lake or Mono Campground.

Lovely rolling mountains create a panorama along the Forbush Flat Trail.

50 RANCHO NUEVO/DEAL CANYON LOOP

Distance: 7.5 miles point-to–point, or 12-mile loop
Hiking time: 4 to 5 hours
Difficulty: Moderate to strenuous
Elevation gain: 1150 feet
High point: 4650 feet
Season: All, road closed during high water runoff
Water: Ample, needs filtering
Fees and permits: Adventure Pass
Maps: USGS Rancho Nuevo Creek, Reyes Peak
Information: Los Padres National Forest, (805) 646-4348, *www.fs.fed.us/r5/lospadres/*

Getting there: From Wheeler Springs drive nearly 33 miles on State Route 33 to Forest Service Road 7N04, signed for Dick Smith Wilderness Access. The road is recommended only for four-wheel drive or high-clearance vehicles. The road forks at just over 0.75 mile; veer left and follow it for another 0.75 mile to the Rancho Nuevo Campground and trailhead at the end of the road. To make this trip a

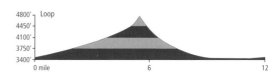

point-to-point shuttle hike, a car must also be parked 3 miles south on SR 33 at the signed Bear Canyon Trailhead.

The Dick Smith Wilderness is a fantastic wonderland.

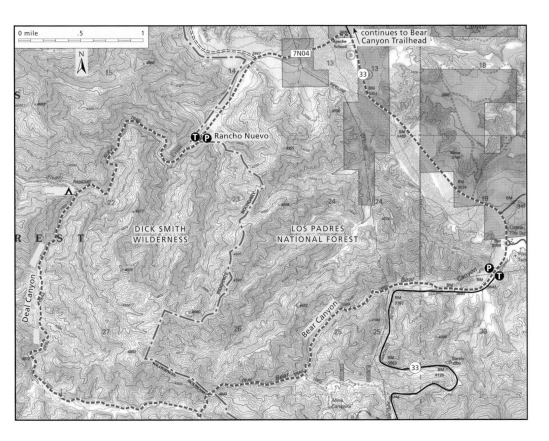

Rancho Nuevo and Deal Canyons are a beautiful way to experience the backcountry of the Ojai district of the Los Padres National Forest and the wild expanse of the Dick Smith Wilderness. Rancho Nuevo Canyon climbs along a creek and skirts narrows, crossing back and forth through lush and vibrant gorges reminiscent of southern Utah. The creek flows year-round during times of heavy rainfall, but will dry up in spots during seasons of low precipitation.

In a little less than 1.5 miles, the trail junctions at a backcountry campsite. Heading west would take you toward upper Rancho Nuevo, which has merits all its own, but for this hike veer left and delve farther into the backcountry. Creek crossings abound, so many they become difficult to count. The trail dips and climbs for at least half a mile, and although it is nothing very strenuous, the up-and-down coupled with

water- and rock-leaping makes this section one to be taken slowly; enjoy it, this is not the place for time trials. Eventually the canyon opens up into a glorious valley where the beauty and tranquility are transcendent.

The trail then drops into a sandy streambed and nearly levels off for over 2 miles through the vale. Here, it becomes more difficult to follow in several places. Watch for cairns and obvious signs of the path; a careful eye is sometimes necessary. At the other end of the canyon, the trail begins a steep unshaded climb to the wilderness exit at a signed saddle. From this point, the trail descends 2 miles and 1000 feet through lovely Bear Canyon and exits at a trailhead on SR 33, 4.5 miles from where this hike began. It is an easy but protracted walk on roads back to the original trailhead, so most groups will want to leave a shuttle car here, making this a point-to-point hike.

51 VINCENT TUMAIIAT TRAIL—PEAK TO PEAK

Distance: 8.5 miles round-trip
Hiking time: 5 hours
Difficulty: Strenuous
Elevation gain: 1300 feet
High point: 8831 feet
Season: Spring to fall
Water: None, bring your own
Fees and permits: Adventure Pass
Map: USGS Sawmill Mountain
Information: Los Padres National Forest, (661) 245-3731, *www.fs.fed.us/r5/lospadres/*

Getting there: From Gorman, take Interstate 5 north for 2.5 miles to the exit for Frazier Mountain Park Road. Turn left and follow the road for nearly 7 miles. Veer right onto Cuddy Valley Road. In another 5 miles veer right onto Mil Portrero Highway. After driving for 8 more miles, turn left onto Cerro Noroeste Road. Follow it for 6.75 miles to the turnout and signed Mount Pinos Trailhead.

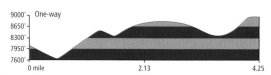

The trail begins right from the road and descends 500 feet in approximately half a mile. From the start, it is clear that what altitude is lost will be just as quickly regained on the other side. Obvious to anyone traveling this way are firebreaks

built and enlarged along the trail during the Day Fire of 2006 to protect the towns below the Mount Pinos area. Thankfully the fire did not reach this far, but it came close to obliterating nearly the entire Los Padres National Forest.

Normally taken as a one-way shuttle trip, this peak-to-peak hike mostly follows a ridgeline. It is a popular outing with three named summits—Grouse, Sawmill, and Mount Pinos—to

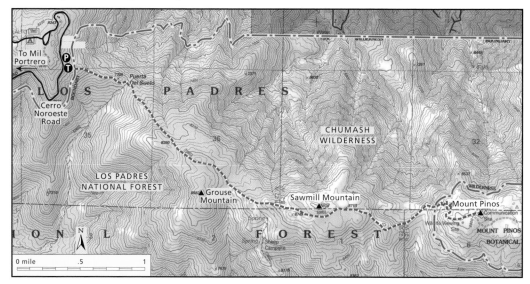

The "Peak to Peak" hike provides fantastic vistas over a great portion of Southern California.

bushwhack to and scramble over, and a lot of tiny, unnamed tops along the way. From any of the overlooks, the views are heavenly and far-reaching. This is the tallest region in the entire forest, so there is nothing in the way to obscure the vistas in any direction.

The Sawmill Mountain and Mount Pinos area is a beautifully lush yellow-pine forest reminiscent of the southern Sierra or the highest reaches of the Angeles and San Bernardino National Forests. Situated nearly entirely within the Chumash Wilderness, this hike is a 4-mile one-way trip. Even with its ups and downs this is a fairly simple outing, but as a round-trip the elevation changes add up to a strenuous hike.

Along the way, two signed trails venture off to the south (right), each making its way down into the Sespe Wilderness to campgrounds that are favorites of backpackers and Boy Scouts. Stay straight and continue up and over ridges to the Mount Pinos area.

There are ups and downs all along the way, so be prepared for gain and loss, and loss and gain. The trail makes enough of these vertical diversions on its own, but it is worthwhile to venture off onto the short (0.25 mile) use trails and ascend both Grouse and Sawmill mountains. There is even the possibility of off-trail exploration and rock climbing. Be on the lookout for condors in the sky above, as the Sespe Wilderness is one of the largest parcels acting as a sanctuary for the endangered birds.

52 PAINTED ROCK

Distance: 10.75 miles round-trip
Hiking time: 5.5 hours
Difficulty: Strenuous
Elevation gain: 550 feet
High point: 5100 feet
Season: All
Water: None, bring your own
Fees and permits: Adventure Pass
Maps: USGS Peak Mountain, Hurricane Deck
Information: Los Padres National Forest, (661) 245-3731, *www.fs.fed.us/r5/lospadres/*

Getting there: From US 101 in Santa Maria, take State Route 166 east for 25.5 miles, then turn right onto Sierra Madre Road. Follow it for 29.5 miles to its completion, and park; do not block the locked gate at the road's end near the McPherson Peak communication towers.

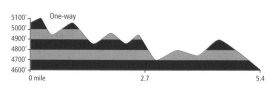

Those wishing to continue farther into Lion Canyon can explore the views and rocky outcroppings near the painted cave.

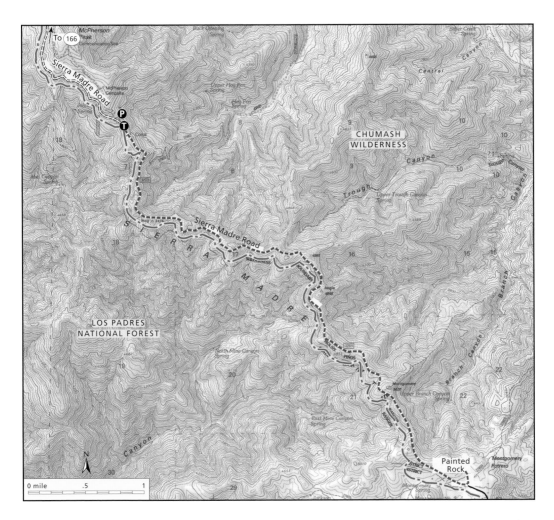

The hike to Painted Rock is as straightforward as they come: walk for 5.25 miles down an old road now used for ranch and fire access, meandering up and down continuously with a general trend that downslopes about 550 feet in total. The elevation gained and lost is substantially more than that, however, but since this hike is on a road, it is not altogether that difficult.

Generally, a hike along a road would not be considered a "classic" in the truest sense of the word, but this hike breaks the mold. Since Sierra Madre Road travels along the crest of the mountain chain, the views are expansive in every direction. The vast Cuyama Valley extends for miles and miles into eroded badlands and higher peaks of the Los Padres, while the San Rafael Wilderness trickles away into the Pacific Ocean to the west. The views along this hike cannot be outdone.

Aside from the views, the hike itself is rather nondescript. However, the large boulder outcroppings of Lion Canyon become apparent rather early on, so the distance to the destination is observable and tangible, even though Painted Rock is a bit closer than the actual canyon itself.

As the hike finally enters the mountaintop vale where the pictographs reside, a magical quality can be felt in the very air. Strange stone formations begin to crop up resembling Celtic standing stones.

There are several rock paintings. An interpretive book describes the natural history of the area and offers interpretations of the art. The large sun disc pictograph in the cave is incredible. Much of the surrounding prehistoric paintings have been eroded either by time, weather, or the heedlessness of humankind. Please obey the posted signs and do not climb into the cave or touch the rock art. This place is a treasure that needs our help to last for posterity.

Return the way you came.

The sun disc is only one of many pictographs at this sacred Native American site.

53 MANZANA SCHOOLHOUSE

Distance: 17 miles round-trip
Hiking time: 9.5 hours or overnight
Difficulty: Strenuous
Elevation gain: 700 feet
High point: 1800 feet
Season: All, very hot in summer
Water: Manzana Creek
Fees and permits: Adventure Pass
Map: USGS Bald Mountain
Information: Los Padres National Forest, (805) 967-3481, *www.fs.fed.us/r5/lospadres/*

Getting there: From US 101 in Santa Barbara take the State Street/State Route 154 exit. Turn right onto SR 154. Continue west for 22 miles, passing Lake Cachuma. Cross the Santa Ynez River, and turn right onto Armour Ranch Road. Drive for 1.5 miles. Turn right on Happy Canyon Road and drive for 14 miles to Cachuma Saddle. Stay straight on Sunset Valley Road at the fork and drive for 4 miles. After crossing a creek, park your car on the left.

Manzana Schoolhouse is an incredible all-day adventure or great beginner overnight backpack. The path is relatively level, shaded, and filled with excitement for the intrepid explorer. The entire trip follows lovely Manzana Creek to its confluence with the mighty Sisquoc Wild and Scenic River. The low elevation of this hike can make it hot and dry during mid- to late summer, and the creek may be too high to cross safely during winter rains and times of high runoff. Early

spring is perhaps the best time to take this hike due to the wildflowers and wildlife in the area, though late fall is just as nice due to the lower frequency of people using the trail.

There are at least sixty creek crossings in all, so be prepared for wet feet if the creek is running high. These crossings can be time-consuming, and will add at least an hour or more to the total amount of time spent hiking. The trail reaches a primitive campsite and junction with the Hurricane Deck Trail at 1.25 miles in. Continue straight and follow the trail as it crisscrosses the creek for the next few miles. Keep an eye out for the trail and the well-placed cairns piled alongside it. The trail is not that difficult to follow, but even

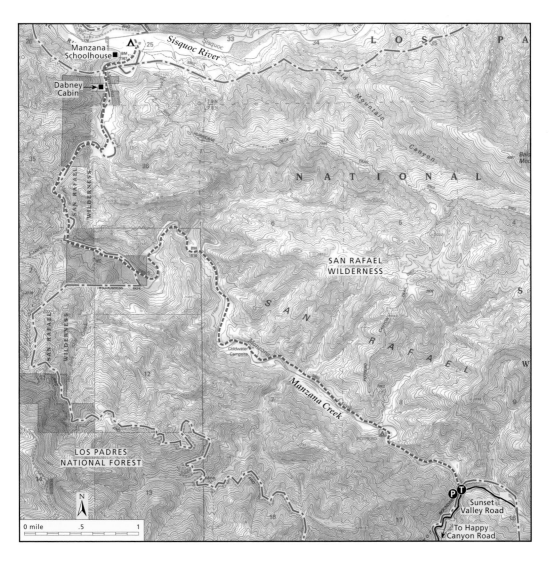

the greatest trail-hardened adventurer may lose sight of the track at a few of the crossing spots.

At nearly 6 miles there is a junction with a road; stay straight and follow the creek. There are posted signs in many places—follow the directions on them and the trail will stay clear. As the trail passes some rusty antique farm equipment and another junction with a road, stay right and hike along the road for a bit. Dabney Cabin, an old rustic hunting lodge, graces the trail at the 7-mile mark, and a historic outhouse is still in service up the hill behind the wooden lodge. A county historical marker and a metal register offer loads of information about the cabin in plastic-protected pages.

Continue hiking along the road and trail for another 1.5 miles to the schoolhouse, which was abandoned in 1901. It too serves as a Santa Barbara County landmark. The schoolhouse sits up the hill from some hitching posts and the campsite. Nearby are some interesting ruins and grave markers that are shown on the topo map, but rarely frequented by day hikers.

Many animals frequent the area, including

The old schoolhouse is in great shape due to its remoteness.

bear. The most interesting might be the endangered arroyo toad. Respect all postings and try not to upset the water or streambeds.

If the weather is nice, the hike can be made into an 18-mile loop by hiking up into the rugged mountains along the Hurricane Deck Trail. If it is hot, though, this is decidedly a bad choice. If backpacking is an option, there are many campgrounds to choose from, and most are very rarely used.

CENTRAL COAST REGION

The Central Coast is a splendid area filled with rolling grasslands, awesome seascapes, and coastal peaks. Where California's Central Coast begins and ends is up for debate, but generally the region is thought of as the section of coastline from Ventura north to San Luis Obispo. The Big Sur region is often included as well. The Pacific Coast Highway (PCH), also known as Highway 1, and US 101 run through this area and generally follow the coast as it winds west and north toward the middle of the state. For the purposes of this book, two hikes have been included that comprise "coastal" regions, and several forest hikes from this region are included in other sections.

54 GAVIOTA HOT SPRINGS AND PEAK

Distance: 5.5 miles round-trip
Hiking time: 3 hours
Difficulty: Moderate to strenuous
Elevation gain: 2100 feet
High point: 2458 feet
Season: All
Water: None, bring your own
Fees and permits: Parking fee
Maps: USGS Gaviota, Solvang
Information: Gaviota State Park, (805) 968-1033,
www.parks.ca.gov/default.asp?page_id=606

Getting there: Take US 101 north from the Gaviota Tunnel for just over 1.6 miles. Exit for HIghway 1. Turn right and then immediately right again. Take the frontage road for 0.25 mile to the parking area for Gaviota State Park.

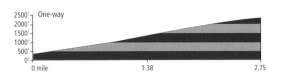

The trail is an old fire road, very well maintained to both the springs and the peak. It begins with a well-signed trailhead at the southern end of the parking lot. The springs enter into a large upper basin and a lower pool. The upper pool is both hotter and clearer than the lower one, which is actually quite milky, but prettier and full of reedy plants. Some people may want to take the half-mile trek into the springs and soak in the hot waters for a generous amount of time before returning to the parking area. Others may wish to hit the peak in the early morning light and then return for a leisurely time at the springs. Either way, the trip is sure to be enjoyable. Many people use the springs in their birthday suits,

so be prepared for nature in a natural setting.

To get to the springs, a short spur trail must be taken from the main trail. At a little less than 0.5 mile into the hike, turn right onto the narrow but well-trodden springs path, marked with a sign by friendly helpers wishing to assist people on their way to the luscious waters. (The sign is a little before the turnoff.)

Continuing on the main trail leads to the summit of Gaviota Peak, which at 2458 feet is the tallest summit around. Ocean views are breathtakingly spectacular: the Channel Islands sit like gemstones upon the crystal blue waters of the Pacific. All of Santa Barbara County is clearly within view, and sights extend all the way

The lower pool at Gaviota Hot Springs

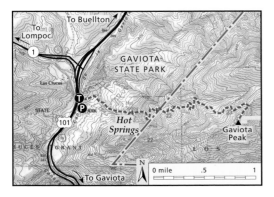

down to the Santa Monica Mountains. If distant coastal views are desired, almost nothing beats Gaviota Peak.

The best way to take this trip is to head to the peak early in the morning to avoid the heat of the day, which can be hot even in the wintertime. Early morning starts also avoid the most severe winds which frequent the Gaviota area. Return to the hot springs while the morning is still fresh, soak and bathe for a while, and then head on out the way you came.

55 OSO FLACO LAKE

Distance: 2.25 miles round-trip
Hiking time: 1 hour
Difficulty: Easy
Elevation gain: 20 feet
High point: 25 feet
Season: All
Water: None, bring your own
Fees and permits: Required
Map: USGS Oceano
Information: California State Parks, (805) 473-7220, *www.dunescenter.org/*

Getting there: From the intersection with State Route 166, drive 3.75 miles north on Highway 1 through Guadalupe to the turnoff for Oso Flaco Road; go left. Drive just over 3 miles to the parking lot at the end.

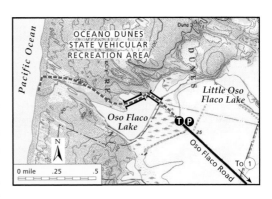

Oso Flaco Lake is part of Oceano Dunes State Vehicular Recreation Area (SVRA), managed by California State Parks. Approximately 2100 acres surrounding Oso Flaco Lake are off-limits to vehicles and managed for plants and wildlife. The lake is a beautiful freshwater reservoir and ecosystem surrounded by towering dunes and nestled beside the Pacific Ocean.

The Guadalupe–Nipomo Dune complex stretches from Pismo Beach in the north to beautiful Point Sal State Beach in the south. Properties within the dune complex that are open to the public include Oceano Dunes SVRA, the Guadalupe–Nipomo National Wildlife

Refuge, and the Rancho Guadalupe County Park. A large area of the dunes and shoreline north of Oso Flaco Lake are closed seasonally to provide breeding habitat for the endangered California least tern and the threatened western snowy plover. In addition to the seasonal restrictions,

The trail at Oso Flaco leads all the way to an unspoiled section of the Pacific Ocean with expansive views.

hiking off existing paths in the surrounding dune habitat is prohibited.

The trail, which begins on the road, heads toward the ocean and some large dunes. Make a left onto the boardwalk and walk across Oso Flaco Lake. More than two hundred different species of birds live within the reserve. Plants such as yellow coreopsis, Indian paintbrush, larkspur, and poppies show off the natural beauty of this area. Some rare and endangered flora found here include the crisp dune mint, beach spectacle pod, and surf thistle. This unique ecosystem is sure to please.

From the end of the lake, the boardwalk continues to the surf. The ocean seems to be ever-forceful here, as the waves hit the sand with violence and vigor. The coast stretches as far as the eye can see in either direction, much of it undeveloped. Sand dollars are commonly found along the beach, as are other types of shells. A walk along the beach can be taken to the south; visitors are free to stroll for as long as they wish.

The area is quite romantic, and bird-watching is a pleasurable activity. Many benches lining the boardwalk offer a quaint setting for putting an arm around a loved one.

Opposite: Mojave National Preserve offers visitors tantalizing peaks and bizarre desert destinations.

MOJAVE DESERT AND TEHACHAPI MOUNTAINS

TEHACHAPI MOUNTAINS

Tehachapi Mountain Park is a lovely wooded area that resides majestically above the desert and the mountain vale of Tehachapi. The mountain range, nestled between the arid starkness of the Mojave Desert and the lush farmlands of the San Joaquin Valley, once served as a wilderness corridor between the San Gabriels, the Sierra Madres, and the Sierra Nevada. Elements of each of these regions are interspersed throughout the park. The desert influence is readily felt, though the hike begins amid lovely oak and laurel.

56 TEHACHAPI MOUNTAIN

Distance: 4 miles round-trip
Hiking time: 2 hours
Difficulty: Moderate
Elevation gain: 2000 feet
High point: 7986 feet
Season: All
Water: None, bring your own
Fees and permits: None
Map: USGS Tehachapi South
Information: Kern County Parks and Recreation, (661) 868-7000,
    www.co.kern.ca.us/parks/index.htm

Getting there: From the town of Mojave, drive northwest on State Route 58 for 21 miles to exit 148, Tucker Road (State Route 202), in the town of Tehachapi. (It is also the exit for the correctional institution located there.) In just over 2 miles, turn right onto Highline Road. Drive for 1.25 miles and turn left onto Water Canyon Road. Drive for another 2 miles and turn right into Tehachapi Mountain Park. Stay right at each fork, and park in the lot next to site number 49.

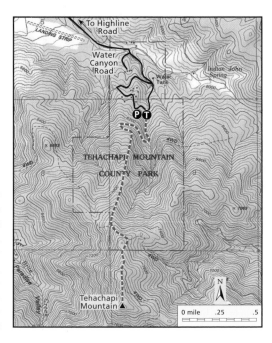

From the Oak Flat Campground at about 6000 feet of elevation, head back to the Nuooah Nature Trail, go up the trail to Marker 13, turn right and walk until the dirt service road. Then turn right and follow it as it wraps around for nearly 2 miles. A use trail leads to the top of Tehachapi Mountain, and some white rocks have been conveniently placed along the road showing hikers where to turn right and ascend the ridge. The use trail is steep and follows the ridge to the summit for the rest of the way. As the trail ascends, the locale looks much like that of the higher reaches of the Angeles, Los Padres, and even Sequoia national forests. The trail is duff-covered with pine needles, and the rocks are mostly granite.

A couple of signs mark the trail along the way, one of which sits high up in a tree and could easily be unnoticed by hikers as they huff and puff up the sharp incline. After 2 miles an old wooden sign marks the summit block, which rests among large pines. A register is hidden in the rocks for hikers to sign their names.

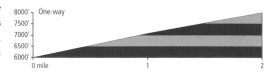

The views are obscured in several directions by tall trees, but not so badly as to say there are no views at all. In fact, the summit is quite nice and the vistas on the way up and down are well worth the effort. Return via the same route.

Sierra and Makaila gather sugar pine cones at Tehachapi Mountain Park.

MOJAVE NATIONAL PRESERVE

The Mojave Desert is a majestic wonderland filled with geologic, historic, and scenic wonders that are quite infrequently visited. Lava tubes, volcanic cinder cones, sonic-booming dunes, the oddly cicular batholith of Cima Dome, a historic rail depot, and many more await within the national preserve. Most Southern Californians zoom by this park on their way to Las Vegas. Many have probably marveled at the oddly named Zzyzx Road, but few ever exit to find out what exactly is behind any of the off-ramps near Baker, California.

Hiking in the preserve is a fantastic experience; many areas and roads are still unsigned and the area retains a very rustic, Wild West feel, unlike most regions in California (and specifically those within a national park unit). Directions to certain areas include such particulars as "turn left after the white tire, continue past the horse trough, and turn onto the rough dirt road after the old corral." Some hikes are difficult to find, but that just adds to the region's adventuresome appeal.

Most hikes taken in the preserve will be tranquil and people-free. A few areas, such as the more popular Kelso Dunes, are frequented more often than others. In many cases, driving to the trailhead is just as fun as the hike itself.

57 KELSO DUNES

Distance: 3 miles round-trip
Hiking time: 1.5 hours
Difficulty: Moderate
Elevation gain: 500 feet
High point: 3050 feet
Season: Late fall through spring
Water: None, bring your own
Fees and permits: None
Map: USGS Kelso Dunes
Information: Mojave National Preserve, (760) 252-6100, *www.nps.gov/moja/*

Getting there: From Baker, drive southeast on Kelbaker Road (State Route 127) for 42.5 miles to the turnoff for Kelso Dunes. Turn right and drive 3.2 miles on the well-graded dirt road to the parking area and trailhead.

The Kelso Dunes are a unique system of dunes that originated from sand deposits in the Mojave River near Afton Canyon. The sand is finely granulated, and no new sand is accumulating. The sand itself has accrued in five waves over the past twenty-five thousand years. Since then, plants have grown into the dunes and stabilized the sand, so there is no need for new alluvium.

The dunes system is one of only a handful in the world to be called "booming" dunes, or "singing sands." The phenomenon occurs when disturbed sand slides downhill, and the sliding sand moves on top of undisturbed sand. If the humidity is right this triggers a low-resonance booming sound that can be both felt and heard.

The trail to the top of Kelso Dunes is a short, moderate one. The sand is not so hard to walk on at first, but as the dune becomes steeper and steeper, the difficulty level amps up a bit.

The Kelso Dunes, the largest in the Mojave Desert, consist of eroded granite from the San Bernardino Mountains.

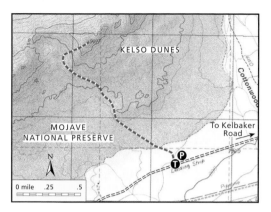

From the parking lot, the trail drops and is level for a short distance before beginning the climb. A lot of typical Mojave vegetation can be found, such as creosote bush and white bursage. Here some of the endemic and rare species native to this desert environment can be seen. The kangaroo rat makes its home here, along with many types of insects, and the fringe-toed lizard.

As the climb continues, evidence of the trail disappears, though it is easy enough to find. There will almost always be footprints to follow; if there aren't any, head for the plateau on the crest, and then continue along the crest for the most difficult portion of the hike to the top. The crest region is the best place to hear the booming sound made by the dunes. Casting sand off the sides of the ridge by pushing footsteps into the sand is enough to cause the effect, if the conditions are right.

The views from the crest and summit of the dunes are both noteworthy and spectacular. The Providence and Granite mountains stretch off into the distance, as does the Devils Playground, where sand seems to spin off into the edges of eternity. Evening to sunset and sunrise to early morning are the best times for photography. Chances of animal sightings are greater during those hours as well. Please do your best not to trample or otherwise walk on vegetation, and leave behind only footprints.

58 LAVA TUBES

Distance: 0.5 miles round-trip
Hiking time: 0.5 hours
Difficulty: Easy
Elevation gain: 150 feet
High point: 3765 feet
Season: Late fall through spring
Water: None, bring your own
Fees and permits: None
Map: USGS Cow Cove
Information: Mojave National Preserve, (760) 252-6100, *www.nps.gov/moja/*

Getting there: From Interstate 15 in the town of Baker, take Kelbaker Road (State Route 127) east toward Kelso for 19.7 miles. There is a large dirt turnout and an easily missed dirt road called Aiken Mine Road; turn left. The road is passable for all vehicles, though it is washboarded and sandy. In 0.5 mile, follow the road as it veers right at a fork. Pass the corral, and continue for a total of 4.5 miles; turn left onto the smaller road. Drive for 0.3 mile and park in the small turnout.

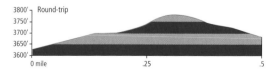

The lava tubes are a very short but incredibly interesting hike, especially for those with children. Lava tubes form when hot lava reaches the earth's surface and cools. The upper layer hardens while lava continues to flow beneath it.

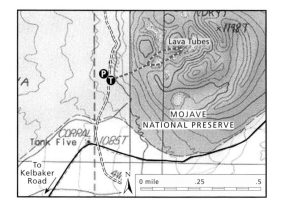

the most visible path from the small parking area and, since it is markedly brief, it is very hard to miss. Walk along the volcanic rock and desert scrub bushes to the upper hole, where a metal ladder has been affixed to the side.

Going into the lava tube is like entering a giant cave; bend down and go beyond the overhanging hardened lava to enter the large chamber. The way is dark, and flashlights or headlamps are a great idea. Once you are in the big room, a set of holes allows sunlight to flood a portion of the cave, and the place feels positively primordial. At first it looks like total darkness as you enter, but it is not.

There are several places in this particular tube where lava continued to flow on top and broke through the upper crust, forming holes that allow light into the now hollow and cavernous formation.

From the parking area, hike up the hillside along a use path that is marked with cairns. It is

There is evidence of animal habitation in the tube. There may be spiderwebs, rat nests, insects, and a host of other desert critter droppings, but nothing too serious, as long as caution is used. Return back down the hill and look for the lava openings on the trail. They are much easier to spot going out than heading in.

The cinder cones left by volcanoes formed caves in their lava tubes.

59 TEUTONIA PEAK

Distance: 3 miles round-trip
Hiking time: 1.5 hours
Difficulty: Easy
Elevation gain: 700 feet
High point: 5700 feet
Season: Late fall through spring
Water: None, bring your own
Fees and permits: None
Map: USGS Cima Dome
Information: Mojave National Preserve, (760) 252-6100, *www.nps.gov/moja/*

Getting there: From the town of Baker, drive north on Interstate 15 for 26.5 miles to the Cima Road off-ramp. Turn right and drive southeast for 12 miles to the turnout and sign for the Teutonia Peak trailhead.

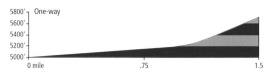

The trail begins on an old mining road near a large outcropping of boulders. It wanders through a sizeable Joshua tree forest and stays relatively flat for nearly a mile. As the trail edges closer to the mountain, it begins to climb upward on a steady incline. The Joshua trees become less and less frequent and the views begin to open up into the Ivanpah Mountains and Valley. In a little more than half a mile, the trail works its way from the base up to the summit block.

Teutonia Peak is not actually a summit, but rather a conglomeration of rocky crags on the northeastern edge of the titanic mound that is Cima Dome. The enormity of the dome is entirely obvious when the trail enters its upper reaches. For as far as the eye can see its rounded structure is apparent, as it spans over 75 square miles in total, making it one of the largest geologic domes on the planet.

The trail peters out before reaching a high point, and some slick Class III and IV climbing skills are needed to proceed any farther—though easier routes are sure to be found for those wishing to explore further. There are three distinct "summit" regions, and all can be scrambled

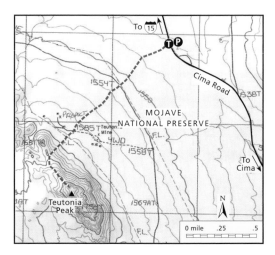

with a bit of fortitude. Just be certain to keep the down-climb in mind when going up; the eroded rocks are slippery and steep, and a fall could mean a serious injury. There are pitches for seasoned rock climbers as well, and anyone wishing to bring along their gear could easily spend a day climbing in relative solitude.

Those wishing to avoid a scramble can enjoy

Opposite: Heading toward Teutonia Peak on the remnants of an old mining road

Heading down the trail from the summit of Teutonia Peak

the vista from trail's end, pointing toward the outposts of Cima and Kelso, with a picnic lunch or just a simple bit of relaxation. Return the same way, and enjoy the scenery on the return trip.

As a side adventure, there are many remnants of mines in the area. Making a right or a left onto the larger dirt road near the trailhead will lead to several.

Opposite: Morro Rock is only one of the many coastal treasures on the route to Big Sur.

PACIFIC COAST HIGHWAY
AND BIG SUR

SANTA LUCIA MOUNTAINS AND BIG SUR

The Santa Lucia Mountains are a coastal range that runs north and south for over 100 miles from the Monterey Peninsula to San Luis Obispo. They are a beautiful chain that sits above the Big Sur region, which is known throughout the world for its lush scenery, picture perfect waterfalls, redwoods, and sylvan canyons. Big Sur is comprised of numerous state parks and beaches, all filled with their own wonders.

The mountains themselves include a large part of the northern reaches of the Los Padres National Forest, and contain several peaks that command amazing coastal views. Cone Peak has the highest coastal prominence in the United States, rising nearly a mile above the Pacific just 3 miles from its shore.

60 VALENCIA PEAK/THE BLUFFS LOOP

Distance: 5 miles round-trip
Hiking time: 2.5 hours
Difficulty: Moderate
Elevation gain: 1250 feet
High point: 1347 feet
Season: All
Water: None, bring your own
Fees and permits: Required
Map: USGS Morro Bay South
Information: Montana de Oro State Park, (805) 528-0513,
www.parks.ca.gov/default.asp?page_id=592

Getting there: From Highway 1 in Morro Bay, take the South Bay Boulevard exit. Turn south toward the ocean and follow the signs for Montana de Oro and Morro Bay State Parks. Stay on South Bay Boulevard for 4 miles. Turn right onto Los Osos Valley Road (which becomes Pecho Valley Road after 1.5 miles) and follow it for 5.25 miles to the turnout for the Valencia Peak Trail. It is the first stop on the left after the campground and visitor center. There is also parking for the Bluffs Trail on the right.

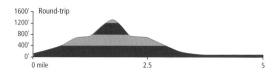

From the parking area, walk east on the Valencia Peak Trail and climb gently for the first 0.75 mile toward the obvious summit, which looms high overhead. Here the trail junctions with the unsigned and slightly overgrown Badger Trail. Continue straight and upward as the trail gains

a steeper grade for almost 1 mile as it reaches the peak.

Atop the summit, the vistas are absolutely astounding. The entire park can be surveyed from this height, as can the nine *morros*, or volcanic outcroppings, of San Luis Obispo County, including Morro Rock protruding from the sea. Wildlife is abundant in this area, including skunk, raccoon, coyote, rabbit, squirrel, badger, deer, fox, bobcat, and mountain lion. Over forty types of birds call the region home, and raptors such as the white-tailed kestrel can commonly be seen along the hiking trail to the summit.

After spending some time enjoying the ample views from the summit, head back down the trail to the aforementioned connection with the Badger Trail. This time, turn left and follow it past an environmental campsite which has the best views on the Central Coast, and across Pecho Road to eventually connect up with the Bluffs Trail near the ocean. The Bluffs Trail travels north and south; turn left and follow it along the wide pathway, examining the majesty of the jetties of white Monterey shale that jut into the Pacific. The trail continues for 0.5 mile to the south, but visitors can backtrack whenever the mood strikes them. In places the trail dips down to the ocean, making great opportunities for a picnic or moments of profound contemplation.

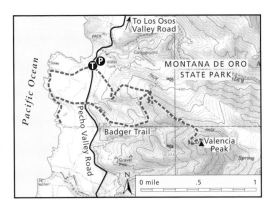

Wildflowers put on a show in the park during the spring and into early summer. Bouquets of white, purple, and red flowers protrude through the orange and yellow of the California poppies that give the park its distinctive color and name, which in Spanish means "mountain of gold." The park and trails are best visited during this time when the grasses are a vernal green and the colors of the mountainside are in full bloom. Head north on the trail and return to the parking area after taking in the serenity of one of the Central Coast's best-kept secrets.

61 BLACK HILL TRAIL

Distance: 1.8 miles round-trip
Hiking time: 1 hour
Difficulty: Easy
Elevation gain: 560 feet
High point: 661 feet
Season: All
Water: None, bring your own
Fees and permits: Required
Map: USGS Morro Bay South
Information: Morro Bay State Park, (805) 772-2560,
www.parks.ca.gov/default.asp?page_id=594

Getting there: From Highway 1 in Morro Bay, take the South Bay Boulevard exit. Turn south toward the ocean and follow the signs for Montana de Oro and Morro Bay State Parks. In less than 1 mile, veer right at the signs for Morro Bay State Park and turn onto unsigned Park View Drive. Veer right again in 0.1 mile, continuing on another 0.25 mile to park at the turnout on the left side of the roadway.

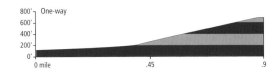

Morro Bay State Park is a highly developed recreational area complete with golf course and a campground equipped with showers. Hiking in the park is limited, but the trail to Black Hill is a

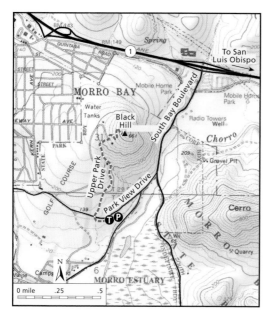

gem hidden amongst the semi-urban surroundings. Eucalyptus trees line the path. There are many offshoots to explore, including a trail by the estuary. Most of the pathways meet up and eventually find their way to the summit which towers above the immediate surroundings.

From the parking area, walk up the road for a couple hundred feet and turn right onto the unsigned trail. The path wanders and climbs gently for the first half-mile, gaining steepness as it nears the apex. Views open up of the beautiful estuary and the sandspit behind you. As the trail climbs around the hill, there are remnants of old structures and a water containment tower. In about 0.75 mile the trail meets with Upper Park Drive, which is an even easier and faster way to climb to the top. Vehicles can drive to within about 0.2 mile from the trail's end at the summit. Those not wanting to spend much time or energy can utilize this option. The trail from the road is not shaded, though, and hikers taking only the last portion will miss the beautiful section lined with eucalyptus.

From the peak, the views are unobstructed in every direction. Morro Rock sits prominently above the bay, towering over the hamlet sharing its name. Three smokestacks nearby pump smoke into the atmosphere from the power plant in the town. Cerro Cabrillo and Hollister Peak, the tallest of San Luis Obispo County's nine morros, reside in the east, while to the south Valencia Peak hovers above Montana de Oro State Park.

Watching the sun set from this vantage point can be divine. Sunrises are not too shabby either. The area is also a haven for bird watchers—from November to February, over 250 species of migrating birds travel through here.

From atop Black Hill, one of nine volcanic morros, Hollister Peak, can be seen.

62 CERRO ALTO

Distance: 4.5 miles round-trip
Hiking time: 2.5 hours
Difficulty: Moderate
Elevation gain: 1600 feet
High point: 2624 feet
Season: All, can be very hot in summer
Water: None, bring your own
Fees and permits: Adventure Pass
Map: USGS Atascadero
Information: Los Padres National Forest, (805) 968-6640,
www.fs.fed.us/r5/lospadres/

Getting there: From US 101 in Atascadero, head west on State Route 41 for 8.75 miles. Turn left on Forest Service Road 29S11, signed for Cerro Alto Campground. Drive 1 mile to the day-use parking area off to the right of the campground.

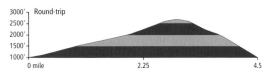

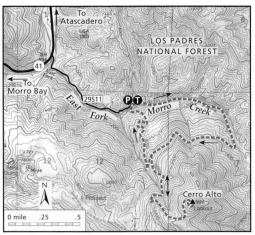

Cerro Alto is one of the taller mountains in San Luis Obispo County, and the highest along the West Cuesta Ridge. The views and scenery from its summit are a spectacular 360-degree panorama of the region, with views extending for miles and miles. In spring expect a show from wildflowers, though the area gets dry and hot toward midsummer. There is shade only on the lower portions of the hike, and as the trail snakes its way up through the canyons, the hillsides are grass-covered with coastal scrub.

Take the loop from the day-use area, as it is not as steep as the campground route. It follows a lovely oak-filled canyon for half a mile before opening up to grass-covered hillsides. In just a little over 1.5 miles, turn left and follow the trail to the top of the peak, which looms obviously overhead. The way is wide—the trail is an old access road for the defunct fire lookout, though now it serves for the utility and telephone lines buried alongside the way. Mountain bikes and horses also use the trail. This path is a favorite of bikers since it is so well graded, so watch out for other trail users who move faster than a walking human.

In the winter, winds and weather can act up at any time. Most afternoons will be windy anyway, since this is a tall mountain near the coast, with a hot inland region on its other side. From the top, enjoy the coastal views stretching from Point Estero to beyond San Luis Obispo into Pismo Beach. The inland scenery is quite nice as well, with several ranges visible, and the green hills of the California Central Coast are beautiful nearly any time of year. Hawks and turkey vultures are commonly seen in the sky here, though there are not likely to be a lot of land animals other than small mammals and lizards.

A black bumblebee gathers pollen from a wooly blue curl.

On the return from the summit, turn left at the main junction to meet up with the shorter trail, signed for the campground, which intersects on the right in less than 0.25 mile down the road. (This is the steeper "campground route" mentioned earlier.)

63 MOONSTONE BEACH TRAIL

Distance: 2.3 miles round-trip
Hiking time: 1.5 hours
Difficulty: Easy
Elevation gain: 10 feet
High point: 35 feet
Season: All
Water: None, bring your own
Fees and permits: None
Map: USGS Cambria
Information: San Simeon State Park, (805) 927-2020,
    www.parks.ca.gov/default.asp?page_id=590

Getting there: From the tiny hamlet of Harmony drive north on Highway 1 a little over 8 miles to the turnoff for Moonstone Beach Drive. Exit left off the highway toward the beach. Drive south along the beach for a little more than a mile and park in the lot for San Simeon Park–Santa Rosa Creek.

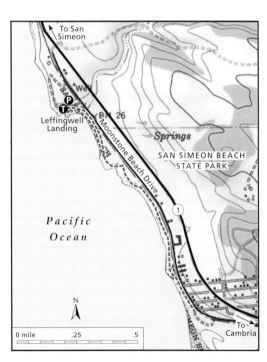

Normally, proximity to a town is not a feature of a "classic" hike, but Moonstone Beach and its seaside town make up a unique experience. The trail along Moonstone Beach is two-fold. A boardwalk runs partially along the road heading out onto the coastal bluffs above the beach, and then there is access to the beach below available in numerous spots. A good way to take this easy trip is to walk along the boardwalk on the way to Leffingwell Landing, and then dip down to the sand as much as possible on the way back.

Moonstone—part tourist attraction, part artist enclave—is a tiny community just north of the growing town of Cambria and south of Hearst Castle and San Simeon. The lovely beach here is only an element of its allure, as there are restaurants, galleries, and shops all within walking distance of the beach and its boardwalk. Though it might not be physically secluded, the trail can feel that way at times, specifically along the beach. The boardwalk has its own magic, especially on a moonlit stroll. Birds of all sorts frequent these shores along with the occasional marine mammal: sea lions, elephant seals, sea otters, and dolphins.

There are tide pools to explore all along the beach, which makes this a great hike for observing marine life. At Leffingwell Landing, there is a picnic area that makes a good stopping and turn-around point, though those wishing to continue can hike into the state park.

After the short hike, head back across the highway on Moonstone Beach Drive (which becomes Exotic Gardens Road); turn left, and

The waves roll in along lovely Moonstone Beach.

eat at the Hamlet Restaurant. The food is second to none, and the exquisite handmade lemon ice cream topped with fresh raspberries is a treat that has driven many travelers, including this author, to make the trip from Los Angeles just to have a taste.

64 LIMEKILN STATE PARK

Distance: 1.5 miles round-trip
Hiking time: 2 hours
Difficulty: Easy
Elevation gain: 300 feet
High point: 350 feet
Season: All
Water: Ample
Fees and permits: Required
Map: USGS Lopez Point
Information: Limekiln State Park, (831) 667-2403,
    www.parks.ca.gov/default.asp?page_id=577

Getting there: From San Simeon, drive 37 miles north on Highway 1 to the turnoff for Limekiln State Park. Turn right and continue to the parking area.

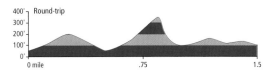

Limekiln State Park is the hidden treasure of the Big Sur region. Many people drive past the park without ever noticing it on their way to the more famous and popular parks farther north. From the highway, it hardly seems more than a stop along the road. Nothing could be further from the truth. The park is a secluded haven of redwoods, tumbling creeks, and historic structures; it even has a beach, though not a very picturesque one. The park has thirty-three campsites available year-round.

This hike combines all three signed hikes within the park; there is a bit of backtracking on each trail, but the hikes are very short and all are worthwhile. From the parking area head up the trail, taking the first fork to the right—signed as the Redwood Trail—which leads up Hare Canyon. The trail climbs gently alongside the creek for about 0.3 mile, and then abruptly ends. Small cascades grace the flowing creek amid the towering trees. Early morning makes for an ethereal experience; rays of light descend through the canopy and illuminate stunning pools of water, which are abundant along the gentle brook. Return to the fork and turn right onto the Limekiln Trail.

After 0.25 mile, the trail forks again just beyond the footbridge. Take the right fork across

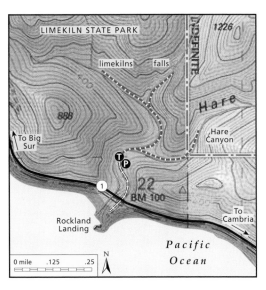

Limekiln Creek, hopping on boulders to avoid wet feet. The trail is well used, though not signed. There are several creek crossings here, though none are difficult. The path leads to a stunning waterfall that cascades over limestone cliffs, dropping more than 100 feet into the canyon. Enjoy the views of Limekiln Falls and then return to the main trail.

Turn right again and climb gently for less than 0.25 mile until reaching the historic limekilns. The four rock and steel towers were used in the late 1800s to extract lime from the rocks, for use in building cement. The raw material was then shipped to San Francisco and Monterey, where it went on to contribute to California's growing economy. Looking like something out of a fantasy novel, the photogenic structures appear out of nowhere, juxtaposed with the natural beauty of the area. The kilns have been cordoned off for safety reasons, and it is wise to stay on the trail at all times as poison oak is ubiquitous in the Big Sur region. Return to the trailhead the way you came.

Limekiln Falls cascade gently over calcium carbonate deposits built up over centuries.

65 CONE PEAK

Distance: 4 miles round-trip
Hiking time: 2.5 hours
Difficulty: Moderate
Elevation gain: 1500 feet
High point: 5155 feet
Season: All
Water: None, bring your own
Fees and permits: Adventure Pass
Map: USGS Cone Peak
Information: Los Padres National Forest, (831) 385-5434,
  www.fs.fed.us/r5/lospadres/

Getting there: From San Simeon, drive 35 miles north on Highway 1 to the turnoff for Nacimiento-Ferguson Road. Turn right and drive for 6.75 miles up the steep and winding road to the turnoff for Cone Peak Road. Turn left and drive just under 5 miles to the barely noticeable turnout and sign for the Cone Peak Trail. There is a section a half mile below the trailhead for which four-wheel-drive vehicles, or at least high clearance, are recommended.

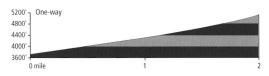

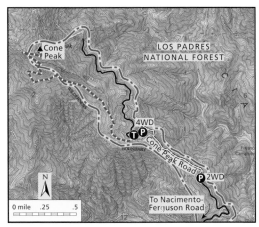

The trail to Cone Peak is a great adventure to the summit of a wondrous peak that affords dramatic views 30 to 50 miles in nearly every direction. The northern skyline is dominated by the highest summit in the region, Junipero Serra Peak, nearly 8 miles away at 5682 feet. While that mountain is higher, it does not command a coastal panorama such as that from Cone Peak where views stretch from horizon to horizon. The beautiful valley of Hunter-Liggett Military Reservation, the Ventana Wilderness, and much of the Santa Lucia Range are within full sight, along with the tremendous Big Sur coastline from Piedras Blanca in the south to Point Sur in the north. Truly nothing short of spectacular, Cone Peak is the very definition of a "classic" California hike.

From the parking area, the relatively short trail climbs rigorously upward toward the summit. The trail is without shade for nearly the entire trip, though Coulter pines, with their widow-maker football-like cones, appear closer toward the apex. Temperatures can be incredibly hot in the summertime, so bring lots of water. Wildflowers are abundant, such as yellow poppies, Indian paintbrush, monkey flower, and penstemon. Butterflies, such as the variable checkerspot, and lizards, such as the western whiptail can also be commonly seen. Poison oak along the trail is frequently eradicated by dedicated volunteers who trim it away, so bare legs are relatively safe along this hike.

Views open up immediately. The trail gains

Beginning the hike back from Cone Peak

nearly 600 feet in the first mile, and then close to 800 feet in the final switchbacking push for the peak. Looking straight down, the bridge above Limekiln State Park can clearly be seen for almost the entire hike. From the lookout on the summit, hikers lord above the immediate surroundings, with a perspective that can only be described as godlike. The heavenly beauty of the area is apparent even during periods when heavy fog rolls in from the coast. Some might even venture to describe fog-bound days as the best time to undertake this excursion. No matter what, visitors to Cone Peak will be moved by the experience. Cone Peak is a summit for the ages.

66 EWOLDSEN TRAIL/McWAY FALLS

Distance: 3 miles round-trip
Hiking time: 1.5 hours
Difficulty: Moderate
Elevation gain: 1000 feet
High point: 1200 feet
Season: All
Water: Ample, needs filtering
Fees and permits: None
Map: USGS Partington Ridge
Information: Julia Pfeiffer Burns State Park, (831) 667-2315,
www.parks.ca.gov/default.asp?page_id=578

Getting there: From San Simeon, drive north on Highway 1 52 miles to the turnoff for Julia Pfeiffer Burns State Park. Turn right and park in the large parking area.

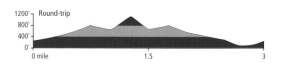

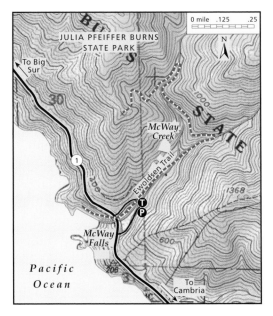

Julia Pfeiffer Burns State Park is home to one of the world's most striking waterfalls. McWay Creek drops 80 feet straight off a cliff and directly onto the beach below. Its visage appears on postcards, pictures, and calendars around the world. Though the name is quite uninspiring, McWay Falls was given its appellation for the pioneer homesteaders who first owned the property, and somehow the moniker has stuck over time. Most people, though, think of the cascade as "that waterfall that pours onto the beach in Big Sur."

This trail encompasses a famous overlook to the falls, and a somewhat less popular though frequented hike along McWay Creek and up through its canyon, known as the Ewoldsen Trail (also named for an early Big Sur entrepreneur). This beautiful canyon is home to many towering redwoods. A babbling brook runs alongside and below the well-shaded trail, which ambles gently for the first half mile until the climb begins for the beach overlook. Wildflowers are common in the spring and during times of runoff.

From the parking area, there are two ways to go. To the west, the road leads to the overlook of McWay Falls; to the east, it heads into the redwood forest. This hike can be started in either direction. Many will want to visit the falls more

McWay Falls make any photo a postcard.

than once, and at different times during the day for optimal photographic opportunities. The trip to McWay Falls is short, easy, and unpaved but accessible to travelers in wheelchairs. Heading into the forest, the trail starts wide but quickly becomes a general use trail. In just over 0.25 mile, take the fork to the left and begin switchbacking up the mountainside to the overlook, which provides a wide view of the Pacific Ocean and Highway 1. Do be careful on this trail, as the way is very steep in parts, and poison oak is nearly omnipresent.

The forest is enchanting and the falls are spectacular. If time pressures do not allow for more than one hike in the Big Sur region, this is the trip to take solely for the experience.

67 PFEIFFER FALLS/VALLEY VIEW

Distance: 1.3 miles round-trip
Hiking time: 1 hour
Difficulty: Easy
Elevation gain: 425 feet
High point: 775 feet
Season: All
Water: None, bring your own
Fees and permits: Required
Map: USGS Big Sur
Information: Pfeiffer Big Sur State Park, (831) 667-2315, *www.parks.ca.gov/default.asp?page_id=570*

Getting there: From San Simeon, drive north on Highway 1 nearly 63 miles to the entrance for Pfeiffer Big Sur State Park. Turn right into the entrance, and then turn left just past the kiosk for the nature center. Park in the lot.

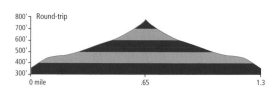

This hike is an easy combination of two hikes. The world-famous Big Sur Lodge is located within the park's confines. This is the most frequented and heavily visited park in the region, making it somewhat heavily trafficked, but still enjoyable.

From the nature center with its friendly, informative staff, head up the road to the trailhead for Pfeiffer Falls. The way is nearly a boardwalk—straight, wide, and gently graded. The trail is fenced in to protect the fragile surroundings from overuse. Strolling through the peaceful redwood forest, it is easy to attain a sense of calm and relish the serenity of the tranquil surroundings. The trees here are some of the tallest and best specimens in the Big Sur area, including magnificent redwoods. An abundance of wildlife frequents

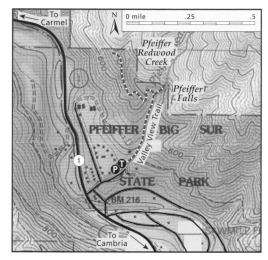

Pfeiffer Falls is a popular destination in Pfeiffer Big Sur State Park.

the area; it is not unusual to see black-tailed deer, and squirrels skirting the trail. Less commonly seen are raccoons and skunks. Bird watchers can spot Stellar's jays, American dippers (formerly known as water ouzels), and belted kingfishers.

The vista point for the falls is reached in a little more than 0.3 mile. Pfeiffer Falls is a 60-foot cascade, beautiful just about any time of year, that drops over limestone. The falls reach their greatest glory after periods of heavy rain, but they are sublime even when their flow is reduced.

Backtrack from the falls less than 0.1 mile to the connector for the Valley View Trail. Turn right and ascend 300 feet in a little more than 0.3 mile. The overlook of the valley is a nice diversion, and this section of the hike is much less frequented than the way to the falls.

68 ANDREW MOLERA STATE PARK BEACH TRAIL

Distance: 2.5 miles round-trip
Hiking time: 1.5 hours
Difficulty: Easy
Elevation gain: 50 feet
High point: 60 feet
Season: All, though Big Sur River is impassable during heavy runoff
Water: None, bring your own
Fees and permits: Required
Map: USGS Big Sur
Information: Andrew Molera State Park, (831) 667-2315,
    www.parks.ca.gov/default.asp?page_id=582

Getting there: From San Simeon, drive north on Highway 1 67 miles to the turnoff for Andrew Molera State Park. Turn left and drive down the access road to the entrance kiosk. Park in the dirt lot.

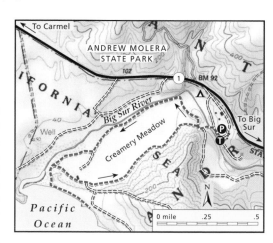

Andrew Molera State Park is unspoiled Big Sur beachfront at its very best. The park, a favorite of hikers and campers, is relatively undeveloped. The park has meadows, the idyllic Big Sur River, a sprawling coastline, and a mountain crest with awe-inspiring ocean views. The Beach Trail, which shows off much of what the region has to offer, can be completed as a loop with the Creamery Meadows Trail, or as an out-and-back hike.

From the parking area, take the signed path for the Beach Trail. Crossing the Big Sur River can be arduous; before the footbridge is installed in summer, be prepared to get wet up to the knees. **Note:** Do not cross in times of high runoff, as the results can be deadly.

Take the first right fork after the crossing and veer right again at the junction with the Creamery Meadow Trail. The trail continues along the river to the beach, passing lovely meadows, shaded under arbors of oak, willow, and bay laurel. Coastal scrub makes up for most of the vegetation, along with grasses and ubiquitous poison oak. In a little over 1 mile the unspoiled and remote beach enters into view.

Take some time to stroll along the beach, and climb up the sandstone to gain a greater appreciation of the surrounding area. The Bluffs Trail sits just a few hundred feet above the line of cliffs, and a bit of bushwhacking can lead to any number of trail combinations for the truly adventurous. Be wary, though, as ticks and poison oak are constant dangers. Those wishing to stick to the guidebook should return to the final junction at the edge of the meadow and take the loop around the lovely meadow back to the bridge crossing.

Banana slugs, millipedes, butterflies, and a variety of other insects and animals can be seen in and around the meadows. Sea otters and sea lions frequent the beaches; the beach is a great place to watch for migrating whales as well. Many varieties of coastal birds can be seen here, including cormorants and California brown pelicans.

A primitive walk-in, first-come first-served campground rests near a eucalyptus grove less than a half mile from the parking lot. This is a choice spot to spend a night on the cheap. At $10 a night, it is the least expensive campground anywhere in the Big Sur region.

The beach at Andrew Molera State Park is a wonderful spot to take a break.

PINNACLES NATIONAL MONUMENT

Pinnacles National Monument is a shining gem of the National Park Service. It is little known, but those who do frequent the park seem to return time and time again. The monument is enjoyed by hikers, bird watchers, rock climbers, tourists, and cave enthusiasts.

Pinnacles received its name from the breccia rock that has eroded into spires and monoliths from the remains of what was once an ancient volcano. Entering the park from the west at first seems unremarkable. The usual grassy and golden brown chapparal-covered hillsides of Central California camouflage the prehistoric landscape that lies behind. When the views of the park begin, it is hard to imagine such a primeval landscape existing anywhere in the twenty-first century, let alone in Southern California. The pinnacles look more like a *Star Trek* backdrop or something out of *Land of the Lost*. At every turn, it feels as if some hairy monster might be lurking ready to pounce.

That aspect of the area might not be completely without merit, however, considering the rare raptors that now frequent the monument's skies. Nineteen endangered California condors released since 2004 now call the monument home, with thirteen of them currently flying and roosting in the High Peaks region. Golden eagles and turkey vultures also build their nests in the park; it is easy to mistake the vultures for condors, so learn the wing patterns before eyeing the sky. Condors have white patches on the leading edges of their wings, while vultures have white patches on the rear area of their wings. Also, condors hold their wings flat while flying, whereas vultures soar in more of a V shape.

69 HIGH PEAKS/BALCONIES CAVE LOOP

Distance: 7.5-mile loop
Hiking time: 4 hours
Difficulty: Moderate
Elevation gain: 1550 feet
High point: 2600 feet
Season: Fall to spring
Water: Water sources are unreliable, bring your own
Fees and permits: Required
Map: USGS North Chalone Peak
Information: Pinnacles National Monument, (831) 389-4485, *www.nps.gov/pinn/*

Getting there: For the west entrance, take US 101 north to the town of Soledad. Exit onto State Route 146/Front Street. Turn right onto East Street/SR 146, and after two blocks turn right onto Metz Road/SR 146. After 2.75 miles turn left onto SR 146 and follow it for 9 miles to the park entrance. Stop and pay the fee at the ranger station, and park in the very large lot.

The Juniper Canyon Trail begins to the southeast of the parking area. The hike starts out along a

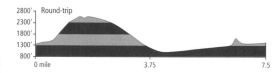

riparian oak woodland streambed, but quickly traverses upward into the spires of the Pinnacles. Getting an early morning start is best to take advantage of the shady side of the mountain and to avoid the warmer temperatures of midday, which can be dreadfully hot even during winter.

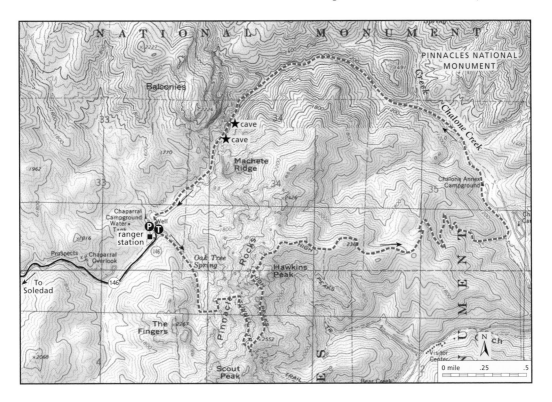

Eerie formations at Pinnacles National Monument look like something out of a science fiction movie.

Portions of this hike may be unsuitable for small children and those afraid of heights.

At the junction with the Tunnel Trail at about 1 mile, stay right to get on the High Peaks Trail, and follow it as it winds up the mountain. Ascend and descend steep steps blasted into the side of the breccia. Continue east toward Chalone along the High Peaks Trail. (Do not descend to the Bear Gulch Visitor Center along the Condor Gulch Trail at about 3 miles, unless you want to add an additional 3 miles to the loop.) At the Chalone Creek riverbed, continue north (left) along the Old Pinnacles Trail and follow it as it gradually ascends to the Balconies area of the park. Flashlights are required to enter the caves below the Balconies, as there is one section that is in near-total darkness. If a flashlight is unavailable, take the Balconies Trail for awe-inspiring views of the Pinnacles formations. Stay on the loop until it reaches the parking lot.

Opposite: The Sphinx is one of many sentinels overlooking the deepest canyon in the United States.

SOUTHERN SIERRA NEVADA AND DEATH VALLEY

TRONA PINNACLES

The Trona Pinnacles are some of the strangest formations on earth. They are well worth a visit for those traveling through the area. Very old by human standards, many date back nearly one hundred thousand years. The tufa formations were created underwater in the now dry Searles Lake bed that was once an interconnected body of water that stretched all the way to Mono Lake in the north. The Pinnacles are made of the same calcium carbonate that birthed the tufa formations in Mono Lake, but they have been exposed for much longer which accounts for the differences in appearance.

In places the towers project over a hundred feet into the air and are great for photography, especially around sunrise or sunset. The full moon contributes to the mystery and eerie nature of the surroundings, but anytime is a great time to explore as long as it is not during the mid-day heat of summer.

70 TRONA PINNACLES

Distance: less than 1 mile round-trip
Hiking time: 1 hour
Difficulty: Easy
Elevation gain: 50 feet
High point: 1825 feet
Season: Very late fall to very early spring
Water: None, bring your own
Fees and permits: None
Maps: USGS West End, Trona East
Information: Bureau of Land Management, Ridgecrest Resource Area,
     (760) 384-5400, *www.blm.gov/ca/ridgecrest/trona.html*

Getting there: From the town of Ridgecrest, drive east on State Route 178 to the signed turnoff for Trona Pinnacles. The road is 7.7 miles from the intersection with the Trona/Red Mountain Road. Turn right and drive for 5 miles on the well-graded dirt road to the parking lot for The Pinnacles. **Note:** The road is sometimes closed after rains in the winter.

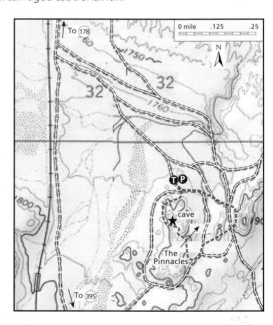

While less of a hike and more of a walk, a visit to the Trona Pinnacles is nonetheless otherworldly. There is a 0.85-mile round-trip trail, but a variety of use paths intersect and climb the towers. Wandering around the tufa spires in no certain way is a rewarding experience in and of itself. Strange caves, unearthly zeniths, and bizarre overlooks are the highlights of this hike. Wildlife frequents the area as well. Even the lizards are fantastic, with long legs and dashing whiptails.

On a cloudy day, Trona Pinnacles is more than just otherworldly.

The Pinnacles area has a strange energy that is almost tangible. Somehow it feels as if this is a land forgotten by time; one can almost imagine vortices that lead to other dimensions. Visiting in the hotter months can be hazardous; the very air seems to suck moisture straight out of the human body. Be sure to bring ample supplies of water even during the winter months.

SOUTHERN SIERRA

Most of the Southern Sierra Nevada is comprised of the Sequoia National Monument, much of which was upgraded from national forest land in the year 2000 to further protect the watershed and surrounding ecosystem of the Kings Canyon/Sequoia National Parks unit. Filled with incomparable beauty all its own, the monument is a haven for all sorts of recreation from mountain biking to hiking, climbing, fishing, and off-roading. There are numerous Giant Sequoia groves here, and acre upon acre of wilderness.

71 MANTER MEADOW

Distance: 6 miles round-trip
Hiking time: 3 hours or overnight
Difficulty: Moderate
Elevation gain: 900 feet
High point: 8000 feet
Season: Spring to fall
Water: Ample, needs filtering
Fees and permits: None
Map: USGS Sirretta Peak
Information: Sequoia National Forest, Giant Sequoia National Monument, (760) 376-3781, *www.fs.fed.us/r5/sequoia/*

Getting there: Drive north from Kernville on Sierra Way (Mountain Road 99) for 20 miles to the junction with Sherman Pass Road (Forest Service Road 22S05). Turn right and drive 6 miles on Sherman Pass Road. Turn right again onto Forest Service Road 22S12, signed for Horse Meadow Campground. Stay on FR 22S12 for just under 12 miles, as the road passes a jumble of intersections. At 4.5, 6.2, and 7.5 miles continue straight at the junctions. Nearly 8 miles in, veer left at an intersection to stay on FR 22S12. In just under 12 miles, turn left onto Forest Service Road 23S07. A trail for the northern loop is signed and intersects the road at 1.5 miles; instead of stopping here, continue for a total of 3 miles

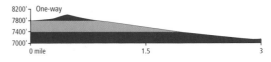

to the southern edge of Big Meadow, and park at the second trailhead for Manter Meadow. There is a parking lot next to an old corral.

The Domeland Wilderness is an isolated, beautiful, and unspoiled piece of Southern California forestland. Named for its looming granite domes, it is a realm of picturesque vales ringed by bald summits. The region's wild nature is apparent even in driving to the trailhead. It is the southernmost wilderness in the Sierra Ne-

A boreal toad rests on a stick near the edge of the Domeland Wilderness.

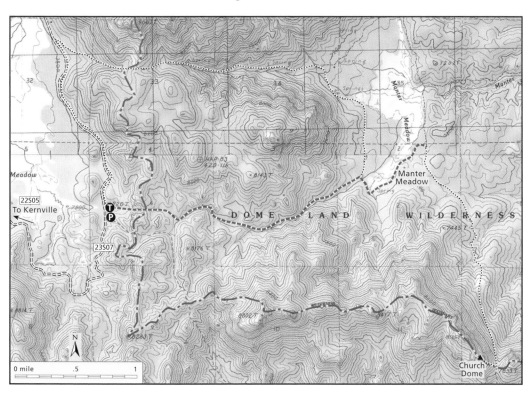

vada Range proper, but its borders encompass a variety of ecosystems that transition into desert in the area's southerly reaches. This is a magnificent place for solitude; making the trip midweek will virtually guarantee it. The Manter Meadow hike makes an excellent introduction to this relatively unfrequented region.

Follow the trail as it climbs abruptly and somewhat steeply in places for 200 feet within the first 0.25 mile to the border of the wilderness, which is marked by a wooden sign. Stunning granite formations dot the trail and make for excellent photographic opportunities. The entire trip is shaded by towering Jeffrey, foxtail, and lodgepole pines interspersed with red fir, though much of the area was devastated in the Manter Fire of 2000.

Look for boreal toads along the trail; in early summer they can be abundant, along with beautiful wildflowers fed by the spring runoff. The trail meets up with a tributary of Manter Creek in 0.75 mile and follows it the remainder of the way to the meadow. The trail here loses nearly 900 feet in elevation that must be regained on the way out. There are a variety of wilderness campsites available in this section of the trail.

Just east of the meadow at 3 miles, a spur trail connects for the side trip to Church Dome, which offers tremendous views of the surrounding area. The dome itself is actually a grouping of separate pinnacles, but several of the spires can be reached by some easy scrambling.

The trip can also be made into a 7.5-mile loop by turning left onto the trail heading north from the creek crossing, with a total elevation gain of 1400 feet.

72 TRAIL OF 100 GIANTS/DOME ROCK

Distance: less than 0.5 mile round-trip for each hike
Hiking time: 1 hour
Difficulty: Easy
Elevation gain: 100 feet
High point: 7225 feet
Season: Spring to fall
Water: None, bring your own
Fees and permits: None
Maps: USGS Sentinel Peak, Johnsondale
Information: Sequoia National Forest, Giant Sequoia National Monument, (559) 784-1500, *www.fs.fed.us/r5/sequoia/*

Getting there: From Porterville, drive 46 miles east on State Route 190. Just past the Quaking Aspen Campground, the road becomes Western Divide Highway; continue straight for nearly 4 miles to the turnoff for Dome Rock. Take the turnoff and continue nearly 0.5 mile to the parking area. To get to the Trail of 100 Giants, continue another 9 miles south on the Western Divide Highway, turn left, and park.

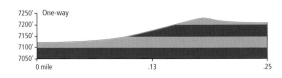

Dome Rock and the Trail of 100 Giants are two very short and easy hikes that can easily be combined

to make for a half-day outing, picnicking included. They are quite different in scope, so doing both gives a sense of the varied wonders of the area.

The hike to the top of Dome Rock, which at 7225 feet is about 100 feet higher than the surrounding land, is a short jaunt up the side of the granite dome. The entire trip is less than a half mile,

Twin sequoias along the Trail of the 100 Giants shares nutrients and a root system.

Sunset atop Dome Rock can be mystical.

and any able-bodied person can attain the summit. From the top of Dome Rock, incredible views of Lake Isabella, Slate Mountain, and The Needles open up, and the vista is truly magnificent, especially at sunrise and sunset. The lookout on top of The Needles can be spotted, perched atop the tallest spire. Spend some time wandering around the dome, but do be careful of loose rocks; rock climbers use the steep side on a somewhat frequent basis.

The Trail of 100 Giants is a short stroll through a lovely and somewhat secluded grove of Giant Sequoia. The world's largest trees have grown in abundance in this grove, with a high percentage of "twin" and "triplet" trees that grow together using the same nutrients in the soil. The way is paved and accessible to wheelchairs and strollers. There are several markers on a self-guided interpretive trail that discuss the ecosystem and its natural history, but the real show is the gigantic trees that seem to grow en masse. At every turn, another colossal tree stands with a base nearly the size of a small house. Those wishing to spend hours marveling at these great wonders of nature can do so in the silence and majesty of a wooded forest of giants.

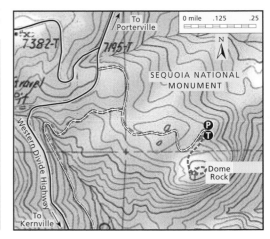

73 THE NEEDLES

Distance: 4.5 miles round-trip
Hiking time: 2.5 hours
Difficulty: Moderate
Elevation gain: 425 feet
High point: 8200 feet
Season: Early spring to late fall
Water: None, bring your own
Fees and permits: None
Maps: USGS Sentinel Peak, Durrwood Creek
Information: Sequoia National Forest, Giant Sequoia National Monument,
(760) 376-3781, *www.fs.fed.us/r5/sequoia/*

Getting there: From Porterville, drive 46 miles east on State Route 190. One half mile past Quaking Aspen Campground, turn left onto Forest Service Road 21S05 and drive nearly 3 miles to the end of the road and parking area which is marked by an informational sign.

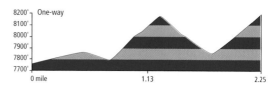

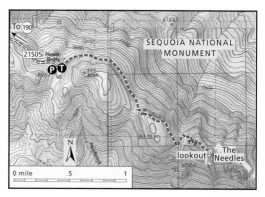

The Needles are a stunning rock formation favored by technical rock climbers. Various routes ascend the series of granite monoliths, and climbers on belay can be spotted on any given day. Hikers and mountain bikers can also enjoy The Needles via a well-graded trail and steep sets of connecting stairs that lead to a lookout tower perched on top of the tallest spire. The lookout itself, still operational, is on the National Historic Lookout Register. It is truly an engineering marvel: seeming to spring straight out of the rock, it appears precariously stationed above the void. Walking around the tower's catwalk is an experience unto itself. The rock drops away hundreds of feet on all sides, and only the boards beneath your feet shield you from the omnipresent pull of gravity.

The well-signed trail begins as a peaceful stroll through a mixed fir and pine forest with expansive views opening up to the north above Freeman Basin, a tributary of the greater Kern River drainage system. The peaks of the Great Western Divide can be seen here, along with the Mineral King area, and as the hike continues, views open all the way over to Mount Whitney

and Olancha Peak. Be wary of mountain bikers, as all of the trails in the Sequoia National Forest (including the Giant Sequoia National Monument) are open to two-wheeled travelers. Most are cautious and courteous, but keep an eye and ear out just in case. The way is wide, well trod, and easy to follow.

Much of the path is forested, and there is ample shade. The trail climbs very gently for the first mile and then begins to climb in a steeper fashion. In a little over 1.5 miles, the lookout comes into clear view. From this spot on the trail, the way appears to be a gentle walk along the

The lookout built in 1937 looks precariously situated, but it is as solid as the rock itself.

same elevation, but the trail actually drops into a saddle and loses 400 feet before climbing back up that same amount to the ascending spires of The Needles.

From the top, the turnaround views are truly breathtaking. Spend a bit of time at the tower, and be sure to thank the friendly host for the hospitality.

74 JORDAN PEAK LOOKOUT

Distance: 1.75 miles round-trip
Hiking time: 1 hour
Difficulty: Easy
Elevation gain: 550 feet
High point: 9115 feet
Season: Late spring to fall
Water: None, bring your own
Fees and permits: None
Map: USGS Camp Nelson
Information: Sequoia National Forest, (760) 376-3781, *www.fs.fed.us/r5/sequoia/*

Getting there: On State Route 190, drive 45 miles east of Porterville. Just before Quaking Aspen Campground, turn left onto Forest Service Road 21S50 and drive for 4.3 miles, then veer left and stay on 21S50 for another 2.9 miles. Veer left onto Forest Service Road 20S71, which is signed for Jordan Peak Lookout. Continue nearly 2 miles to the end of the road and the parking area for the trail. (The road is closed in winter.)

Jordan Peak Lookout was built in 1934 and is still operated by paid staff during the fire season. At 9115 feet, it has the distinction of being one of the highest lookouts in California. It also affords one of the most dramatic 360-degree views the region has to offer. Near the summit grows a cluster of beautiful fawn lilies. The wildflowers, quite rare in these parts, can provide a stunning display in early spring.

The trail has recently been reworked by a volunteer and is in great repair. It traverses a sparse but shady forest and gains 500 feet in about half a mile. The air is a bit thinner above 8000 feet, so some may experience a bit of shallowness in breathing here. Still, the way is nicely graded with many switchbacks that traverse back and forth to the peak. Some recent logging activity is present in the area, but it does not detract from the inherent beauty of the surroundings.

Visitors can approach the lookout tower and visit, should the host allow it. The tower's catwalk imparts the best viewpoints; the vista of the Great Western Divide to the north is

Fawn lilies near the lookout on Jordan Peak

Views from Jordan Peak extend to Farewell Gap in Sequoia National Park and the Tehachapis in the south.

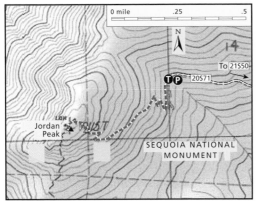

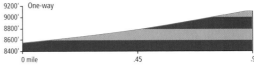

stunning, to say the least. The Coast Range and the Tehachapi Mountains can also be seen, along with many local peaks such as Maggie, Slate, and Moses mountains. Chatting with the host can provide you with information on the surrounding area and its history, and also on the lookout itself. Return the way you came, and treasure the memories of a great hike.

SEQUOIA AND KINGS CANYON NATIONAL PARKS

Like Yosemite, Sequoia and Kings Canyon national parks contain some of the most beautiful scenery on the planet. The two units are administered together, comprising the largest parcel of federally protected land in the Sierra Nevada Range. No roads cross the combined parks from east to west, and the high altitude views are beyond compare anywhere in the state. The passes on the parks' eastern side open up into lake-dotted alpine wonderlands complete with fine fishing, surreal mountain splendor, and stunning sunsets.

Sequoia National Park takes its name from the giant trees that are the largest living things (by volume) on earth. The trees were named in honor of the Native American who invented a system of writing for the Cherokee language. There are many groves of the gigantic trees, several of which are so large that it would take more than twenty people holding hands to circle the trees at ground level. This behemoth species is truly a sight to behold, and wandering among these ancient giants, which live as long as two thousand years, is enough to lead anyone into meditative contemplation.

Kings Canyon National Park was named for the deep glacial canyon carved out by the mighty Kings River. It is the deepest canyon in the United States, with a maximum depth of over 8000 feet. Truly, the scale of these two parks is majestic. While neither park is known for having waterfalls like Yosemite's, their granite magnificence, alpine lakes, backcountry tableaus, and towering conifers offer visitors a type of beauty that exists nowhere else.

75 FRANKLIN LAKES

Distance: 13 miles round-trip
Hiking time: 7 hours or overnight
Difficulty: Very strenuous
Elevation gain: 3000 feet
High point: 10,500 feet
Season: Late spring to late fall
Water: Plentiful
Fees and permits: Required
Map: USGS 7 Mineral King
Information: Sequoia/Kings Canyon National Parks, (559)565-3341,
www.nps.gov/seki/

Getting there: From Bakersfield, head north on State Route 99 about 75 miles. Exit onto State Route 198 and drive 34 miles east to the town of Three Rivers. Continue east for nearly 4 miles to the turnoff for Mineral King Road. Turn right and drive for 23 narrow, winding miles to the Mineral King Ranger Station. Those afraid of marmots might want to park here— marmots eat anything, tires, wires, hoses, bumpers, rubber molding, etc.

(no kidding). The yellow-bellied varmints have done a lot of damage to cars at the trailhead! The brave (or those with chicken wire to place around the car, like a fence) can cut this hike shorter by driving on another 1.3 miles to the trailhead parking lot across the wooden bridge.

This hike begins at the ranger station with a walk up Mineral King Road. Doing this adds 1.3

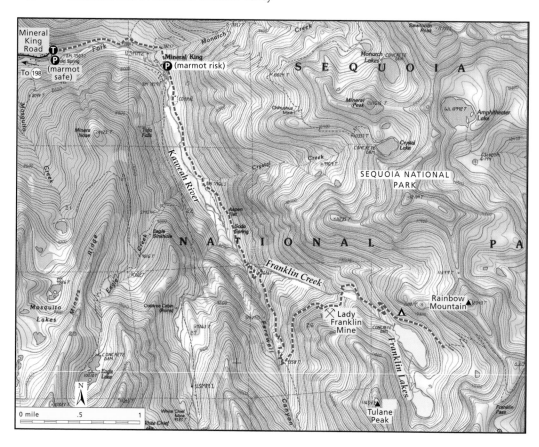

miles to the trip each way, but the peace of mind gained by avoiding the marmots at the trailhead parking is well worth it.

From the ranger station, continue east along the road. Turn left onto a dirt road that appears just before a bridge, and follow it until it becomes the trail shortly beyond a pack station. Skirt the Kaweah River through beautiful dwarf aspens as the trail crosses three creeks and eventually heads up the mountainside. The crossings can be hip-deep and swift in early spring due to runoff, so be prepared with dry socks and even a walking stick to use while fording.

As in many areas of the park, wildlife is abundant on this trail. It is not unusual to see

several of the creatures that call the region home. At the very least, marmots will be present, as they are ubiquitous here. A long backpacking trip will have even vegetarians wondering about the possibilities of marmot stew. The critters are protected, so that is not a prospect, and the idea would be truly unappetizing to most, excepting those souls hardened on freeze-dried packaged foodstuffs.

As the trail climbs, Farewell Gap looms ever closer, and the views of its stunning scenery are breathtaking. Tree cover is sparse in this alpine terrain, though many solitary pines grow along some sections of the trail. Snow remains in the canyon until late in the summer, and mule deer routinely graze on the alpine shrubbery.

In just over 4 miles, the trail junctions to the gap; turn left and continue around the mountainside toward Lady Franklin Mine, which sits a couple hundred feet above the trail at the 5-mile

The snow and ice on high-altitude Franklin Lake can stick around until after midsummer.

marker. The route in is clearly discernable from these heights, as are the majestic unnamed summits that ring the outer basin of the lake. A quarter mile farther brings you to the final crossing of Franklin Creek, which can be accomplished by stepping on rocks when the water levels have subsided with summer melt. Earlier in the season, the creek must be forded.

The campsite sits 30 feet above the creek at almost 10,300 feet. It is a nearly flat area complete with metal bear container, though marmots are the bigger threat to any misplaced food. Always take proper care with edible and scented items. The campsite is well within view of Franklin Dam, and the lake can be explored by climbing higher. The trail continues up over Franklin Pass, and any extended backpacking trip should include a hike to the top. The lake is ringed by the venerable peaks of Tulare, Florence, and Rainbow mountains.

76 HAMILTON LAKES

Distance: 34 miles round-trip
Hiking time: 3–5 days
Difficulty: Strenuous
Elevation gain: 1600 feet
High point: 8235 feet
Season: Late spring to late fall
Water: Plentiful
Fees and permits: Required
Maps: USGS Lodgepole, Triple Divide Peak
Information: Sequoia/Kings Canyon National Parks, (559)565-3341,
www.nps.gov/seki/

Getting there: From Bakersfield, head north on State Route 99 about 75 miles, then exit on State Route 198 and head east toward Visalia. Continue for 53 miles into Sequoia National Park. Pass the turnoff for Crystal Cave, go 2 miles, and then turn right for Crescent Meadow, Moro Rock, and Tunnel Log. Park in the Crescent Meadow parking lot.

The High Sierra Trail makes a wonderful introduction to the backcountry wilderness of Sequoia National Park. Any number of shorter or longer trips can be taken along this trail, but Hamilton Lake, 17 miles into the trail, is the perfect destination to take in all the splendor that this section of the park has to offer. Wildlife is abundant, from smaller rodents such as squirrels and marmots, to larger mammals like mule deer and black bear. The myriad stream and creek crossings along the way are home to many insects and birds.

Views on this hike start early and never stop. The trail begins by wandering in and around a grove of sequoias. As the trail climbs up out of wooded Crescent Meadow, the magnificent subrange of the Sierra known as the Great Western Divide enters into view and provides the backdrop for the entire remainder of the trip. Its sculpted granite supplies an ethereal tableau, a masterwork of nature's stunning palette that no human touch or photograph can truly capture.

There are many junctions to navigate on this trail, but the way is well signed. Stay on the High Sierra Trail the entire way. The first half mile through the meadows can be a bit confusing,

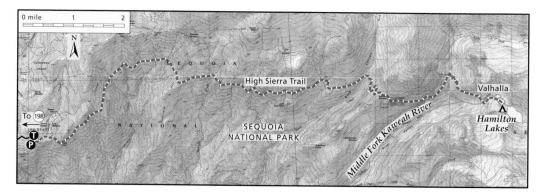

Heading back along the trail toward Ninemile Creek

as many side trails circumnavigate the meadow and head toward other regions. After crossing the second footbridge and the Sugar Pine Trail, follow the sign for the High Sierra Trail and climb up out of the meadow. At the four-way junction 0.5 mile in, take the trail to the right and continue toward Eagle View, where the expansive vistas open up that make this a must-do, classic hike.

The trail, which is quite open and exposed, narrowly skirts the mountainside for much of the way. Some may find the experience a bit disconcerting, as there are precipitous drop-offs into the valley below, though the trail is itself wide enough to safely navigate without fear of falling. Continue on the High Sierra Trail past junctions with the Wolverton Cutoff, Seven Mile Trail, and Redwood Meadow Trail. Mehrten Creek at 5.5 miles is the only creek crossing that has to be navigated with the possibility of wet

feet. At Bearpaw Meadow, veer left and head toward High Sierra Camp. At 12 miles, cross the footbridge over Lone Pine Creek and continue straight on the High Sierra Trail as it switchbacks below the lofty formation known as Valhalla. Continue climbing beyond Lower Hamilton Lake to a campsite beside the shores of Upper Hamilton Lake.

Ideally, this trip is suited for a several-day adventure, to allow time to camp along the way. People yearning to rest their weary heads far from the confines of civilization should spend a couple of days nestled beside Hamilton Lake, underneath the godly spires of Valhalla. There are several campgrounds along the High Sierra Trail, all of which are equipped with bear boxes. Bears do frequent the area and are a common sight along the trail. They know where the campsites are as well, so take care with food at all times.

77 CONGRESS TRAIL

Distance: 2.3 miles round-trip
Hiking time: 1.5 hours
Difficulty: Easy
Elevation gain: 300 feet
High point: 7100 feet
Season: All
Water: None, bring your own
Fees and permits: Required
Map: USGS Lodgepole
Information: Sequoia/Kings Canyon National Parks, (559)565-3341,
www.nps.gov/seki/

Getting there: From Lodgepole in Sequoia National Park, drive 1.5 miles south on the Generals Highway to Wolverton Road. Turn left and follow the signs for the General Sherman Tree Trail. Park in the large lot.

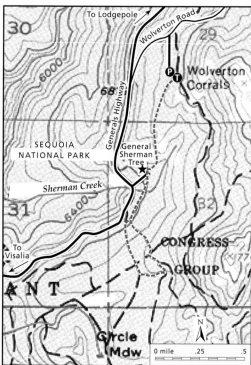

The highlight of this trail is the enormous General Sherman Tree, the world's largest living organism by volume. It stands nearly 275 feet tall, and is over a hundred feet in circumference at its base. The tree itself, named for General William Tecumseh Sherman, is estimated to be over two thousand years old. A protective fence has been erected around the towering sentinel to protect its fragile root system. Giant Sequoias have relatively shallow roots—the biggest natural danger to their health is high-velocity winds that can topple the behemoths.

The trail descends from the parking lot on a paved path for about 0.25 mile to the General Sherman Tree. Several stairways must be descended here (and again ascended on the way out). A wheelchair-accessible parking lot and paved path are a little farther down the Generals Highway for those unable to climb stairs. Near the General Sherman Tree itself, the Congress Trail connects with the Sherman Trail; follow the well-signed loop. There are many young sequoias along the way, and quite a few larger ones—some named, others not.

Follow a slight descent and cross a bridge which then commences into an easy uphill grade. Half a mile into the Congress Loop the way crosses a cutoff trail, and a short distance farther reaches a junction with the Alta Trail.

Makaila and Sierra await the enormous trees of the Congress Trail.

Stay on the Congress Trail. Several offshoots will be encountered, but the way is very well signed and easy to follow. The President is the first of the larger named trees that will be encountered, followed by a grouping named The Senate and then another grouping named The House (hence the denomination of the trail). The General Lee is next, followed by the gigantic McKinley Tree. A photo point sits just off the trail where an enor-mous spectacle, the McKinley Tree, will barely fit into one photograph. Continue on the loop until the junction with the main Sherman Trail, and return to the parking lot.

All manner of animals are often seen on this trail, up to and including bears; springtime wildflowers can be abundant and beautiful. The path is verdant and shady. There are many benches for resting, and several nice spots for an impromptu picnic.

78 ALTA PEAK

Distance: 13 miles round-trip
Hiking time: 7 hours or overnight
Difficulty: Extremely strenuous
Elevation gain: 4000 feet
High point: 11,204 feet
Season: Late spring to early fall
Water: None, bring your own
Fees and permits: Required
Map: USGS Lodgepole
Information: Sequoia/Kings Canyon National Parks, (559)565-3341, *www.nps.gov/seki/*

Getting there: From Lodgepole in Sequoia National Park, drive 1.5 miles south on the Generals Highway to Wolverton Road. Turn left and follow the road for 1.5 miles to the large parking lot at the end.

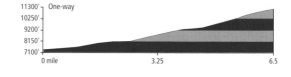

Alta Peak is a magnificent and popular Sierra summit. It is well liked and well traveled, with good reason. From its superior perch, the entirety of Sequoia National Park can be observed. "Breathtaking" is an understatement for the views from Alta Peak; to comprehend this

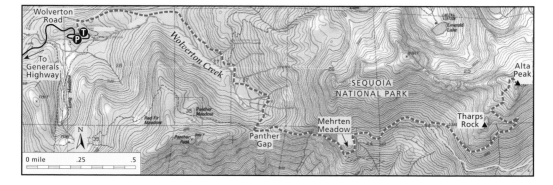

Tharps Rock sits high above the trail to Alta Peak for a good majority of the lower trail.

place's majesty, try standing atop the peak and breathing in the 360-degree view. If your schedule allows for only one tough all-day hike in the park, this is the trail to take. Its central location provides views of some of the most magnificent scenery in the park. The way will not be crowded, but there will almost always be fellow like-minded individuals enjoying the vistas and forested trail.

From the parking area, follow the pine-shaded Lakes Trail through lovely forest and wooded meadows. Stay straight at the crossing with the connector for the Lodgepole Trail, which occurs very near the start of the hike. In just under 2 miles the trail reaches a junction; continue straight toward Panther Gap. At the gap, veer left onto the Alta Trail toward the peak and meadow. The Seven Mile Trail intersects at a little over 3.5 miles and drops toward the lower High Sierra Trail; stay straight on the Alta Trail and continue through Mehrten Meadow. In 4.5 miles the path splits again; take the left fork and head up the final leg of the trail to the summit. There are several small, easy creek crossings along the way

where water can be filtered if necessary, with the last one being about 1 mile from the top.

The trail wanders beneath dominating Tharps Rock and eventually wraps around the formation, gaining 2000 feet of elevation in the last 1.5 miles. The final push is steep, shadeless, and strenuous at this high elevation, but more than worth the effort. The rewards are myriad. Wildlife is ubiquitous in the region, including marmots, coyotes, bears, and deer. Wildflowers are ever-present during the early summer and provide a dazzling display during times of high runoff.

Views of the Great Western Divide are abundant for most of the trip beyond Panther Gap, so those not up for the strenuous final trek to the top can enjoy the best that the trail has to offer without venturing farther than Mehrten Meadow. Those not feeling up to the altitude can take the short 1.5-mile-long side trip to lovely and secluded Alta Meadow. There is a wilderness campsite near the meadow, and the two trips can be combined for a moderate overnight or two-day backpacking trip.

79 BIG BALDY RIDGE

Distance: 4.25 miles round-trip
Hiking time: 2.5 hours
Difficulty: Easy
Elevation gain: 650 feet
High point: 8211 feet
Season: Late spring through early fall
Water: None, bring your own
Fees and permits: Required
Map: USGS General Grant Grove
Information: Sequoia/Kings Canyon National Parks, (559) 565-3341,
www.nps.gov/seki/

Getting there: From Fresno, head east on State Route 180; follow it 54 miles to the turnoff for the Generals Highway, just 1.5 miles beyond the Big Stump Entrance Station. Turn right and drive 6.75 miles to the turnout on the right-hand side of the road signed for Big Baldy.

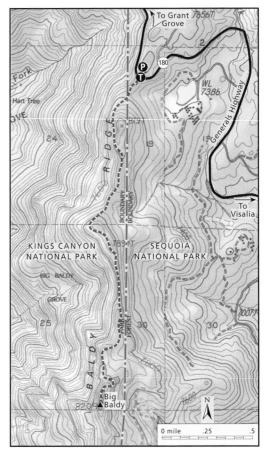

Big Baldy Ridge is an exhilarating hiking destination. The trail is short enough to complete in a couple of hours, and relatively unfrequented for a hike in a national park. A great spot to watch sunrises and sunsets, the trail follows a ridgeline skirting Redwood Canyon, which drops precipitously—nearly 3000 feet below—for most of the trip. The trail wanders, not quite precariously, up and over some sections that resemble a granite dome sliding into oblivion. The trail is safe, though those with an extreme fear of heights may be uncomfortable in a few spots.

The trail begins in a lovely wooded pine forest with large, centuries-old trees that loom overhead. Nearly all of the pines reach heights hundreds of feet above the trail.

The climb starts early. Within the first 2 miles, the trip summits and descends over two unnamed peaks that are worthy destinations in and of themselves for people with small children or limited time. Each peak affords wonderful vantage points and near-360-degree views, but the real stunner is Big Baldy itself.

Big Baldy is a beautiful piece of granite that provides views of Kings Canyon, the Great Western Divide, the lower reaches of Sequoia National Park, and lovely Redwood Canyon. Wildflowers

Precipitous drop-offs into Redwood Canyon are common all along the trail to Big Baldy.

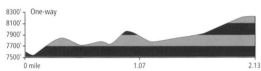

abound throughout early summer, and the area is great for catching glimpses of local fauna as well. The final summit push is nearly trailless and some minor scrambling is involved, though it is easy enough to be attainable by anyone who has made it this far.

For those wanting more, a use trail continues for an additional 1.5 miles along the ridgeline, dropping 500 feet to another wonderful overlook called Chimney Rock. This part of the trail is not maintained, nor heavily used. There is a good chance that no other people will be traveling on it, but it does add an additional 3 miles to the trip and changes the difficulty level to "strenuous." But the unique viewpoint offered by Chimney Rock is decidedly fantastic.

80 SUNSET TRAIL LOOP

Distance: 7.5-mile loop
Hiking time: 4 hours
Difficulty: Moderate
Elevation gain: 1100 feet
High point: 6600 feet
Season: All
Water: Sequoia Creek, Azalea Campground
Fees and permits: Required
Map: USGS General Grant Grove
Information: Sequoia/Kings Canyon National Parks, (559) 565-3341, *www.nps.gov/seki/*

Getting there: From Fresno, head east on State Route 180. Follow SR 180 for 54 miles into the park. (Once inside the park, veer left at the junctions with the Generals Highway to stay on SR 180 heading north.) At the 55-mile mark, turn left into the turnoff for Sunset Campground, just after the settlement of Wilsonia, and continue 0.25 mile to the Grant Grove Visitor Center. Park in the designated trail parking areas.

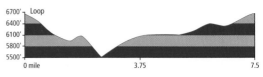

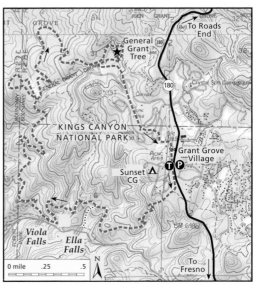

The Sunset Trail is so named because it begins in the Sunset Campground. As to why the area is named after the sunset, it is not so hard to guess. The campground sits on the edge of the western Grant Grove portion of Kings Canyon National Park; it is said that some of the campgrounds provide dramatic vistas of the sun's nightly descent, or perhaps the trail is simply more beautiful in the waning hours of the evening.

The loop follows several trails and one forest road to connect some of the best scenery and hiking in the Grant Grove region. While part of the trail is very popular—the General Grant Loop is the most frequented trail in this section of the park— most of it is only lightly traveled. Sequoia and Kings Canyon are not known for waterfalls, but this hike passes two quaint and secluded cascades. Wildflowers such as azalea and tiger lilies abound. The trail also winds through one of the most beautiful sequoia groves the park has to offer.

From Sunset Campground, head toward the highway. Find the wide and well-marked Sunset Trail, and turn right (south). The trail leads past a short side trail to Ella Falls, a beautiful series of several small waterfalls. Continue on and follow the South Boundary Trail. Return to the main trail, then continue on the South Boundary Trail and head left as it meanders toward Viola Falls.

Viola Falls is spectacular, but difficult to photograph due to slippery rocks, a quick-flowing creek, foliage in the way, and no true vantage point from which to capture the entirety of the cascade. Sitting within earshot of the roar of the water, this is a wonderful spot to enjoy lunch or a snack. When the break is over, continue on the South Boundary Trail until it becomes a nondescript road. Follow the winding road north

and northeast, remaining on the main road for 1.5 miles. Do not head toward Sequoia Lake on any of the side roads. Views of Sequoia Lake will open up in spots, but this hike's destination is the Dead Giant Loop.

After 1.5 miles on the main road, turn (left) north onto an unsigned but obvious trail and follow it past lovely Lion Meadow. The Dead Giant Sequoia tree is quite impressive, and the overlook of Sequoia Lake is also splendid.

Return to the main trail and a short distance later take the left turn into the North Grove Loop. There are amazingly beautiful trees along this loop, with quite a few instances of twins and even triplets that share the same nutrients and root systems.

This area of the park is just a little out of the way, so it gets surprisingly few visitors. Most tourists hit the General Grant Loop and then, having seen the biggest tree this side of the park has to offer, get back in their RVs instead of walking another 1.5 miles to explore the big-tree forest further. Because of that human reality, this is the place to enjoy the majesty of the big trees in

Azaleas grow near the cascades of Ella Falls, presenting a beautiful tapestry.

Tiger lilies have a distinctive, easily recognizable shape.

relative solitude, even on the weekends. However, the occasional hiker or horseback rider will make their way past.

After you complete the North Grove Loop, turn left at the Sunset Trail and continue 0.15 mile to the parking lot for the crowded and highly frequented Grant Grove. This region certainly has merit, and incredibly large trees. Undoubtedly, it is worth a look and the short, paved walk. Follow the loop and the interpretive guidebook with a smile, secure with the secret knowledge of the solitude shared simply a short ways away from all the hustle and bustle. Enjoy the biggest trees and then walk an additional mile on the trail through the campgrounds back to your starting point.

81 BOOLE TREE LOOP

Distance: 2.4-mile loop
Hiking time: 1 hour
Difficulty: Easy
Elevation gain: 550 feet
High point: 6830 feet
Season: Early spring to late fall
Water: None, bring your own
Fees and permits: Required
Map: USGS Hume
Information: Sequoia National Forest, (559) 338-2251, *www.fs.fed.us/r5/sequoia/*

Getting there: From Fresno, drive east on State Route 180 for 54 miles. Once within the park, veer left at the junction with the Generals Highway to stay on SR 180 headed north. Drive for 5.5 miles from the entry gate and turn left on Forest Service Road 13S55, signed for Stump Meadows. Stay on this dirt road for 2.5 miles and park at the trailhead, which is the road's end.

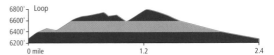

Boole Tree Loop is a short jaunt that leads to the largest tree within Sequoia National Forest boundaries. Follow the right fork at the trailhead and climb the shady way; the entire first mile is under cover of large yellow pines. At 1 mile, a use trail leads down to the Boole Tree, a gigantic specimen at 269 feet tall and nearly 35 feet in circumference at its base. After walking the tree's perimeter, it is humbling to stand next to an arboreal giant alive since before the advent of the Common Era. If the bugs are not particularly bad, this makes a wonderful rest and snack spot, conducive to timeless contemplation.

From the tree, take the use trail back to the main trail. The Boole Tree Loop Trail ascends slightly higher and enters a clearing. From here,

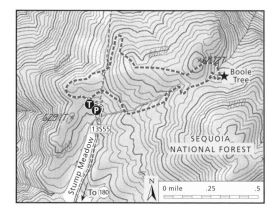

the views across to Monarch Divide and into Kings Canyon are nothing short of spectacular. This too is a great spot for a rest break, though it offers no protection from the sun. The loop continues on, crossing a private dirt road, until it circles around and descends back to the parking lot. There are cattle gates that need to be opened and closed on the trail as well; please close them after you have crossed through.

Interestingly enough, the Boole Tree is named after the lumber mill owner who cut down most of the sequoias in the Converse Basin, which just happened to hold the largest grove of the trees in the world. The road to the trailhead crosses the accurately named Stump Meadow, where some of the mill owner's handiwork can be seen. It is hard to imagine that anyone could have ever dreamt of cutting down such wonders of the natural world. At least he left the largest tree as a sentinel that could represent a specimen of majesty for all to see. The meadow itself is a worthy stopping and photo point, one that clearly illustrates the potential of the destructive hand of mankind.

The immense Boole Tree

82 MIST FALLS

Distance: 6.5 miles round-trip
Hiking time: 3.5 hours
Difficulty: Moderate
Elevation gain: 550 feet
High point: 5600 feet
Season: Spring to fall; road closes in winter
Water: Kings River
Fees and permits: Required
Maps: USGS Cedar Grove, The Sphinx
Information: Sequoia/Kings Canyon National Parks, (559)565-3341,
www.nps.gov/seki/

Getting there: From Fresno, drive east on State Route 180 for 54 miles. Once inside the park, veer left at the junction with the Generals Highway to stay on SR 180 headed north. Drive for over 30 winding miles to Roads End.

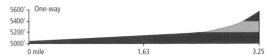

In the canyon of the king, there lies a mystical cascade that is not too tough, not too far, nor too steep. The hike is relatively easy, but at 6.5 miles it may be a long distance for beginners. Unlike Yosemite, Kings Canyon is not known for its spectacular waterfalls. Nevertheless, Mist Falls is a true gem. While not incredibly photogenic, the falls have a raw power and potency; during heavy runoff, being even half a mile away from the falls can be a dripping experience. Even when subdued, the falls retain their grandeur among the gorge's ramparts, unleashing their mist upon visitors to the viewpoint.

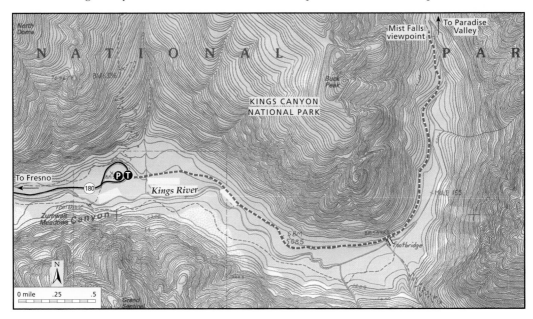

The Sphinx guards the trail on the way back from Mist Falls.

Hike past the ranger station onto the trail. Hiking in to the falls is an awe-inspiring journey in a rainforest environment. There are several creek crossings coming from Roads End, and the ever-present, glacier-scarred granite looming above makes this an idyllic walk. The trailhead is the most popular in this section of the canyon due to its easy access; backpackers and day hikers alike travel the well-worn and wide, road-like trail, so it is best to get an early start. Mosquitoes can be present here, so bring quality bug repellent.

At 2 miles the trail branches left at a footbridge, and can be soggy and a little boggy in spots. Please stay on the path as it narrows—the surrounding area is very fragile, and any deviation from the trail can have lasting impact on this pristine natural treasure.

Hike upward as the trail climbs into the water-sculpted canyon. The rushing of the Kings River is omnipresent as the ascent nears the viewpoint for the falls. The falls are beautiful and voluminous, but they are difficult to photograph well, due to the namesake mist that bathes onlookers at the viewpoint.

Return the way you came, basking in the glory of the return views of The Sphinx, and marvel at the change in perspective.

Those feeling eager to see more after a trip to the falls may wish to venture more than 3 miles farther into Paradise Valley, where canyon walls loom well over half a mile above on both sides. This addition adds significant distance (6.5 miles total) and elevation gain (nearly 1800 feet) to your round-trip—well worth it for those wishing to spend a whole day seeing this section of Kings Canyon.

DEATH VALLEY NATIONAL PARK

Death Valley is one of the hottest spots on the planet. It is also one of the strangest. Even the park's name conjures up fascinating and somewhat horrifying images—skeletons, or gravestones. There is almost no end to the bizarre scenery one encounters within the confines of this park. The monikers given to local landmarks are as amusing as the park's scenery: the Funeral Mountains, Devils Golf Course, Furnace Creek, and Dantes View, just to name a few.

Laying claim to the lowest elevation in the Western Hemisphere, the Badwater Basin acts as a natural furnace, with the high mountain ranges on either side reflecting and trapping heat within the valley. Telescope Peak in the Panamint Range is the highest point in the park at over 11,000 feet.

Simply driving through the immense landscape (the park is a little bigger than Connecticut, one quarter the size of Belgium, and twice the size of Rhode Island) is an adventure all its own. Death Valley is best visited in winter when the temperatures are manageable. The higher mountains are perfect for hiking in the summer, but the lower elevations are absolutely deadly and should not be attempted by anyone. Summer temperatures in the valley itself rarely drop below triple digits, even at night.

83 TELESCOPE PEAK

Distance: 12 miles round-trip
Hiking time: 7 hours
Difficulty: Very strenuous
Elevation gain: 2950 feet
High point: 11,049 feet
Season: All, road closed during heavy snows in winter
Water: None, bring your own
Fees and permits: Required
Map: USGS Telescope Peak
Information: Death Valley National Park, (760) 786-3200, *www.nps.gov/deva/*

Getting there: Death Valley is far from civilization, no matter from which direction it is approached. Drive northbound on US 395. Just north of the tiny burg of Red

Mountain, take the slight right (signed for the town of Trona) onto Trona Road headed north and follow it for 21.5 miles to State Route 178. Turn east (right) and stay on SR 178 for 45 miles, past the park entrance. At the junction, take the right fork signed for Wildrose Campground. Continue past the campground; at 9.5 miles keep straight and pass the Charcoal Kilns. At this point the road becomes very rough and suited for four-wheel-drive vehicles, or high-clearance at the very least. If your vehicle isn't suitable to continue, park here and hike the rest of the way. Another 2 miles leads to the Mahogany Flats Campground; those with high-clearance vehicles can park here. **Note:** Check the web page or inquire at the Furnace Creek Visitor Center about the status of the road, which sometimes closes in winter.

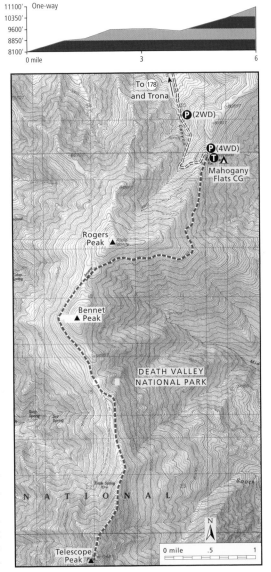

Telescope Peak is the showcase summit in Death Valley. It is the national park's highest point, and a place that gets a fair amount of snow in the wintertime. Since this region is known as one of the hottest places in the world, many people don't realize there are also snow-covered mountains here, let alone ones that boast winter conditions. The massif possesses pinyon, bristlecone, and limber pines, though none of these trees offers much protection from the sun—they are all rather short and stubbly, and most are sparsely spaced off the trail.

The trail begins at the northern end of the campground. There is a register for signing in a few hundred feet from the trailhead marker. The way to the top has recently been reworked by volunteers and is in good shape. The ascent begins at a steady and somewhat steep clip along an angled slope. For 2.5 miles the elevation gain is considerable until the trail reaches the saddle between Bennett and Rogers peaks. The route then plateaus and descends slightly over the course of 2 miles until the final push for the summit, which begins 2.5 miles away from the top. The hike is perfectly balanced in that respect; but the final gain is difficult and drawn out over thirteen very long switchbacks.

The views can be truly magnificent from the summit. Sadly, smog has greatly increased here, blown in from the Central Valley through Tehachapi Pass. Occasionally in winter it can be difficult to see Mount Charleston directly east in the Spring Mountains, a mere 80 miles away. The Sierra summit of Olancha Peak sits less than 60 miles directly west and is easily visible, while San Gorgonio resides almost 140 miles to the south. The White and Inyo mountains are readily identifiable, as is Badwater and the salt flats that

Charcoal kilns present an odd introduction to the higher reaches of Death Valley National Park.

run through the main corridor of Death Valley National Park. This can be a hot, dusty, and dry desert peak—bring ample amounts of water, and a hat. During wintertime the slopes and angles can be treacherous when iced over, so be sure to bring along proper winter mountaineering tools, including ice ax and crampons—and the skills to use them.

84 BADWATER

Distance: 0.5 to 2.5 miles round-trip
Hiking time: 0.5 to 1.5 hours
Difficulty: Easy
Elevation gain: 20 feet
Low Point: -280 feet
Season: All, very hot in summer
Water: None, bring your own
Fees and permits: Required
Maps: USGS Badwater, Devils Golf Course
Information: Death Valley National Park, (760) 786-3200, *www.nps.gov/deva/*

Getting there: There are many ways to approach Death Valley, all of which are far from civilization of any sort. From US 395 half a mile north of the town of Red Mountain, turn right onto Trona Road and drive for 21.5 miles. Then turn right onto State Route 178 and follow it for 58.5 miles to State Route 190. Turn right onto SR 190 and drive for 52.5 miles to the Furnace Creek Visitor Center. Head south on SR 190 from the Furnace Creek Visitor Center for 1 mile, then turn right onto State Route 178 south and continue for 16.5 miles. At Badwater there is a turnout, parking area, interpretative signs, and a boardwalk.

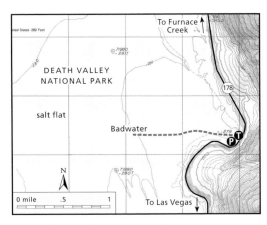

Badwater is less of a hike and more of a must-do walking excursion for visitors to Death Valley. There is no trail here, but visitors can walk as far as they wish. This is the transcendent and devilishly hot place from which the area's hellish moniker is derived. In the summertime, the desert heat is trapped and recirculated by the encompassing mountain walls that keep it within the low elevation of the valley. At night, the high altitude of the surrounding ranges does not allow hot air to escape. In many ways, the area acts like a convection oven.

The salt flat, 282 feet below sea level, is the lowest elevation in the Western Hemisphere.

In summer at midday the area is deadly if proper precautions are not taken, but in the winter it can be pleasantly mild, or frigid, or even a balmy 80-plus degrees Fahrenheit. Regardless of weather, the area is beautiful, austere, and eerie at the same time. From the center of the salt flat the basin extends for miles and miles to the north and south, while east to west the depression spans a little over 6 miles. The area is bounded on the north by the surreal Devils Golf Course, which is a maze of jagged crystalline rocks. To the west, the Panamint Mountains rise to just over 11,000 feet. The aptly named Funeral Mountains stand to the east, while the Owlshead Mountains complete the valley's walls to the south.

Many people come to the area to visit the lowest spot in North America. The actual point where the elevation dips to 282 feet below sea level is a couple of miles walk into the valley. Should hitting that point be desirable, it is easy to mark the spot on a Global Positioning System (GPS), or follow a bearing on a compass, using a topo map. Chances are very good that there will be nothing there but solitude. Wandering more than a half mile out onto the basin will leave other, more casual visitors behind.

The salt flat itself is very interesting. When there has been little precipitation, the crust of salt gets to be between 5 and 10 inches thick and the heat causes huge polygonal plates to crack and bulge up from the surface of the ground. Dropping little pieces of rocklike salt onto the plates gives off a distinctly metallic sound. Conversely, when there has been a high level of precipitation, the salt flat levels off and the cracking in the crust appears as jagged interlocking lines reminiscent of a turtle shell.

85 THE RACETRACK

Distance: 0.5 to 2.25 miles round-trip
Hiking time: 2 hours
Difficulty: Easy
Elevation gain: 20 feet
High point: 3725 feet
Season: Late fall to early spring
Water: None, bring your own
Fees and permits: Required
Map: USGS Ubehebe Peak
Information: Death Valley National Park, (760) 786-3200, *www.nps.gov/deva/*

Getting there: Approaching Racetrack Valley is an adventure all in itself. The way is rutted, rough, and remote. The park service recommends a high-clearance vehicle with truck tires and a full-size spare due to the many sharp rocks which tend to easily puncture regular street tires. (Tows from the area are not usually covered by insurance and can easily cost more than $500.) Allow at least an hour and a half to two hours one-way on the dirt road from Ubehebe Crater; the road is extremely washboarded for almost its entire length. Do not attempt the drive in the summer, or in a vehicle that is not in excellent repair. Always check with the ranger about road conditions before visiting.

From Stovepipe Wells in Death Valley National Park, drive east on State Route 190 for nearly 7.5 miles to the turnoff for Scotty's Castle, signed for Ubehebe Crater. Make a left and drive northbound for 33.5 miles. Veer left at the junction for Scotty's Castle and continue north and west for nearly 6 miles, past Ubehebe Crater. The dirt road leads 20 miles to Teakettle Junction; stay right for 7 more miles, past Teakettle Junction, to Racetrack Valley. Park at a pullout.

Rocks on the Racetrack Playa can move hundreds of feet, leaving mysterious tracks behind.

The Racetrack is more of an experience had by walking than by hiking. There is no real trail here, other than where visitors decide to go. **Note: Do not walk onto the Racetrack or its surroundings if there is even the slightest bit of moisture on the ground! Careless footsteps can leave traces that take decades, even centuries, to clear away. The footwork of at least a couple of thoughtless visitors can be clearly seen near some of the sliding stones.**

Once the first footstep is taken onto the playa, there is almost no way to visit this remote and fascinating region without being intensely affected. This dried, oval-shaped Death Valley lakebed is unique; nowhere else on the planet is like it. At the northern end of the playa, an island of bedrock, appropriately named The Grandstand, rises above the surface and provides incredible vistas of the entire valley.

The playa receives its moniker from the bizarre tracks left by rocks which have sailed across it, leaving blazed paths and trails in the earth. Somehow the rocks—which vary in weight from a few pounds to several hundred—move. No one has seen them do so, or recorded their movements, but the tracks are there, some hundreds of yards long. Many of the grooves run parallel, while others cross and crisscross. Some tracks abruptly change direction at right angles, while others meander in curvy patterns. Theories to explain how the rocks move run the gamut from aliens and magnetic forces to more scientifically acceptable explanations.

Currently, two competing theories are the most plausible and widely accepted, though scientists disagree on which is predominant. The lakebed is composed of a strange, spongy sort of clay, and although Death Valley as a whole gets very little rainfall, the mountains do occasionally get some precipitation. The dry Racetrack Playa is nearly level. After these small traces of moisture flow down into the valley, the lakebed can be filled with as much as 2 inches of water. Extreme temperatures in the national park sometimes cause this water to freeze into ice sheets. It has been theorized that these ice sheets are affected by the high winds that sometimes occur in the

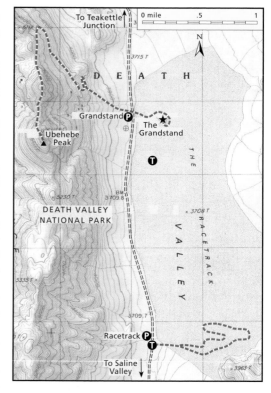

basin; perhaps the ice moves along the surface of the Racetrack, pushing the rocks through the clay in similar patterns. Conversely, others believe that water saturates the porous clay surface and the high-powered winds drive the rocks across the muddy depression, leaving behind fantastic striations.

Stop first at The Grandstand, an obvious rock outcropping on the playa, then drive to the southern parking area and walk to the black peak at the southern end of the playa—the source of the rock deposits. Should the playa be wet, there are worthy alternate adventures in the area. A four-wheel-drive trail leads into Saline Valley, a remote and austere valley rarely seen by anyone. Ubehebe Peak is easily reachable via a 2.8-mile trail. Sitting 2000 feet above the Racetrack, it provides excellent 360-degree views of the park and its outlying regions. On the drive back out the way you came, Ubehebe Crater is a short but worthwhile trip to walk around and into the caldera.

Opposite: The Eastern Sierra is full of beautiful passes, mountains, and lakes such as Long Lake.

EASTERN SIERRA NEVADA, WHITE MOUNTAINS, AND YOSEMITE

EASTERN SIERRA NEVADA AND THE WHITE MOUNTAINS

The Sierra Nevada is among the most beautiful mountain ranges in the world. From stunning alpine battlement summits lording over rocky views, to the hypnotic grandeur and magnitude of Yosemite, Sequoia, and Kings Canyon national parks, the mountain range stretches more than 400 miles from Tehachapi Pass in the south to Fredonyer Pass in the north. It is bordered by the San Joaquin Valley on the western side and the Great Basin in the east.

While not technically Southern California, most Southern California travelers have made at least one journey up US 395 to Mammoth Lakes and beyond. The Eastern Sierra—the one range where true alpine conditions exist in California—are a great travel destination. The passes in the East Sierra, amazingly steep, lead into some of the world's most beautiful landscapes.

The mountain wall is an amazing barrier not only to humankind, but also for weather. Weather can be unpredictable at all times of year, though snow typically moves in by mid- to late October. During summer afternoons, it is common for thunderheads to appear high in the Sierra. It is wise to get up early, get an early start, and be safely back down again before lightning threatens in the upper reaches of the atmosphere.

Unusual geography abounds in the desert to the east of the Sierra. Mono Lake's alkaline strangeness offers a unique adventure filled with picturesque displays. Volcanic activity has produced its share of oddities, including the wonderful Devils Postpile. The White Mountains sit in the rain shadow of the mighty Sierra Nevada, but they hold their own share of adventure with the world's oldest living trees and the third-highest mountain in California.

Note: The wilderness permitting process has gotten stricter for hiking and camping in the Sierra Nevada. To protect your trip from unexpected delays, make sure to call ahead and find out the latest permitting requirements.

86 OLANCHA PEAK

Distance: 14 miles round-trip
Hiking time: 7 hours
Difficulty: Extremely strenuous
Elevation gain: 4100 feet
High point: 12,123 feet
Season: Early summer to late fall
Water: Unnamed stream and several springs, may dry up by late summer
Fees and permits: Wilderness permits required for all backpacking. Reserve in advance
Maps: USGS Olancha, Monache Mountain
Information: Sequoia National Forest, (559) 784-1500, *www.fs.fed.us/r5/sequoia/*

Getting there: Take US 395 north 11.6 miles from Coso Junction to Kennedy Meadows Road. Turn left onto Kennedy Meadows Road and follow it for approximately 24 miles. At the fork for Kennedy Meadows Campground,

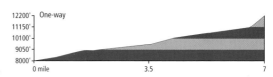

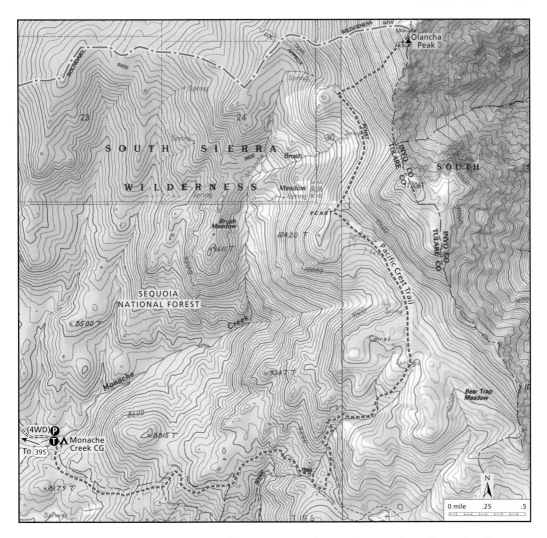

turn left and drive for another 12.5 miles to the turn for Blackrock Visitor Center. Turn right and follow the road for nearly 3.5 miles. Then veer right and drive another 3.5 miles until the junction for Monache Meadows; turn left. Go almost another mile (the road is still passable to this point for two-wheel-drive vehicles), and veer left. If you have a four-wheel-drive vehicle, continue as the road gets very rough, dropping down into a valley. In 0.2 mile the road forks; stay right. Continue for 5.3 miles to the junction with the Kern River. A little over 0.5 mile after crossing the river, turn left onto an unsigned road. Stay right, continue nearly 1 mile, and park at Monache Creek Campground. Allow at least an hour and a half driving time from the Blackrock Visitor Center.

Half the fun of getting to Olancha Peak is driving there. A four-wheel-drive vehicle is necessary to navigate the roadway to Monache Meadows. There are very good jeep trails, and all are well signed going in. Still, it is important to call the ranger, get a map, use a topo map, and Global Positioning System (GPS), and follow the signs. For detailed driving directions, see also *www.climber.org/DrivingDirections/monache.html.*

The PCT climbs through a grand valley with towering summits on all sides as it approaches the summit.

For the most part, the way to the Kern River and Monache Meadows is easy to follow, but it is wise to call ahead and get directions from the brochure at the visitor center.

Note: The wilderness permitting process has gotten stricter for hiking and camping in the Sierra Nevada. To protect your trip from unexpected delays, make sure to call ahead and find out the latest permitting requirements.

From the parking area, the road continues a bit up the hill and quickly turns into an unmaintained trail; the trailhead is marked with a register. The first 2 miles are steeper than the

remainder of the trail until the final summit push. Sierra cattle hands still use this trail to move livestock, so let the herds pass if or when they come through. A little over 2 miles brings the trail to an intersection with the Pacific Crest Trail (PCT). Turn left onto the PCT; from here, stay on the PCT and follow the trail signs that point to Gomez Meadows. At this point the gain also eases to a gentle gradient. However, the PCT is so underused through this area that in spots it is almost difficult to follow. Most of the trail travels through nicely shaded pine forest, occasionally opening up into meadows.

As the trail ascends, it wanders through a spring-filled canyon overflowing with wildflowers and corn lilies. Here it seems as if the trail will continue upward forever. Just as it climbs up and out of a valley, another climb appears. Eventually, views open up into Monache Meadows, and the trail follows along an exposed mountainside.

The first views of Olancha Peak come into sight as the trail rounds a corner. There is no trail to the summit, not even a mountaineer's route or a use trail. Instead, the final 0.75 mile is a straight-up scramble. Most of the climbing is Class II, but some Class III moves can be attempted near the summit if one chooses. The summit can be reached just as easily by avoiding any dangerous maneuvers, though.

Olancha Peak is one of fifteen Sierra Club Sierra Peaks Section emblem peaks, meaning that it dominates the area around it and can be clearly seen towering above the rest of the peaks in the region. Olancha is the southernmost California peak reaching over 12,000 feet in height, and is pictured on every bottle of Crystal Geyser drinking water. The summit provides incredible views of the entire southern Sierra, the Great Western Divide, Death Valley, and other peaks and valleys to the south.

87 MOUNT WHITNEY

Distance: 22 miles round-trip
Hiking time: 15 hours or overnight
Difficulty: Extremely strenuous
Elevation gain: 6200 feet
High point: 14,494 feet
Season: Summer to fall
Water: Lone Pine Creek and several lakes; no water after Trail Camp
Fees and permits: Wilderness permits required for all backpacking. Reserve in advance
Maps: USGS Mount Whitney, Mount Langley
Information: Inyo National Forest, (760) 873-2400, *www.fs.fed.us/r5/inyo/*

Getting there: Take US 395 to Lone Pine. In the center of town is Whitney Portal Road. Turn left (west) and drive nearly 12 miles to the stadium-sized parking lot at the end of the road.

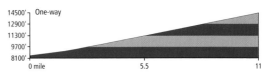

The Mount Whitney "freeway" is definitely a classic hike in the truest sense of the word. The tallest peak in the contiguous forty-eight states has long been a life-list destination for hikers. Many people still dream about climbing its flanks and standing atop it as a once-in-a-lifetime achievement. It is California's "going to Disneyland" mountain, but that doesn't mean it is without difficulty or merit. It is hard not to be drawn to the spiky, dominating summit. Even from the Portal Road, its spires and obelisk-like profiles give Whitney an ethereal appearance as it commands the skyline from its lofty perch behind several towering summits that are formidable in their own right.

Note: The wilderness permitting process has gotten stricter for hiking and camping in the Sierra Nevada. To protect your trip from unexpected delays, make sure to call ahead and find out the latest permitting requirements.

The approach is very steady; there isn't a mile on the trail that gains more than 800 feet in elevation, and most ascend at an even 500–600-foot

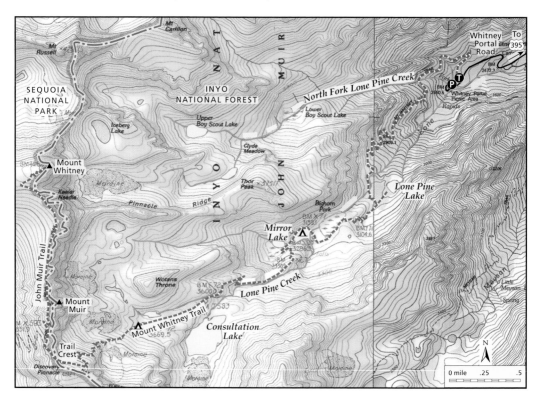

pace. Of course, at such altitude the hike is difficult nonetheless.

The 3 miles to Lone Pine Lake is a great adventure and a worthy destination in and of itself. Most of those miles traverse through manzanita and chaparral scrub, though some large trees present occasional shade. From May 1–November 1, hikers need a day-use permit to continue onto the Whitney Main Trail above Lone Pine Lake. (In addition, a Wilderness Permit is required for camping at Trail Camp.) Those who cannot get a permit may find the lake itself a worthy alternative. The lake is a piece of perfection, resting above a precipice with a stunning view down into the Owens Valley.

From the lake, hikers with a permit can continue upward, passing places with mythological names such as Wotans Throne and Thor Peak. More people appear on the trail between two campsites, Outpost Camp and the higher Trail Camp, which lies just beyond Consultation Lake. Supposedly there are only sixty camping spots and a hundred day-use permits available per day. One hundred and sixty people is still a large amount of traffic for one route (and when hiking, it may seem like more than that). Make sure to filter water at Trail Camp, as it has the last reliable source of water along the trail.

Trail Camp sits at the base of the infamous "96" switchbacks, which also go by the names "97," "98," and "99" switchbacks, depending upon who is counting. The trail twists and turns again and again with the most drastically exposed spots bastioned by railings, occasional steps, and chains. At the top of the seemingly endless coils, some of the most spectacular views in the world open up. The sky is endless here, and so is the Sierra Nevada Range. The entire Great Western Divide stands jaggedly above lakes too numerous to name, creating a bountiful panorama like no other.

From Trail Crest, elevation 13,600 and the entry into Sequoia National Park, the path loses 300 feet of elevation and joins the John Muir Trail on its way to the summit of Whitney. The walking, and especially climbing, is difficult at very high altitude; the last 2 miles is by no means an easy stretch. After the switchbacks have taken a toll on one's energy reserves, there is still a steady slog to the peak itself. The area is very exposed and rocky. Here the trail follows a ridgeline, and care should be taken in watching the sky for signs of thunderstorms. This is not a stretch to be caught on in an electrical storm.

The way in is long and tough, though many make the journey every day. Atop the highest point in the Lower 48, the views are commanding, though it is nearly impossible to get a full 360-degree, because the summit is so angular, and there is much of the bulk of the mountain behind you when you are on top. The perspective is similar to that from Trail Crest. In some ways, this makes the Mount Whitney summit a bit anticlimactic, but it is still an experience not to be missed. Mount Muir, another fourteener, can be scaled from near Trail Crest by ascending just a few hundred feet off the main Whitney Trail. The way is obvious for the trained eye, but be careful, as it is Class III climbing: falls and mistakes can be deadly.

Clouds roll in over Mount Whitney. Afternoon thunderstorms are common in the Eastern Sierra during summer.

88 KEARSARGE PASS TO MOUNT GOULD

Distance: 12 miles round-trip
Hiking time: 7 hours or overnight
Difficulty: Extremely strenuous
Elevation gain: 3900 feet
High point: 13,005 feet
Season: Late spring through fall
Water: Independence Creek, Little Pothole, and Gilbert Lakes
Fees and permits: Wilderness permits required for all backpacking. Reserve
    in advance
Map: USGS Kearsarge Peak
Information: Inyo National Forest, (760) 873-2400, (760) 876-6200 for
    wilderness permits, *www.fs.fed.us/r5/inyo/*

Getting there: Take US 395 to Independence. In the very center of town, make a left onto Onion Valley Road. Follow it for 13 steep, winding miles to the large trailhead parking lot next to the Onion Valley Campground. **Note:** Adhere to all bear-box guidelines, and do not leave any food or scented items in your vehicle.

Kearsarge Pass is one of the most popular backpacking entry points into the Sequoia/Kings Canyon National Parks region. It is popular because of its relatively steady grade and short distance.

Note: The wilderness permitting process has gotten stricter for hiking and camping in the Sierra Nevada. To protect your trip from unexpected delays, make sure to call ahead and find out the latest permitting requirements.

Beginning at 9200 feet, this trip starts in high altitude. For those acclimated to the higher elevations and used to hiking with less oxygen, the climb to the pass could be classified as easy, or at least easy in relation to other Eastern Sierra passes like Taboose or Olancha. The trailhead begins a little ways west down the road from the

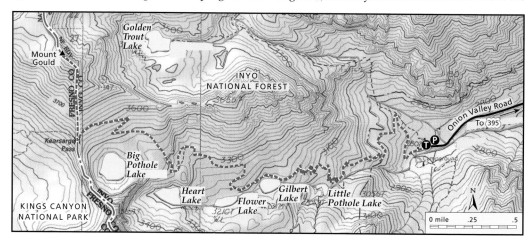

Views of Kearsarge Lakes and the High Sierra from just below the summit of Mount Gould

parking area. The way is shadeless for most of the outing, but due to its high starting elevation the trip is still relatively cool, even in the early afternoon. Some people prefer to hike to the pass in the afternoon. There is a lot of water in the area, and while bugs are not as huge a problem as they can be in other places, the mosquitoes here bite just like anyplace else. Generally, an easy wind blows up the pass, which helps to reduce the numbers of pesky insects. The hike passes numerous beautiful alpine lakes along the way; the scenery is magnificent. There are overlooks, towering spires, and an abundance of photo opportunities for both the novice and the professional.

The trail constantly ascends, branching near the beginning for Golden Trout Lake, and again, farther on, near Matlock Lake. Stay straight each time. (Due to the lakes, this trail is also popular with fishermen.) As you ascend, the pass comes into clear view. The way meanders a bit and switchbacks up the mountain, making the distance appear less than it actually is. At 6 miles, the top of the pass affords incredible views of University Peak, Pothole Lake, the Kearsarge Lakes Basin and the Great Western Divide. Rest and have some lunch atop the many boulders that mark the top of the pass.

After lunch, the truly bold can extend this hike by continuing directly north on a cross-country mountaineer's path up to the summit of Mount Gould. Gould is a 13,000-foot peak; hikers should watch everyone in their party for signs of elevation sickness. The half mile to the top from Kearsarge Pass is deceiving; it takes at least an hour to an hour and a half to ascend the rocky escarpment, which is steep and Class II most of the way. There are sections of severe exposure, so this side trip is not for the faint of heart. Near the top, there is some open Class III climbing to reach the top of a false summit. The actual summit block requires a nontechnical and easy Class IV move. Any mistake, however, means a fall of several hundred feet, and then perhaps a tumble of thousands of feet onto sharp and jagged rocks. Errors would certainly prove to be fatal. Return carefully down the route to the trail and then back to the trailhead.

89 BISHOP PASS

Distance: 11 miles round-trip
Hiking time: 7 hours or overnight
Difficulty: Strenuous
Elevation gain: 2300 feet
High point: 11,960 feet
Season: Late spring through fall
Water: Bishop Creek and numerous lakes
Fees and permits: Wilderness permits required for all backpacking. Reserve in advance
Maps: USGS Mount Thompson, North Palisade
Information: Inyo National Forest, (760) 873-2400 for wilderness permits, *www.fs.fed.us/r5/inyo/*

Getting there: Take US 395 to the town of Bishop. Make a left turn onto Line Street/ State Route 168. Follow SR 168 for 15 miles to the turnoff for South Lake Road. Make a left and follow South Lake Road for 7 miles to the parking lot at its end. **Note:** Adhere to

all bear-box guidelines, and do not leave any food or scented items in your vehicle.

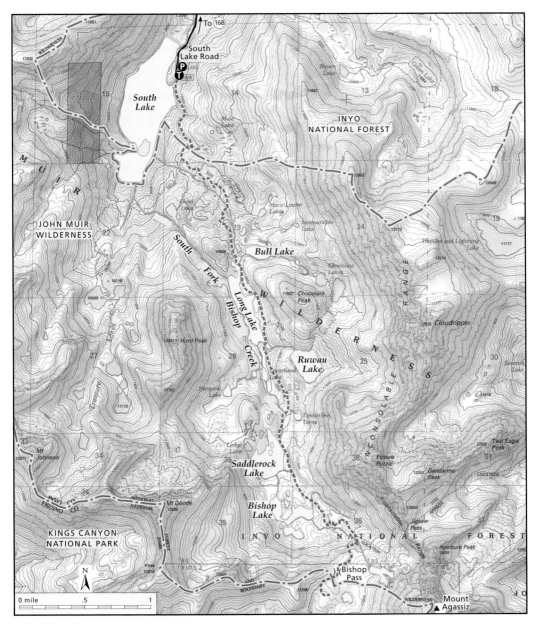

The scenery on this trip is without compare. Eastern Sierra alpine beauty figures prominently at every twist and turn. The traverse touches the borders of seven named lakes which can all be photographed from a variety of angles, with prominent peaks reflecting off the waters in the background. *Dazzling, exquisite, heavenly* are merely words which fail to capture the contrasting beauty of the granite and water of the region. Treeline does not occur until nearly 11,500 feet, though the stands of trees do begin to thin out quite a bit lower on the trail, along with the shade that they provide. There is still plenty of greenery and flora, though, to make the area a virtual color cornucopia. Wildflowers dominate the surroundings in times of high water. From the pass, Mount Agassiz and the jagged sawteeth of the Inconsolable Range dominate the skyline. Dusy Basin sits below the pass and is a popular backpacking destination within the northern reaches of Kings Canyon National Park.

The trail to Bishop Pass should be classified as a butt-kicker in more ways than one. It isn't that the way is particularly steep or long. In fact the trail is fairly short, relatively easy, well traveled, and very well graded, with a gradual incline for an eastern Sierra pass. The main challenge of this hike is its high elevation from beginning to end. Merely driving to the trailhead from sea level can cause altitude sickness. Hiking at high altitude is a strenuous activity at best for those who are not properly acclimated.

Note: The wilderness permitting process has gotten stricter for hiking and camping in the Sierra Nevada. To protect your trip from unexpected delays, make sure to call ahead and find out the latest permitting requirements.

The trail begins at the south end of the lot near South Lake. After leaving South Lake, the trail gains elevation for 2 miles before reaching the stunning jewel known as Long Lake. The scenery alone makes this a worthwhile destination for those who want to go no farther.

From the lake, water is constant as the trail passes several more lakes. There are a nearly limitless number of ponds and unnamed tarns in close proximity as well. As a result of all this standing water, the mosquitoes here are often very pronounced during certain months of the year, especially early summer after winters of high precipitation. Sierra mosquitoes are

Navigating across Bishop Creek near Bishop Pass

notorious for their ability to turn bug spray into a condiment. Make sure to bring the strongest stuff available, you just might need it.

High-country trout are abundantly stocked in the lakes and streams, so the area is a paradise for fishermen as well.

The ascent is very gradual except for the final push to the pass. From the top, the views are quite memorable. For those who want to extend the hike, a short quarter mile and a few hundred feet of gain to the west lead to the top of an unnamed peak that offers views of superior quality, while the truly brave and unwearying can summit the steep, rocky talus of Mount Agassiz.

90 SCHULMAN GROVE

Distance: 3.75-mile loop
Hiking time: 2 hours
Difficulty: Easy
Elevation gain: 550 feet
High point: 10,160 feet
Season: Late spring through early fall
Water: None, bring your own
Fees and permits: Wilderness permits required for all backpacking. Reserve in advance
Map: USGS Blanco Mountain
Information: Inyo National Forest, (760) 873-2400, *www.fs.fed.us/r5/inyo/*

Getting there: From US 395 in Big Pine, turn east onto State Route 168 and drive for approximately 13 miles toward Westgard Pass. Turn left onto paved White Mountain Road (Forest Service Road 4S01) and follow it for 10 miles to the Schulman Grove turnoff; turn right and park.

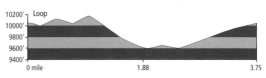

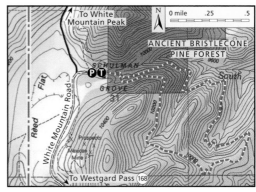

The oldest living things in the world grow on this trail. Bristlecone pines (*Pinus longaeva*) are a hardy and otherworldly species. They grow throughout the West, but none grow as old as the trees on this trail and its environs. The area's harsh soil and climate are what allow these trees to become so robust. The environment is brutal, but bristlecone pines are specifically adapted to such extremes. Insects, disease, and fire do not harm the trees, due to their sinewy and resinous wood. When a part of the tree dies, other parts continue to grow. The more bent, twisted, and gnarled the tree, the older it is.

The Methuselah Tree, named for a biblical figure renowned for his long life, is nearly five thousand years old. To put the tree's age into historical perspective: It is a contemporary of Stonehenge, the Great Pyramid, and Gilgamesh. When the tree's life began, England, Greece, and Italy were populated with people living in mud huts. The Methuselah Tree reportedly has only one branch that still produces pinecones. The rest of it has died off, a husk clinging to existence through its remaining stem of life.

In terms of trees, these arboreal ancients are millennia older than sequoias and giant red- woods. Much of the undecayed dead wood lying near the trail is also thousands of years old.

Thankfully, this monarch of all trees is not marked. This is so that people don't hang on it, damage it, or trample its roots, and to keep it safe

Bristlecone pines live to be thousands of years old, clinging to life in difficult environs.

from the love-struck who might thoughtlessly carve initials and a heart onto its bark. Still, many trees in the grove are over four thousand years old, which still puts them ahead of the majority of human civilization. The grove's older trees have existed longer than most of the world's major religions.This gives infinite fodder for the mind while strolling among these otherworldly trees. Once this hike is completed, it will not be forgotten.

A relatively new visitor center sits at the end of the parking lot. The trail begins near the visitor center. The hike is a well-marked loop on a nature trail with signs that correspond to a guide-book that can be purchased for a nominal fee or borrowed from dispensers. There are no other trails intersecting the trail; simply follow the loop as it undulates up and down until it returns to the parking lot. The high-elevation scenery is magnificent, and the starkness of the surroundings leaves visitors awestruck.

For those who want to explore further, the Discovery Walk is a shorter 1-mile option that also begins near the visitor center; these two loops can be combined for a longer hike. Patriarch Grove, a less-frequented alternative, involves an additional drive along White Mountain Road, but provides a similar, transcendant experience.

91 WHITE MOUNTAIN PEAK

Distance: 15 miles round-trip
Hiking time: 8 hours
Difficulty: Very strenuous
Elevation gain: 2400 feet
High point: 14,246 feet
Season: Late spring through early fall
Water: None, bring your own
Fees and permits: Wilderness permits required for all backpacking. Reserve in advance
Maps: USGS Mount Barcroft, White Mountain Peak
Information: Inyo National Forest, (760) 873-2400, *www.fs.fed.us/r5/inyo/*

Getting there: From US 395 in Big Pine, turn east onto State Route 168 and drive about 13 miles toward Westgard Pass. Turn left onto paved White Mountain Road (Forest Service Road 4S01) and follow it for 10 miles to the Schulman Grove turnoff. Instead of taking the turnoff, continue straight onto the unsigned gravel road. In another 12 miles veer left (away from the entrance to the Patriarch Grove). Follow the road another 4.5 miles to a makeshift parking lot on the left just before a locked gate. **Note:** The trip from Big Pine, which you will pass on US 395 on the way in, will take you close to two hours in a four-wheel-drive or high-clearance vehicle. A passenger car can make it, but at greatly reduced speeds. **Also note:** There is a lot of

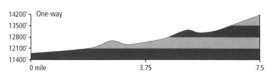

marmot activity in the area, and they have reportedly done some damage to cars parked at the trailhead. Take precautions.

The White Mountains are largely ignored due to their proximity to the greener and more inviting Sierra Nevada Range. In fact, the Whites lie in the rain shadow of California's most storied and popular mountains, so the only precipitation they receive is from snow in the wintertime, which endows the range with its namesake. These mountains are no slouch in the height

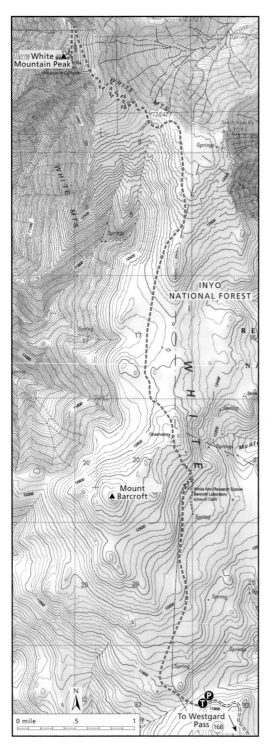

department; they cast their own formidable shadows. White Mountain Peak, at 14,246 feet, just happens to be California's third tallest summit. It is the only "fourteener" that can be reached via a relatively "easy" road walk-up—not that any hike can be truly easy at this elevation. It is also home to the University of California's high-altitude research station.

The austere beauty of the White Mountains is dazzling. This landscape has a lunar eeriness, which is pronounced by its makeup of mul-ticolored rock piled on more rock. The area is home to wildflowers, bees, all sorts of rodents, and bighorn sheep. The Sierra Nevada sparkles across the Owens Valley, and once you start gain-ing views into Nevada, the panoramic tableau is unobstructed for hundreds of miles. There is a tangible tranquility in the White Mountains; it is impossible not to be affected by the mountains' serenity and stark magnificence.

Once you park, the trail is the road; you walk on it the whole way to the summit. In a little under 2 miles, the trail passes the Barcroft Research Station, a stalwart outpost complete with animal pens and a telescope. Nearing Mount Barcroft (an easy side jaunt), the climb opens up to jaw-dropping vistas of the summit. The next 3 miles lead down and up across a plateau to the base of the mountain, where the remainder of the hike ascends some very long switchbacks. The road is the only trail, so it is impossible to miss it or get lost.

From the apex, the views' range and perspec-tive is unrivaled. Sensory overload may set in, so take a good amount of time to enjoy it. This is one of the greatest wraparound views in the entire western United States. You've earned it; despite the road, this mountain is anything but easy.

If time allows, just below the trailhead, in the Schulman and Patriarch Groves, reside the old-est living things on the planet. Bristlecone pines thrive in this barren, desiccated realm, but almost nothing grows above the trailhead except some scattered, hardy, but beautiful flora and a few specimens of grass.

Be particularly wary of certain dangers on this hike. None are particularly hazardous, but being aware is a sure way to avoid trouble and get the most enjoyment out of this amazing place. Alti-tude sickness is a real possibility; the trailhead

After a dusting, it is obvious how the high-altitude White Mountains came by their name.

is located above 11,600 feet, and the trail climbs above 14,000. The rays of the sun can burn skin in minutes at this elevation, so cover up, and wear sunblock. Look out, too, for afternoon thunderstorms. The weather on top is normally windy and cold.

92 DEVILS POSTPILE/RAINBOW FALLS

Distance: 3.5 miles round-trip
Hiking time: 2 hours
Difficulty: Easy
Elevation gain: 350 feet
High point: 7700 feet
Season: May through November
Water: San Joaquin River
Fees and permits: Required. Wilderness permits required for all backpacking. Reserve in advance
Map: USGS Crystal Crag
Information: Devils Postpile National Monument, (760) 934-2289, *www.nps.gov/depo/*

Getting there: Take US 395 north to Mammoth Lakes Junction (State Route 203). Turn west and continue through the town for nearly 4 miles. Turn right onto Minaret Road and follow it for 4 miles to the Mammoth Mountain Ski Resort main lodge. Park here and purchase tickets for the shuttle. Between the hours of 7:00 AM and 7:30 PM, all

The hexagonal basalt columns of Devils Postpile draw scores of visitors.

summertime visitors must ride the shuttle. (Only campers, Reds Meadows resort-goers, people with disabilities, and those with stock trailers can drive in throughout the day, but there aren't enough parking spaces and the road is very narrow.) The road is generally closed and unplowed in winter.

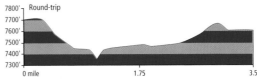

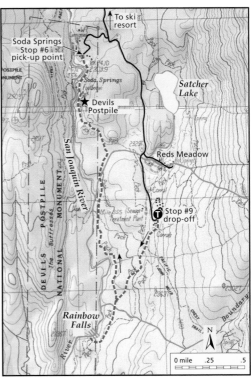

Devils Postpile and Rainbow Falls, both beautiful destinations, are popular draws in the town of Mammoth Lakes. Tourists fill shuttle busses every twenty to thirty minutes and stream out onto the trail heading for both attractions. It is impossible to avoid people on this trail, but it is quite easy to get started without the throng. Most people stream off the bus at Soda Springs and head straight for the short walk to the Postpile. From there they take the trail to Rainbow Falls, and finish the point-to-point hike beyond Reds Meadow. Instead of exiting with the masses, stay on the bus and continue to stop number 9 after Reds Meadow. Head backward down the hike.

From here the trail winds through areas devastated by the Rainbow Fire of 1992. Nearly a century of fire suppression helped to build up dense undergrowth. Many dead, dying, and living trees were burned up in a crown fire of epic proportions. Little regrowth has occurred since then, but the majority of the trail crosses through regions virtually untouched by the fire.

In almost no time the wide and well-signed walkway wanders within listening distance of the cascade. There are several overlooks that provide vistas of the spectacular falls. Getting down to the falls is a bit trickier; a lengthy series of steps descends to the base of the falls, where at times of low water it is possible to swim underneath the downrushing water. After enjoying the rainbows that nearly always glisten from the prismatic mist, climb up the steps and backtrack a ways on the trail to the junction that leads to the Postpile.

The Devils Postpile is a fascinating piece of geology. The columnar basalt that erupts wickedly from the earth formed during a cooling lava flow. As the lava cooled, cracks formed on the surface, creating what is known as a *tessellation*. (This is a formation where no gaps or overlaps occur in the surface.) Most of the columns appear hexagonal, with precise 120-degree angles caused by the heating and cooling of the magma. Glacial ice uncovered the formation as it now stands for posterity.

There is a side trail to the top of the Postpile that is a worthy detour. The columns here look like natural tile flooring, and the view from the front edge is nothing short of spectacular. Be wary of the columns, though; they still break off occasionally. Walk back down to the front of the formation and take in the view while striking a pose for some excellent pictures, and return to shuttle stop number 6.

For those who want to see more, the side trip to Lower Rainbow Falls is a worthy venture with a lot less pedestrian traffic. The same goes for the trip to Minaret Falls, which is just north of the Postpile on the John Muir Trail.

93 SAN JOAQUIN MOUNTAIN

Distance: 7.3 miles round-trip
Hiking time: 3.5 hours
Difficulty: Strenuous
Elevation gain: 1700 feet
High point: 11,601 feet
Season: Late spring through fall
Water: None, bring your own
Fees and permits: Wilderness permits required for all backpacking. Reserve
    in advance
Map: USGS Mammoth Mountain
Information: Inyo National Forest, (760) 873-2400, *www.fs.fed.us/r5/inyo/*

Getting there: Take US 395 north to Mammoth Lakes Junction (State Route 203). Turn west and continue through the town for nearly 4 miles. Turn right onto Minaret Road and follow it for 4 miles to the Mammoth Mountain Ski Resort main lodge. Continue on toward Devils Postpile to the entrance booth, and make a right turn onto the paved road for the Minaret Summit overlook. Four-wheel-drive vehicles should turn immediately right onto the jeep trail and continue for nearly 2.25 miles along the ridge to Deadman Pass. There is an obvious spot to stop and park. Two-wheel-drive vehicles will have to stay on the paved road signed for Minaret Summit, and park in the large unsigned lot. The access road behind the bathroom at the paved parking lot is gated and locked, but this road connects with the jeep trail and eventually the hiking trail to the summit. **Note:** Parking in the lot adds 5 miles round-trip and 1050 feet of elevation gain in addition to the length and elevation shown above for this hike.

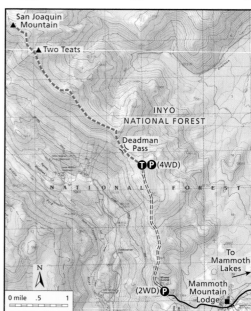

San Joaquin Mountain is an overlooked summit in the Mammoth Lakes region. Most hikers and tourists line up to visit Devils Postpile, while this incredible spot goes relatively unnoticed. The dramatic peaks of the Minarets overshadow this lofty high point, taking the focus off it entirely, even though the summit is part of the ridgeline that connects Mammoth Mountain to June Lake.

There are more prominent peaks along the skyline, but none provide San Joaquin's easy access to high vistas and solitude. From the trail's outset the jaw-dropping views begin; they only get better as the climb progresses.

One reason this peak sees fewer visitors than

others in the area is that there is no maintained trail to the rocky peak. However, a use route is easily distinguishable for the entire trip, simple to follow and unmistakable. If for some reason you do lose the trail, follow the high spine of the mountain. The trail always connects back up to and follows the ridge. Due to this being a ridge hike, there are many ups and downs, some steeper than others. There are a few Class II sections that require a bit of scrambling, but no inherently dangerous drop-offs or extreme vertical exposure to scare off the acrophobic. There are some rocky spots, especially between the Two Teats at 3.2 miles and the final push to the summit. "Two Teats" is the official name for a double peak that only remotely resembles its namesake. Evidently, some lonely miner, mountaineer, or mapmaker gave the peaks that designation with other things in mind.

The summit offers an incredible 360-degree view, with spectacular vistas of Banner and the entire Ritter Range, along with the valley below and a myriad of lakes below the spirelike summits. The Inyo and White mountain chains are visible across the Owens Valley, as are the high-country Yosemite peaks to the north. Many of the summits in the High Sierra continue to glisten with snow even late in the summer. Mono Lake seen in its entirety, sits like a shimmering blue jewel buttressed by volcanic craters. Butterflies and bees dance on the summit, where the register rests in an old ammo box waiting for a signature and lofty words of wisdom for such a beautiful peak.

For those who would like to explore this region further, there are many fine hiking trails and destinations between the ridgeline and June Lake, including Yost, Fern, and Rush creeks.

Looking for a spot to take a lunch break atop San Joaquin Mountain

94 PARKER LAKE

Distance: 4 miles round-trip
Hiking time: 2 hours or overnight
Difficulty: Easy
Elevation gain: 600 feet
High point: 8320 feet
Season: All (road may be closed in winter)
Water: None, bring your own
Fees and permits: Wilderness permits required for all backpacking. Reserve
in advance
Map: USGS Kolp Peak
Information: Inyo National Forest, (760) 924-5500, (760) 873-2483 for
wilderness permits, *www.fs.fed.us/r5/inyo/*

Getting there: Take US 395 north from Mammoth Lakes. From June Lake Junction, drive 6 miles to the northern turnoff for the June Lake Loop. Turn left and drive for nearly 1.5 miles, then turn right onto Forest Service Road 1S25 and follow the signed dirt road to the Parker Lake Trailhead.

Parker Lake may be the easiest-to-reach "secluded" alpine lake in the eastern Sierra. It is a haven for local fishermen, and a good starter hike for older children and people new to the Sierra Nevada. The elevation gain, while tough in spots, is minimal; the distance is also minor for such an amazingly beautiful destination. The trail gets a lot of usage because of the lake and streams and their plentiful fishing opportunities, but it is

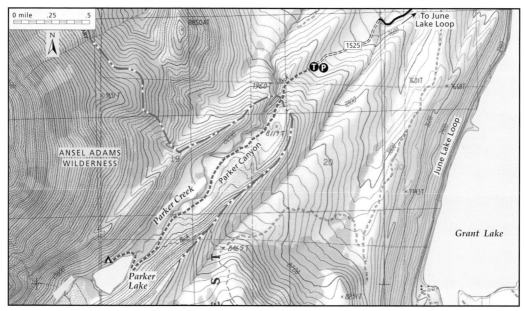

Pure mountain splendor reflected in the beauty of Parker Lake

The trail leading out of Parker Lake takes in outstanding views of Mono Lake.

relatively underused in comparison with other areas around the June Lake Loop. A hike here can feel like a great escape from civilization, even if only for a little while.

It is best to get an early start on this one, as the trailhead begins amid sagebrush in an area that looks like a scene out of *High Plains Drifter*. (The Clint Eastwood movie was filmed not far away, near Mono Lake's South Tufa.) The sun and heat can clamp down very early, and much of the climb is gained in this desert environ. As the trail ascends 500 feet in the first mile it climbs out of the sage and enters lush Parker Canyon, flirting with the edge of Parker Creek, beautifully lined with quaking aspens. The trees here in the Ansel Adams Wilderness have unfortunately suffered under the many hands of vandals with pocket-knives. The graffiti is thick, some of it nearly fifty years old. The trees have rebounded with knotty fibers covering the wounded bark; it is, however, a bit unsightly. Unfortunately, due to this trail's easy access, new scars appear every season. Luckily, the damage ends before the trail reaches the lake.

The lake itself is surrounded by towering walls of granite. Enormous unnamed waterfalls cascade from the upper reaches of Kolp Peak and feed the oval perfection of Parker Lake. A small use trail continues all the way around the lake to a campsite area within the wilderness. (Permits are necessary for all camping in this region, but not for hiking.) The creek can also be crossed on the eastern side or forded during times of high runoff, though the waters are nearly always chilling. The lake is ideal for fishing. Those brave enough may attempt to swim, but the waters are mighty icy until at least late August, if not September.

Return the way you came, and enjoy spacious views of Mono Lake that are normally overlooked on the trip up canyon. The way out is easy, and all downhill.

95 MONO LAKE—SOUTH TUFA

Distance: 0.5- to 1.5-mile loop
Hiking time: 0.5 to 2 hours
Difficulty: Easy
Elevation gain: 40 feet
High point: 6420 feet
Season: All
Water: None, bring your own
Fees and permits: Required. No backpacking allowed.
Map: USGS Lee Vining
Information: Mono Lake Committee, (760) 647-6595, *www.monolake.org/*;
Inyo National Forest, (760) 873-2400, *www.fs.fed.us/r5/inyo/*

Getting there: From Los Angeles take State Route 14 north to US 395 north. Follow US 395 north past the town of Mammoth Lakes to the turnoff for June Lake. From June Lake Junction, continue north for another 5.5 miles to State Route 120. Turn right and drive east for 4.8 miles to the left turn (Test Station Road) for South Tufa. Park in the large lot.

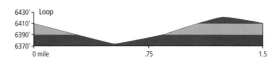

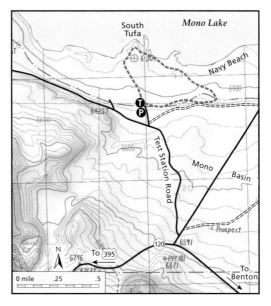

To visit Mono Lake is to enter another world. The landscape is reminiscent of a science fiction movie or a walk on the moon. The tufa towers stand above the water like eerie sentinels guarding the massive salt lake. Tufa towers are made of ancient deposits of calcium carbonate that once seeped up from springs under the water and over millennia evolved into the distorted towers that exist today. Sand flies blanket the water's edge and scatter at the approach of humans, creating a moving blanket of blackness. It sounds alarming, but they avoid all contact with human flesh. Brine shrimp ply the waters, the only life form capable of surviving in the lake's harsh salinity, which is several times saltier than the ocean's.

For most of the twentieth century, Los Angeles County diverted the stream water that fed Mono Lake, and many of the colossal stands of tufa were uncovered. The lake's importance to migratory bird patterns was also threatened. As the water level dropped, a land bridge connected one of the islands with the mainland, making nesting sites vulnerable to predators. An agreement has been reached with Los Angeles County, and Mono Lake is in the process of being restored to earlier sustainable levels. Much of the tufa that can now be walked around will be partly or wholly underwater in the near future.

Tufa towers stand sentinel above the lake at South Tufa.

South Tufa, one of the largest tufa stands on the lake, used to be free to visitors, but the area was also relatively unprotected, open to vandalism, refuse, and the extreme danger of becoming overused without proper management. The number of visitors to the lake is growing, and South Tufa gets the lion's share. For those who visited the lake's most photogenic and popular destination in the days of old, it has lost something of its rustic charm, and the Wild West allure has definitely been tamed by the fees due at the entrance kiosk. However, the amenities and improvements were necessary. The clean restrooms in the parking lot are a welcome addition, as is the interpretive trail, the wonderfully constructed boardwalk, and the friendly and knowledgeable rangers.

From the parking lot, head toward the lake. The trail itself is made up of a boardwalk and walking paths; the parking lot is easy to spot at all times, so feel free to wander. There really is not an official loop, though there is a connector to Navy Beach where fragile sand tufa provides a different perspective. The lake is rising rapidly. With the rainfall of 2004 and 2005, the waters have risen. The surge of water has surrounded many tufa formations that could be walked around just a couple of years ago. Even though much has changed, the lake retains its otherworldly beauty.

YOSEMITE NATIONAL PARK

Yosemite National Park is renowned as one of the world's most beautiful locations. From its granite domes, dazzling waterfalls, backcountry peaks, and illustrious valley, the Range of Light known as the Sierra Nevada puts on its greatest display here. Listed as a UNESCO World Heritage Site, the park is undeniably beautiful.

Yosemite is a highly sought-after tourist destination, as it has been since the turn of the twentieth century. The Sierra Club, started by John Muir, grew out of his love for the natural surroundings of Yosemite and the rest of the Sierra Nevada. The National Park Service was also created in large part due to the grandeur of the area. Famous photographs of its landscapes by Ansel Adams have only increased its appeal, not only to photographers but to travelers and nature lovers alike.

Yosemite has something to offer everyone. It is a great family attraction and an incomparable hiking destination. Undoubtedly, some of the greatest views in the world can be obtained from its peaks and vista points. It is easily accessible from anywhere in Southern California, and the memories made will be indelible.

96 SENTINEL DOME/TAFT POINT LOOP

Distance: 5 miles round-trip
Hiking time: 2.5 hours
Difficulty: Easy
Elevation gain: 800 feet
High point: 8122 feet
Season: Late spring through early fall
Water: None, bring your own
Fees and permits: Required
Map: USGS Half Dome
Information: Yosemite National Park, (209) 372-0308, *www.nps.gov/yose/*

Cameron stretches his legs to climb up the last steps to Sentinel Dome.

Getting there: From State Route 41 at Chinquapin between Yosemite Valley and Wawona, turn east onto Glacier Point Road and follow it for 13.2 miles to the turnout and parking area for Sentinel Dome and Taft Point.

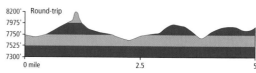

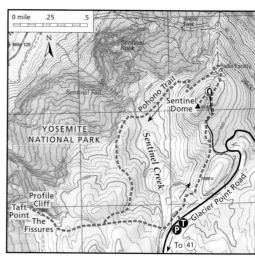

Sentinel Dome was named for the lone Jeffrey pine that until recently adorned its summit. It may have been the most photographed yellow pine in the world. Ansel Adams made it famous, though pictures of it first appeared as early as 1867. The tree stood until 2003, even though it had died due to drought in 1976. Humanity may have had more than a hand in the tree's demise, though that is not the official claim. Signs had warned people away from the tree, but people disregarded the placards entirely; children climbed on it, vandals hacked at it.

Even without the famous tree the view is still spectacular, and without a doubt it is one of the easiest to attain and most remarkable in Yosemite National Park. The tree's skeleton endures at the apex, a redoubtable remnant of the steadfast sentry that once guarded the vista spreading out toward the horizon. It is only a 1-mile walk to the popular summit, and from there most people turn around and head back to their cars. This hike's remaining loop wanders away from the crowds and into a serene forest nestled along the valley's edge.

The trail begins right at the parking area. Follow it northeast and up. It eventually meets an old road. Continue up the mountain; there are various routes to the top of the granite dome. Walk up the rock and enjoy the views.

On the way down, head northeast on an old road/connector trail toward the radio towers and shed, which are clearly visible when descending. The connector trail is not well marked, but it is a few hundred yards past the towers once it intersects the Pohono Trail. Turn left and follow it along the ridge for sweeping vistas of Yosemite Valley and especially Yosemite Falls. This section of the trail is not frequented by most visitors. It will not necessarily be empty, but the crowds

will be substantially reduced until you reach the junction for Taft Point and The Fissures. There will be a few more people along this section, but nowhere near as many as on Sentinel Dome.

At about 3.5 miles turn right at the junction for the Taft Point Trail, and continue 0.5 mile to The Fissures, Taft Point, and Profile Cliff. The Fissures are five splits in the granite that yield views and drops all the way down to the floor of the valley 3000 feet below.

Taft Point offers heart-stopping drop-off views with no guardrails. Visitors need to be careful of their footing near Taft Point, though reasonably well-balanced people have nothing to fear. The superb view offers a unique perspective on El Capitan and the valley. Half Dome is not visible, but that hardly matters. Profile Cliff is the place for acrophobics—there is a guardrail in place that aids in vertical orientation and prevents disastrous loss of equilibrium.

Follow the Taft Point Trail back to the junction and then to the parking area to complete the loop.

97 HALF DOME VIA GLACIER POINT TO HAPPY ISLES

Distance: 18.5 miles round-trip
Hiking time: 12 hours or overnight
Difficulty: Extremely strenuous
Elevation gain: 3000 feet
High point: 8838 feet
Season: Late spring through early fall
Water: Merced River, several springs and water fountains along the Mist Trail
Fees and permits: Required; reserve backpacking permits in advance
Map: USGS Half Dome
Information: Yosemite National Park, (209) 372-0308, (209) 372-0740 for
    Wilderness Permits, *www.nps.gov/yose/*

Getting there: From State Route 41 at Chinquapin between Yosemite Valley and Wawona, turn east onto Glacier Point Road and follow it for 17 miles to the Glacier Point parking area.

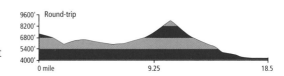

This is a brutal point-to-point hike. You will need at least four liters of water per hiker, and

possibly more. A concessionaire shuttle system transports riders to Glacier Point from Yosemite

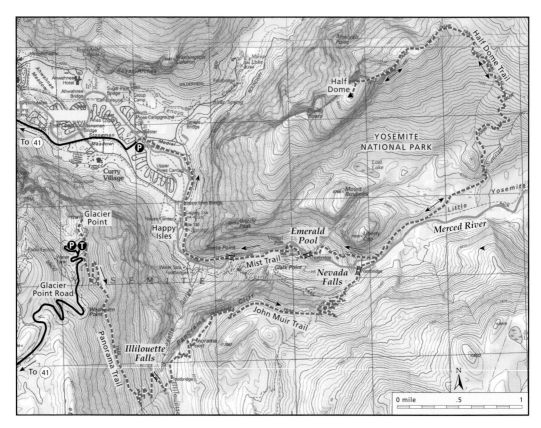

Valley, but spaces must be reserved in advance. There is a fee, and the first bus leaves kind of late at 8:30 AM with stops along the way. Another option is to leave one car at Happy Isles and drive another to Glacier Point. It takes at least an hour to do the drive, as the road is narrow and winding. Either way, adhere to all bear-box guidelines and do not leave any food or scented items in your vehicle.

Half Dome is the most visible and recognized symbol of any national park. The trip to its top is *the* hike in Yosemite. Many people dream of it as a once-in-a-lifetime adventure. A lot of people only look up in awe, but the epic journey is the most popular hike in the park. Hundreds climb it every day from the valley floor. This trip takes you away from the crowds and omits the very steep initial 2000-foot elevation gain on the Mist Trail by starting at Glacier Point, but it does add 4.5 miles to the total distance hiked.

From Glacier Point, take the Panorama Trail as it gently loses 1200 feet of altitude in a little more than 2 miles. On this trail, hikers are treated to rarely visited vistas of the ribbonlike Illilouette Falls. Cross a bridge over the creek that shares its name and begin hiking steeply up Panorama Cliff. The trail then climbs and descends 700 feet over 3 miles to a junction; turn onto the John Muir Trail.

A bridge crosses the mighty Merced just above Nevada Falls. This is where a lot of other people begin entering the picture. A little past Nevada Falls is a junction with the Mist Trail. You can stop for a snack here and take a stomach-churning look over the edge, where millions of gallons of water surge in torrents toward the valley floor. Continue on the John Muir Trail toward Little Yosemite Valley. There is a restroom here. Anywhere along the river is a good place to filter water should you need some.

Here the real climb begins. The John Muir Trail hits the junction with the Half Dome Trail

Get started early or the cable trail to Half Dome can become overcrowded on weekend afternoons.

with 2 miles to go and 2000 feet of elevation yet to gain. Turn left onto the Half Done Trail. The last leg of the hike is no joke. Steps were blasted out of Quarter Dome, which sits in front of the monolith. The steps were quarried in giant fashion; large strides are needed to get up them. Many people of all abilities turn around here, convinced that they can go no farther. The way onward is steep and exposed in sections, but easy for those who have no fear.

There are cables to hold onto as you ascend the last 800 feet to the top of Half Dome. These cables are mind-blowing. They ascend the last 800 feet nearly vertically. Most people are exhausted by the time they reach the base of Half Dome, which makes clambering up a daunting task. Since all sorts of people make the climb, some have no regard for others and will cling to both sides of the cables, refusing to let quicker climbers pass. By mid day the lines and waits can be ridiculously long, so get as early a start as possible to avoid crunches; go on a weekday if you can. Bringing gloves is also a good idea, at least for the descent.

From atop the dome, the view cannot be described in words. It is surprising how enormous the top is; the area could cover several football fields. Have fun, you've earned it, but do be careful—the valley floor is a long ways down.

Return to Nevada Falls and descend the Mist Trail. As you enjoy the beauty of the falls, the mastery of the trail builders, and the spray from Vernal Falls, ponder just how good it feels to be walking down, not up, this steep trail. Be confident that you have enjoyed the best of all possible worlds.

98   CLOUDS REST

Distance: 12 miles round-trip
Hiking time: 7 hours or overnight
Difficulty: Strenuous
Elevation gain: 1800 feet
High point: 9926 feet
Season: Late spring through fall
Water: None, bring your own
Fees and permits: Required; reserve backpacking permits in advance
Map: USGS Tenaya Lake
Information: Yosemite National Park, 209-372-0309, (209) 372-0740 for wilderness permits, *www.nps.gov/yose/*

Getting there: Take State Route 120 west from just outside the town of Lee Vining. Drive for 12 miles to the entrance for Yosemite National Park. Drive an additional 16 miles through Tuolumne Meadows to Tenaya Lake. The parking area is marked for the Sunrise Trail. **Note:** Adhere to all bearbox guidelines and do not leave any food or scented items in your vehicle.

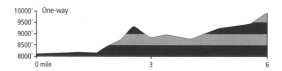

This summit not only has the loftiest name of the mountains that overlook Yosemite Valley, but it also has the most commanding view over the grandeur that is Yosemite. The popular, much-photographed waterfalls sadly are just out of view, but Half Dome sticks out like a large granite thumb to the west, its imposing dominance reduced to baby-brother status when seen from atop the commanding height of nearly 10,000 feet. Half Dome sits well below the

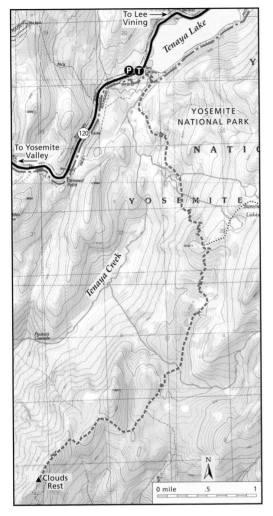

Tenaya Canyon appears to be a massive and spectacular painted backdrop.

apex of Clouds Rest, and the jaw-dropping 360-degree view encapsulates some of the finest vistas in the entire Sierra Nevada Range. Toward the trailhead, Tenaya Canyon adorns a tableau that resembles an ethereal painting more than reality. One might expect to see the colossal hand of god reaching down to create brushstrokes when staring into the east toward the canyon, the high Tuoloumne area, and Tenaya Lake.

This trail is nowhere near as crowded as the one to Half Dome (Hike 97), but expect to see people even on weekdays. This is a popular hike, but since it is out of the valley the great bulk of tourists stay away. Get a very early start and

enjoy the summit before anyone else. Sunrises and sunsets are magical here. If either is an option, be sure to carry headlamps or flashlights and extra batteries; it is a good distance back to Tenaya Lake.

The trail begins by wandering past Tenaya Lake, with minimal elevation gain in the first 1.5 miles. The flat terrain serves as a good warm-up for the steep, steady climb that gains 1000 feet in the next mile. At the top of the climb, the trail meets a fork for the three Sunrise Lakes, which are beautiful destinations on their own. The trip to all three lakes is only 1 mile beyond the junction. This can be a wonderful destination for those less inclined to high elevation, or a side trip on the return for those who are looking for a bit more adventure.

Follow the signs for Clouds Rest and descend 300 feet before resuming a much more gradual climb. Here the trail passes through lovely meadows and unnamed lakes that glimmer with morning reflections. The trail maintains a gradual climb until the final summit push, but the altitude can definitely take a toll on those used to sea level.

The last 100 yards to the top follow a rocky ridge, with some very minor scrambling involved. The gut-wrenching drops to either side can be difficult for acrophobics, but the blocks are several feet wide even in the narrowest section, and any hiker can make it to the top as long as care and caution are exercised.

99 CATHEDRAL LAKES

Distance: 8 miles round-trip
Hiking time: 4 hours or overnight
Difficulty: Moderate
Elevation gain: 1000 feet
High point: 9600 feet
Season: Late spring through fall
Water: Cathedral Creek and Lakes
Fees and permits: Required
Map: USGS Tenaya Lake
Information: Yosemite National Park (209) 372-0309, (209) 372-0740 for wilderness permits, *www.nps.gov/yose/*

Getting there: Take State Route 120 west from just outside the town of Lee Vining. Drive for 12 miles to the entrance of Yosemite National Park. Drive an additional 8 miles through Tuolumne Meadows until you see a large parking area on both sides of the roadway for Cathedral Lakes. Park here.
Note: Adhere to all bear-box guidelines; do not leave any food or scented items in your vehicle.

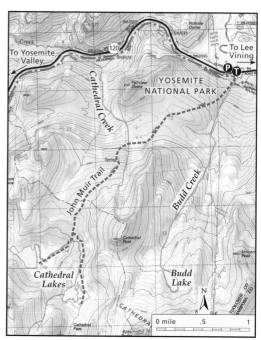

Cathedral Lakes are a popular hiking destination along the John Muir Trail in Tuolumne Meadows. Just about anyone with a little gumption can reach one or both of these alpine lakes, though the average person might be tired after the trek to both. The trail, frequented by horses and backpackers as well as day hikers, follows an even gradient. Most of its ups and downs are relatively gentle, and there are plenty of large trees, rocky dome spires, and even spots of lightning damage to look at. The initial 0.75 mile of elevation gain is the toughest part, but the trail steadily evens out and plateaus in several sections, making most of the trip relatively easy. The rewards of the hike are exquisite for such a "short" walking distance. Both Cathedral Lakes nestle beneath high peaks reflecting the celestial countryside. The Sierra scenery is truly peerless.

Following the trail is simple; it is well trod and clearly marked. Near the lakes at 3.25 miles, a fork is signed for the lower lake. Take the upper trail (the left fork) first and get the climbing out of the way; breaking up the elevation gain is a much more pleasurable way to sample this high country. The lower lake sits below the right fork.

In the early months of summer, especially during years of heavy precipitation, mosquito repellent is mandatory here, though the voracious little suckers sometimes treat 100-percent DEET like insect ketchup. It is best to apply and reapply due to all of the standing water in the area.

A trail has been carved out of the meadow in order to get to the lower lake. In times of high water there are deep channels or rivulets that can expand to waist-deep and several feet across. You will not have to ford any of them, but don't expect dry feet if you do want to cross to the lake.

In many of the swampier areas, the trail has become braided as people have tried to avoid the muddiest and wettest areas by walking to one or both sides of the trail. They may have avoided wet feet, but the damage done to the wilderness becomes irreparable. In some instances the trail looks like several paths all running parallel. Eventually, the secondary paths become inundated with mud and runoff as well, so hikers continue to create unsightly new paths, tantamount to vandalism. Always stick to the main trail, even if it is wet and muddy. Hiking boots will eventually dry, but continued trampling of a meadow results in the eventual loss of the meadow. The reason people hike is to experience nature in its rugged splendor, not to see the destruction wreaked by humankind. Please take care of the wilderness and encourage others to do the same.

There is wilderness camping along the John Muir Trail for those who want to make an overnight trip. Either way, return the way you came.

In rainy years, pools present awesome photo opportunities in and around Cathedral Lakes.

100 MOUNT DANA

Distance: 5.5 miles round-trip
Hiking time: 4 hours
Difficulty: Very strenuous
Elevation gain: 3075 feet
High point: 13,057 feet
Season: Late spring through fall
Water: None, bring your own
Fees and permits: Required
Maps: USGS Tioga Pass, Mount Dana
Information: Yosemite National Park 209-372-0309 *www.nps.gov/yose/*

Getting there: From US 395 just south of the town of Lee Vining, turn west onto State Route 120/Tioga Pass. Follow this roadway for 12 miles to the entrance station for Yosemite National Park. Park as close to the ranger kiosk as possible; there are at least three parking areas nearby. The trail begins just south of where the rangers park their cars. The trailhead is unsigned, but the rangers can point it out to you.

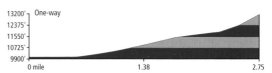

The Mount Dana Trail is an unmaintained trail that begins in lovely Dana Meadows. The trail is wide, flat, and well traveled for the first half mile—an easy stroll past lakes, wildflowers, and an assortment of wildlife. When the trail reaches the base of the mountain, the climb begins. In a little more than 2 miles of climbing, you gain over 3000 feet of elevation. The way to the top is a strenuous scramble. The route passes through rocks, boulders, snow runoff, and even ice fields if you make the trek early enough in the season.

A false summit plateau sits between the bottom of the trail and the upper reaches of the peak. The last half mile of the trail is spent

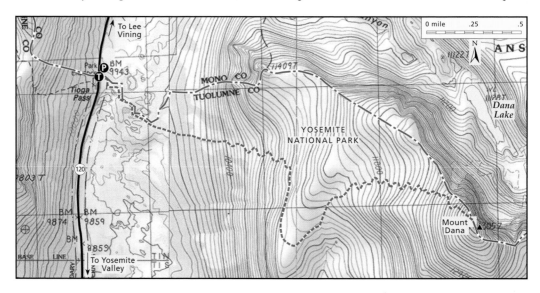

Numerous alpine lakes dot the meadows at the foot of Mount Dana.

bouldering 1000 feet to the top. There is a trail through the boulders, but it is hard to follow; it may be easier to find your own route to the top in many places.

At 13,057 feet, Mount Dana is the second-highest mountain in Yosemite National Park. It is also the most accessible high point along this part of the Sierra Crest. Mount Lyell, the park's highest point (13,114 feet), can be seen from Dana's summit, but Lyell's peak is not easily reached, so Dana gets the greater share of traffic.

The view from the summit is nothing short of heavenly. The horizon seems to stretch endlessly as your gaze extends hundreds of miles east into the state of Nevada. Mono Basin in its entirety is visible below, and the lake's salty waters reflect a cobalt blue equaled only by the Nevada sky. Tuolumne Meadows and the Yosemite high country complete the 360-degree panorama that will be etched into memory forever, as the upper elevation winds speak directly to the psyche of all those who attain this lofty perch.

Use caution when climbing this high. Elevation sickness can be a factor on this hike, as the trailhead is already well within high-altitude range before the trail climbs into *very* high altitude. Another caveat for this summit is: watch for summer thunderstorms. Above treeline at 13,000 feet is the last place you want to be during an electrical storm. If turning around is the best option, take it, and come back another day; the mountain will wait.

APPENDIX

NATIONAL PARKS

Cabrillo National Monument
1800 Cabrillo Memorial Drive
San Diego, CA 92106-3601
(619) 557-5450

Channel Islands National Park
1901 Spinnaker Drive
Ventura, CA 93001
(805) 658-5730

Death Valley National Park
P.O. Box 579
Death Valley, CA 92328
(760) 786-3200

Devils Postpile National Monument
P.O. Box 3999
Mammoth Lakes, CA 93546
(760) 934-2289

Joshua Tree National Park
74485 National Park Drive
Twentynine Palms, CA 92277
(760) 367-5500

Mojave National Preserve
2701 Barstow Road
Barstow, CA 92311
(760) 252-6100

Pinnacles National Monument
5000 Highway 146
Paicines, CA 95043-9762
(831) 389-4485

Santa Monica Mountains National Recreation Area
401 West Hillcrest Drive
Thousand Oaks, CA 91360
(805) 370-2301

Sequoia/Kings Canyon National Parks
47050 Generals Highway
Three Rivers, CA 93271-9700
(559) 565-3341

Sequoia National Forest/Giant Sequoia National Monument
1839 South Newcomb Street
Porterville, CA 93257
(559) 784-1500

Sonny Bono Salton Sea National Wildlife Refuge
906 W. Sinclair Road
Calipatria, CA 92233
(760) 348-5278

Yosemite National Park
P.O. Box 577
Yosemite National Park, CA 95389
(209) 372-0200

CALIFORNIA STATE PARKS

Andrew Molera State Park
Big Sur Station #1
Big Sur, CA 93920
(831) 667-2315

Anza Borrego Desert State Park
200 Palm Canyon Drive
Borrego Springs, CA 92004
(760) 767-5311

Cuyamaca Rancho State Park
12551 Highway 79
Descanso, CA 91916
(760) 765-3020

Gaviota State Park
#10 Refugio Beach Road
Goleta, CA 93117
(805) 968-1033

Julia Pfeiffer Burns State Park
Big Sur Station #1
Big Sur, CA 93920
(831) 667-2315

Limekiln State Park
Highway 1
Big Sur, CA 93920
(831) 667-2403

Malibu Creek State Park
1925 Las Virgenes Road
Calabasas, CA 91302
(818) 880-0367

Mono Lake Tufa State Reserve
P.O. Box 429
Lee Vining, CA 93541
(760) 647-3044
(760) 647-6331

Montana de Oro State Park
1 Pecho Valley Road
Los Osos, CA 93402
(805) 528-0513

Morro Bay State Park
Morro Bay State Park Road
Morro Bay, CA 93442
(805) 772-2560

Oceano Dunes Off Highway Vehicular Recreation Area District Office
340 James Way, Ste. 270
Pismo Beach, CA 93449
(805) 773-7170

The Dunes Center
1055 Guadalupe St.
Guadalupe, CA, 93434
(805) 343-2455

Pfeiffer Big Sur State Park
Big Sur Station #1
Big Sur, CA 93920
(831) 667-2315

Point Dume State Beach
(805) 488-1827
(818) 880-0350

Point Mugu State Park
9000 W. Pacific Coast Highway,
Malibu, CA 90265
(818) 880-0350

San Simeon State Park
Van Gordon Creek Road at San Simeon
    Creek Road
Cambria, CA 93428
(805) 927-2020

Torrey Pines State Reserve and State Beach
12600 N. Torrey Pines Road
San Diego, CA 92037
(858) 755-2063

NATIONAL FORESTS

Angeles National Forest
701 N. Santa Anita Ave.
Arcadia, CA 91006
(626) 574-5200

Big Pines Information Center
Angeles Crest Highway (Hwy 2)
Wrightwood, CA 92397
(760) 249-3504

Chilao Visitor Center
Angeles Crest Highway (Hwy 2)
La Canada, CA 91011
(626) 796-5541

Clear Creek Information Center
Angeles Crest Highway (Hwy 2)
La Canada, CA 91011
(626) 821-6764

Grassy Hollow Visitor Center
Angeles Crest Highway (Hwy 2)
Wrightwood, CA 92397
(626) 821-6737

Mount Baldy Visitor Center
Mount Baldy Road
Mount Baldy, CA 91759
(909) 982-2829

San Gabriel River Ranger District
110 N. Wabash Avenue
Glendora, CA 91741
(626) 335-1251

Cleveland National Forest
10845 Rancho Bernardo Rd.
Suite 200
San Diego, CA 92127
(858) 673-6180

Descanso Ranger District
3348 Alpine Boulevard
Alpine, CA 91901
(619) 445-6235

Palomar Ranger District
1634 Black Canyon Rd.
Ramona, CA 92065
(760) 788-0250

Trabuco Ranger District
1147 East Sixth Street
Corona, CA 92879
(951) 736-1811

Inyo National Forest
351 Pacu Lane, Suite 200
Bishop, CA 93514
(760) 873-2400
Wilderness Information Line: (760) 873-2485
Reservation Line: (760) 873-2483
Fax: (760) 873-2484

Eastern Sierra Interagency Visitor Center
Visitor Services/Wilderness Permits
Junction Highway US 395 & SR136
    (1 mile south of Lone Pine)
Lone Pine, CA 93545
(760) 876-6222

**Mammoth Ranger Station and
    Welcome Center**
P.O. Box 148
Mammoth Lakes, CA 93546
(760) 924-5500

**Mono Basin Scenic Area
Ranger Station & Visitor Center**
P.O. Box 429
Lee Vining, CA 93541
(760) 647-3044

Mount Whitney Ranger Station
Administrative/Business Office
640 S. Main Street
Lone Pine, CA 93545
(760) 876-6200

White Mountain Ranger Station
798 North Main Street
Bishop, CA 93514
(760) 873-2500

Los Padres National Forest
6755 Hollister Avenue
Suite 150
Goleta, CA 93117
(805) 968-6640

Mount Pinos Ranger District
34580 Lockwood Valley Rd.
Frazier Park, CA 93225
(661) 245-3731

Ojai Ranger District
1190 E. Ojai Ave.
Ojai, CA 93023
(805) 646-4348

Santa Barbara Ranger District
3505 Paradise Rd.
Santa Barbara, CA 93105
(805) 967-3481

Santa Lucia Ranger District
1616 N. Carlotti Dr.
Santa Maria, CA 93454
(805) 925-9538

San Bernardino National Forest
602 South Tippecanoe Avenue
San Bernardino, CA 92408
(909) 382-2600

Mountaintop Ranger District
Arrowhead Ranger Station
28104 Highway 18
P.O. Box 350
Skyforest, CA 92385
(909) 382-2782

Big Bear Ranger Station
41397 North Shore Drive, Highway 38
P.O. Box 290
Fawnskin, CA 92333
(909) 382-2790

Front Country Ranger District
Cajon Ranger Station
1209 Lytle Creek Road
Lytle Creek, CA 92358
(909) 382-2850

Mill Creek Ranger Station
34701 Mill Creek Road
Mentone, CA 92359
(909) 382-2881

San Jacinto Ranger District
San Jacinto Ranger District
54270 Pinecrest
P.O. Box 518
Idyllwild, CA 92549
(909) 382-2921

**Santa Rosa and San Jacinto
     National Monument**
51-500 Highway 74
Palm Desert, CA 92260
(760) 862-9984

BUREAU OF LAND MANAGEMENT
Ridgecrest Resource Area
300 South Richmond Road
Ridgecrest, CA 93555
(760) 384-5400

COUNTY PARKS
Kern County Parks and Recreation
1110 Golden State Avenue
Bakersfield, CA 93301
(661) 868-7000

INDEX

ABOUT THE AUTHOR

Allen Riedel is a teacher and award-winning author, journalist, and photographer. His first guidebook, *Best Hikes with Dogs: Southern California* (The Mountaineers Books, 2006) was a 2006 Outdoor Writers Association of California Best Guidebook Award winner and has been well received by readers and critics alike. He attained his bachelor's degree in English with honors from the University of California at Santa Barbara, and holds a master's degree in education from Chapman University. Allen authors a biweekly hiking column for the Inland Empire newspaper *The Press-Enterprise* and is the top reporter for *www.localhikes.com*. In his spare time, he loves to travel, hike, go camping, take photographs, and play bass guitar. Allen is married to his wife, Monique, and has twin daughters, Sierra and Makaila, and a stepson, Michael. He has volunteered as a fire lookout host in the San Bernardino National Forest and appeared on the game show *Jeopardy!*

The author and his daughter, Makaila, have a wonderful time together in the Great Outdoors. (Photo by Monique Riedel)

THE MOUNTAINEERS, founded in 1906, is a nonprofit outdoor activity and conservation club, whose mission is "to explore, study, preserve, and enjoy the natural beauty of the outdoors...." Based in Seattle, Washington, the club is now the third-largest such organization in the United States, with seven branches throughout Washington State.

The Mountaineers sponsors both classes and year-round outdoor activities in the Pacific Northwest, which include hiking, mountain climbing, ski-touring, snowshoeing, bicycling, camping, kayaking, nature study, sailing, and adventure travel. The club's conservation division supports environmental causes through educational activities, sponsoring legislation, and presenting informational programs.

All club activities are led by skilled, experienced instructors, who are dedicated to promoting safe and responsible enjoyment and preservation of the outdoors.

If you would like to participate in these organized outdoor activities or the club's programs, consider a membership in The Mountaineers. For information and an application, write or call The Mountaineers, Club Headquarters, 300 Third Avenue West, Seattle, WA 98119; 206-284-6310. You can also visit the club's website at www.mountaineers.org or contact The Mountaineers via email at clubmail@mountaineers.org.

The Mountaineers Books, an active, nonprofit publishing program of the club, produces guidebooks, instructional texts, historical works, natural history guides, and works on environmental conservation. All books produced by The Mountaineers Books fulfill the club's mission.

Send or call for our catalog of more than 500 outdoor titles:

The Mountaineers Books
1001 SW Klickitat Way, Suite 201
Seattle, WA 98134
800-553-4453
mbooks@mountaineersbooks.org
www.mountaineersbooks.org

The Mountaineers Books is proud to be a corporate sponsor of The Leave No Trace Center for Outdoor Ethics, whose mission is to promote and inspire responsible outdoor recreation through education, research, and partnerships. The Leave No Trace program is focused specifically on human-powered (nonmotorized) recreation.

Leave No Trace strives to educate visitors about the nature of their recreational impacts, as well as offer techniques to prevent and minimize such impacts. Leave No Trace is best understood as an educational and ethical program, not as a set of rules and regulations.

For more information, visit *www.LNT.org*, or call 800-332-4100.

OTHER TITLES YOU MIGHT ENJOY FROM THE MOUNTAINEERS BOOKS

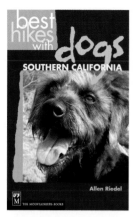

**Best Hikes with Dogs:
Southern California**
Allen Riedel
Take your four-legged friend
on an adventure.

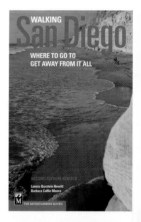

**Walking San Diego,
2nd Edition**
Hewitt & Moore
San Diego's friendliest
guidebook, fully updated!

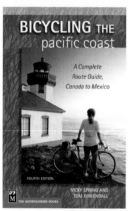

**Bicycling the Pacific Coast,
4th Edition**
Kirkendall & Spring
Ride from Canada
to Mexico!

Backcountry Betty
Jennifer Worick
Hit the trail in
comfort and class!

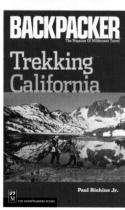

Trekking California
Paul Richins
"There's a lot for your money
in this book...Just get this book
and go along!"
—*Los Angeles Daily News*

Outdoors Online
Erika Dillman
The only honest
evaluation of all things
outdoorsy on the web!

Find The Mountaineers Books' entire catalog of outdoor titles online at *www.mountaineersbooks.org.*